NEW GOVERNANCE PARADIGM

NEW GOVERNANCE PARADIGM
Issues in Development

Edited by
T.M. Joseph

PUBLICATIONS

KALPAZ PUBLICATIONS

New Governance Paradigm: Issues in Development

Rs. 890

ISBN: 978-81-7835-715-7

Published in 2008 in India by
Kalpaz Publications
C-30, Satyawati Nagar,
Delhi-110052
E-mail: kalpaz@hotmail.com
Phone: 9212729499

Laser Type Setting by: Quick Media, Delhi
Printed at: Singhal Print Media, Delhi

CONTENTS

Preface and Acknowledgements

This collection of 17 essays is partly the result of the national seminar titled *Paradigm Shift in Governance: The Emerging Challenges and Strategies* organized by the Department of Political Science, Newman College, Thodupuzha, Kerala during 28th and 29th March 2007 with the financial support of University Grants Commission, New Delhi. The seminar evoked good response from different parts of the country. As many as 28 papers were presented in the two-day deliberations. But due to thematic constrains, only six of such papers could be included in this issue. The other 11 papers were invited.

Most of the paper contributors were quick enough to submit their full length papers in time enabling the publication of this documentation. The contributors are quite known for their scholarship and experience. I thank all authors for generously collaborating with this humble project.

The production of this book stands testimony to the promotion of academic activities in the college from the part of our Principal Rev. Fr. Paul Nedumpurath which is, again, vindicated by the accreditation of the College at 'A' grade by the NAAC this year. But for his constant and positive interventions, this project would not have been completed. I have also benefited a lot from my friendly encounters with Prof. Jojo Joseph, Vice Principal and Rev. Fr. Sotter Peringarappillil, the Bursar.

The organization of the national seminar was an effective teamwork put up by my colleagues in the college. Their relentless enthusiasm and sincerity of purpose made the programme a memorable event in the college. I must remember, with thanks, a few of them: Dr. P.A. Jose, Prof.

Joseph Augustine, Prof. K.M. Mathew, Dr. Stephen Joseph, Prof. M.J. Jacob, Prof. R.K. Pillai, Prof. K.A. Benny, Prof. Joseph Daniel, Rev. Fr. Raju Jacob, and Ms. Jomol George.

My research students: Prof. Reji Varghese Mekkaden, Mr. Abhilash C. Kumar and Kum. Anila C. Parackal also have extended a helping hand in the smooth conduct of the seminar.

I remember with gratitude all my teachers especially Dr. S.N. Sangita, Dr. B.S. Bhargava, Dr. G. Gopakumar and Dr. K. Raman Pillai for having promoted me. I also owe a lot to my academic friends: Dr. Jos Chathukulam, Dr. M.S. John, Dr. N. Sivanna, Dr. Shaji Varkey, and Dr. Raju Abraham for the necessary cross fertilization of ideas.

Last, but not the least, I thank my wife, Dr. Beena, and children, Ajay and Vijay, for the much needed moral and emotional support they have extended to me.

T. M. Joseph

Date: 19th December, 2007

List of Contributors

1. Dr. Abhijith Das is Lecturer in Economics at Kandi Raj College, Kandi, Murshidabad, West Bengal
2. Mr. Akshayakumar Panigrahi is Research Scholar, Population Research Centre, Institute for Social and Economic Change, Bangalore-560 072
3. Dr Amarkant Pandey is Reader in Economics, Pt. R.S. University, Raipur
4. Mr. Harinam Singh is Research Scholar in Economics at Bharatiyar University, Coimbatore
5. Dr. K. Gireesan is Senior Fellow, Centre for Rural Management, Kottayam, Kerala
6. Jayaseelan Raj is currently pursuing an Honors programme in Political Economy and Development Anthropology at Central College, Iowa, U.S.A
7. Dr. Jos Cathukulam is Director, Centre for Rural Management, Kottayam, Kerala
8. Dr. T.M. Joseph is Reader and Head Department of Political Science, Newman College, Thodupuzha, Kerala - 685 585
9. Dr. G. Lakshmi is Faculty (HR) at ICFAI National College, Mysore
10. Mr. A.D. Manikandan is M.Phil. Scholar, Centre for Development Studies, Thiruvananthapuram.
11. Mr. V.J. Manikumar is associated with Poverty Learning Foundation (PLF), Secunderabad
12. Dr. B. Mohanan is Professor, Department of Politics and International Studies, Pondicherry University, Pondicherry-605 014

13. Mr. Narasimha Rao is associated with Poverty Learning Foundation (PLF) Secunderabad
14. Dr. N.L. Narasinha Reddy is associated with Poverty Learning Foundation (PLF), Secunderabad
15. Ms. Nisha Velappan Nair is Research Scholar, School of Gandhian Thought and Development Studies, Mahatma Gandhi University, Kottayam, Kerala
16. Dr. Panchanan Das is Senior Lecturer in Economics at Taki Government College, West Bengal and doing research under the guidance of Prof. Amiya Kumar Bagchi
17. Dr. (Smt.) Radha Pandey is Professor, Govt. Sanskrit College, Raipur
18. Shri K. Rajasekharan is the Librarian, Kerala Institute of Local Administration (KILA), Thrissur, Kerala
19. Dr. Ram Krishna Mandal is Selection Grade Lecturer in Economics at Dera Natung College, Itanagar, Arunachal Pradesh- 791 113
20. Sajan Thomas is an Mphil scholar in Anthropology of Development in Department of Social Anthropology at University of Bergen, Norway.
21. Mr. Sambit Kumar Mishra is Research Scholar in Economics at Pt. R.S. University, Raipur
22. Mr. N.V. Shivaiah is associated with Poverty Learning Foundation (PLF) Secunderabad
23. Shri. Toms K. Thomas is a Development Practitioner associated with the Evangelical Social Action Forum (ESAF), Thrissur, Kerala
24. Ms. Vandana Kashyap is Research Scholar in Economics at Pt. R.S. University, Raipur
25. Dr. S. B. Yadav is Head, Department of Economics, Govt. College, Thanagazi, Alwar, Rajasthan

Introduction

T.M. Joseph

The term 'good governance' continues to be a significant part of our political lexicon for the last one and a half decades. Though there is little unanimity with regard to the meaning of the term, the general understanding is that it refers to the way in which cities, provinces, or whole countries were being governed or should be governed. It could mean different things to different people in different contexts. For a banker financial accountability might form the crux of good governance, while for majority of ordinary citizens it could mean protection of their life and property, freedom from hunger or corruption free administration.

The good governance agenda underlines the curbing of the role of state and expanding the space for market and competition. It further places emphasis on civil society institutions to strengthen democracy and in constructing an informal sector that can harness people's entrepreneurship through community institutions and inter-personal relationships. That is, governance encapsulates government but it also encompasses non-governmental mechanisms to meet the demands, and aspirations of citizens. In this way, the state and civil society are co-responsible for citizen welfare (Oommen 2003:128-9). In the good governance discourse, democracy emerges as the necessary political framework for successful economic development, and within this discourse democracy and economic liberalism are conceptually linked: bad governance equals state intervention; good governance equals democracy and economic liberalism. (Abrahamsen 2000:51)

In its current usage 'good governance' always includes the following core elements: people-centered, equity, accountability, transparency, participation and consultation in planning and decision-making, effective and efficient public sector management, and civil society involvement. In other words, good governance is pro poor and gender-conscious, is legitimized by participatory processes, undertakes anti-corruption efforts, is bureaucratically accountable, is efficient and effective in the use of resources, and promotes the active involvement of the private sector and the civil society to counteract vested interests. Box 1 provides a full list of properties which have been associated with good governance developed by a UNDP Workshop on Good Governance for Sustainable Development in 1996.

Box 1: Characteristics of Good Governance

- Participatory
- Sustainable
- Legitimate and acceptable to the people
- Transparent: Promotes equity and equality
- Able to develop the resources and methods of governance
- Promotes gender balance
- Tolerates and accepts diverse perspectives
- Able to mobilize resources for social purposes
- Strengthens indigenous mechanisms
- Operates by rule of law
- Efficient and effective in the use of resources
- Engenders and command respect and trust
- Accountable
- Able to define and take ownership of national solutions
- Enabling and facilitative
- Regulatory rather than controlling
- Able to deal with temporal issues
- Service-oriented

The style of governance has far reaching consequences for people's behavior. Participatory governance gradually leads to more egalitarian institutions which will substitute the rigid hierarchical institutions which captured the thinking and behavior of people.

Implications of new governance paradigm for development

A country with several socio, economic, political and administrative maladies, India presents itself a typical scenario to test the indicators of good governance. With large scale prevalence of poverty, unemployment, illiteracy, malnutrition, corruption, nepotism, communalism etc, the citizens of this country look forward to better governance in all respects. Going by the broader connotations and the potential of the concept for unfolding paradigmatic changes, the concept of governance is likely to have major consequences on the whole developmental process. Since governance as is emerging has a crucial bearing on the manner of exercise of power and control over societal resources, its implications are also immense for tackling the problems of poverty and inequality. However, predicting the real outcomes of the phenomenon is problematic. As such, there is no clear experience of any country which has gone through the new paradigm with all its features. Moreover, the paradigm is still evolving. Hence, the emerging results or outcomes of the new approach are uncertain and ambivalent (Jayal and Pai 2001). This could be a cause of concern for those countries including India which still have a long way to go in eradicating poverty. However, the major concern comes from the argument that the new paradigm of governance being advocated is basically an instrument for pushing forward the western neo-liberal economic ideology which supports capitalistic mode of development using market as the dominant agency of development (Jayal and Pai 2001). Hence there is also an argument that the governance paradigm itself needs to be assessed before all its ramifications could be analysed (Chandhoke 2003).

The pluralisation of state apparently has multiple implications for development (Shylendra 2004). On the positive side, it means that development which is a complex problem can be tackled in a more efficient and effective manner by combining the strengths of all the diverse players who have been given due space. On the negative side, the major implication of such plurality is how and on whom to fix the clear responsibility and accountability for tackling the problems like poverty alleviation. Further, the relationship between different agencies involved under governance has to be harmonious and predictable. If such a harmonious and predictable relationship cannot be evolved or ensured, potentially there could be a scenario of conflict rather than one of smooth co-ordination among the actors. Such a scenario of conflict may pose difficulties for realising the synergy for development expected of the plurality.

Therefore, in the light of the prevailing socio-economic conditions in India, the new paradigm of governance poses some difficulties for our efforts to reduce poverty and inequality. First, how is it possible to achieve perfect harmonisation between the multiple actors involved in development process? Second, how is to ensure that these actors are sensitive towards the poverty ridden people? The poverty stricken people have no mechanism to overcome the failures of state, civil society or market. Hence, it is rather impossible to make all the actors responsible for poverty reduction and achieving an egalitarian society. Third, what role do we anticipate for the state in the new governance paradigm? Can the market be effectively controlled by the state under the new paradigm? When the state becomes weak how can we utilise the resources of civil society for removing poverty and inequality. These are some of the concerns that emanate from the discussions on the new paradigm of governance.

This book contains 17 chapters, each of which has a direct bearing on some aspect of the emerging paradigm of governance in fostering development in India. In the first chapter Harinam Singh sought to examine the various dimensions of economic reforms in India. His study has examined two groups of reforms; the first one involving redrawing of state-market boundaries, including changes in ownership and regulation, and the second one concerned with reconfiguring federal institutions in the country. Further, he has highlighted the challenges of greater openness to the world economy, and of growing regional disparities. In the second chapter, A.D. Manikandan analyses the relative contribution of foreign and domestic firms in India's regime of economic globalisation during the period 1993/94-2004/05. His finding is that there is no significant statistical difference between foreign and domestic firms in India in terms of globalisation variables over the reference period.

In the third chapter, Panchanan Das examines the incidence of wage inequality among skilled and unskilled workers across various manufacturing industries in two Indian States, namely West Bengal and Gujarat, over the period 1979-80 to 2002-03. His main point is that the wage inequality among unskilled workers is substantially higher than the inequality among skilled workers. In the fourth chapter Vandana Kashyap and her associates look at the differential impacts of income inequality within a single firm in Chattishgarh. Their finding is that the salary inequality among workers in the same firm or workgroup can affect the group's output by altering the incentives workers get, in both positive and negative ways. The fifth chapter is authored by Satya Bhan Yadav who deals with the magnitude and dimension of poverty in India and the strategies adopted by Government of India in combating it. He explains that there is immense need and scope for improving the efficacy of poverty alleviation programmes by more funding, better targeting, reducing waste and corruption and creating institutional conditions for greater accountability. In the next chapter Dr. N.L. Narasinha

Reddy and his associates seek to understand the changing role of District Rural Development Agency (DRDA) in the poverty reduction strategies in Andhra Pradesh.

Akshaya Kumar Panigrahi, depending on the available secondary data, looks into the role of the state in maintaining the overall health status in India. Basically he examines the rates of fertility, mortality, and infant mortality and achievement in family planning from 1950 to 2000. Ram Krishna Mandal in his chapter on "Forest and its Sustainability in Arunachal Pradesh" makes an attempt to examine an in-depth study about the degradation of common property resources, poverty and sustainable development in Arunachal Pradesh. The 9th chapter is by Abhijith Das who shares his apprehensions over the success of extending the full sanitation coverage to the entire population in West Bengal by the government set deadline of 2010.

In the next chapter, Sajan Thomas and Jayaseelan Raj outline the grassroot level changes in Kerala associated with the subsequent bottom-up, community based, participatory and decentralized approaches to the process of development. They have explained the transition in the practice and conceptualization of Kerala's development as a transition from *old Kerala model*, which was characterized by socially sustained redistributive policies of the native and democratic state, to a *new Kerala Model* that 'seeks reconciliation of social, productive and environmental objectives at the local level, and tries to develop synergies between civil society, local governmental bodies and the state government'. In the 11th chapter, G. Lakshmi gives an account on the decentralization experiments in Kerala to achieve greater local economic development. In the process, she demands the increasing dependence on local resource mobilization as well as innovative methods of financing projects.

The 12th chapter is a critical evaluation of the Kerala model of decentrlisation authored by B. Mohanan. He argues that the politics of democratic decentralisation and campaign for people's planning initiated in Kerala was the outcome of the quest for a new agenda for action in response to the development challenges of the State. The point he makes in his chapter is that the Kerala society's attitude towards economic production and productivity has changed tremendously after the implementation of People's Plan Campaign. Previously there was organised resistance against private investment as it was considered a means of exploiting the workers. But an attitudinal change has surfaced on the horizon of Kerala society which is evidenced through the widespread promotion of private sector investment.

The 13th chapter is by the editor himself. It focuses on the emerging pattern of governance in Kerala with special attention on the drinking water sector which has been implemented in the state with the increased involvement of the people and civil society organisations. The particular drinking water scheme is called 'jalanidhi', a project implememted with the support of the World Bank, Village Panchayat, Beneficiary Groups and NGOs. The chapter seeks to examine what kind of synergy and harmony is achieved among these multiple players. It also looks into the impact this new paradigm has created in solving the problems of the rural people.

Jos Chathkulam and K. Gireesan in yet another chapter makes an attempt to assess the pre-launch preparedness of the National Rural Employment Guarantee Scheme in Palakkad district of Kerala. The scheme provides for the enhancement of livelihood security of the households in the rural areas by providing at least one hundred days of guaranteed wage employment in every financial year to every household whose adult members volunteer to do unskilled manual labour.

K. Rajasekharan in his chapter makes an attempt to report the recommendations of the II Administrative Reforms

Commission headed by Mr. Veerappa Moily with regard to reforming the local governance structure in the country. The paper highlights the strengths and deficiencies of the recommendations which would help evolve a vibrant rural and urban local governance system in India.

In the 16th chapter, Toms K. Thomas talks about the Panchayati Raj Institutions as an effective mechanism to take the people along the democratic route. In contrast to central and state legislations, the PRIs allow citizens not only to participate in elections but also to post election monitoring of the elected representatives. Since most of the elected candidates are known very personally to all the electorates, the accountability is much higher in this tier of governance when compared to the central and the state legislatures.

In the last chapter Nisha Velappan Nair explores the role played by Gram Sabhas in promoting the women's participation based on her study in two wards of a Village Panchayat in Kerala. It looks into the nature and extent of women's participation in Gram Sabhas, the motivating and constraining factors of such participation, the degree to which the Gram Sabha acts as a democratic support structure and the perceptions of the Panchayat members to the prospect of greater participation in the Sabha. The study indicates a general trend of declining participation in absolute terms and an increasing feminisation of the Gram Sabha.

References

Abrahamsen, Rita (2000): *Disciplining Democracy: Development Discourse and Good Governance in Africa*, Zed Books, London

Chandhoke, Neera (2003): 'Governance and the Pluralisation of the State: Implications for Democratic Citizenship,' *Economic and Political Weekly,* 38(28): 2957-68.

Government of India (2002): Tenth Five Year Plan (2002-2007): Dimensions and Strategies, Vol. I., Planning Commission, New Delhi.

Jayal, Niraja Gopal and Sudha Pai (eds.) (2001) *Democratic Governance in India: Challenges of Poverty, Development, and Identity.* New Delhi: Sage Publications.

OECD (1995): *Participatory Development and Good Governance*, development Co-operation Guidelines Series, Paris

Oommen T K (2003): 'Civil Society and the Goal of Good Governance' in Rajesh Tandon and Ranjita Mohanty ed. *Does Civil Society Matter?* Sage, New Delhi, pp125-144.

Shylendra, H.S. (2004): 'The Emerging Governance Paradigm and its Implications for Poverty Alleviation and Equity', Working Paper 182, Institute of Rural Management, Anand.

UNDP (1997), *Governance for sustainable development,* A UNDP policy document, New York

World Bank (1992): *Governance and Development*, Washington DC.

World Bank (1994): *Governance: The World Banks's Experience*, World Bank, Washington D.C.

World Bank (1997): *World Development Report*, Washington DC.

1

Economic Reforms in India Since 1991 : Recent Changes and Future Challenges under Globalization

Harinam Singh

Introduction

India is a large and relatively poor developing country. After independence in 1947, it pursued economic policies that gave the government a primary role in promoting economic development. While the country's size dictated some kind of federal structure, the arrangements that were adopted in the Constitution (ratified in 1950), and their subsequent evaluation gave the central government a dominant position vis-à-vis the constituent units of the nation (states and territories).

India's economic reforms began in 1991 when a newly elected Congress government, facing an exceptionally severe balance-of-payments crisis, embarked on a programme of short-term stabilization combined with a longer-term programme of comprehensive structural reforms. The reforms initiated in 1991 were different precisely because they recognized the need for a system change, involving liberalization of government controls, a larger role for the private sector, and greater integration with the world economy.

The 1991 economic reforms lifted India from decades of slow growth under socialist rule and offered an opportunity to improve the living conditions of the poor. And the recent growth has been impressive–among the highest growth rates in the world. A great portion of the world's poor lives in India, and will depend on its future growth to overcome poverty. But the recent progress is not enough. Certainly, great steps have been taken toward reform on trade, industrial policy, and the financial system; substantial progress has been made in reducing poverty; and India has a growing and thriving middle class.

There are two major groups of reforms, such as micro economic, and macroeconomic reforms in India. The first group includes the industrial deregulation, assignment of regulatory powers, financial sector reforms, capital-market deepening, agricultural reforms, infrastructure reforms and development, and privatization. The second group includes the fiscal policy, monetary policy, trade policy and exchange rate, and management. The present study includes tax reforms, reform of center-state fiscal transfer mechanisms, and local government reforms. To some degree, these reforms in federal governance hold the key to opening the door to further reform elsewhere, by reducing the fiscal burden placed on the private sector by government deficits. This study has highlighted the challenges of greater openness to the world economy, and of growing regional disparities.

Microeconomic Reforms

A microeconomic reform includes the industrial deregulation, assignment of regulatory power, financial sector reforms, Capital-market deepening, agriculture reforms, infrastructure reforms and development, and privatization.

Structural Reforms

The structural reforms were medium and long-term policies for bringing in changes in the broad structure of Indian economy to promote efficiency in industrial sectors as well as external sector along with exchange rate policies to take the economy on high growth path. The main trust of structural reforms was on liberalization, privatization and globalization. The structural reforms were aimed at transfer of resources from unproductive to productive areas, increasing the element of competition in the economy and making the economy outward looking from an inward looking one.

India's efforts at structural reforms covered the familiar gamut of decontrol of private investment, opening up the economy to foreign trade and foreign investment, financial sector reforms, etc. This familiar package of market-oriented reforms was supplemented by efforts to strengthen various anti-poverty programmes reflecting a widely shared perception that liberalization by itself would not provide adequate flow of benefits to the poorest sectors of population at least in the short run. In this section the extent of change actually implemented in the critical areas of structural reform, indicating the degree of consensus on each of these issues across the political spectrum is evaluated. Multifaceted reforms also raise issues of sequencing because the effectiveness of reforms in one area depends upon the implementation of reforms in other areas. These issues where they are especially important, or have been the focus of public debate are touched upon.

Industrial Sector Reforms

Massive deregulation of the industrial sector, in fact, constituted the first major package of reforms in July 1991. The new Industrial policy was initiated in 1991. With it new industrial policy was also drafted for increasing productivity and growth in the sector. The government of India has announced a series of initiatives of the new industrial policy, which are given below: (i) Abolition of industrial licensing; (ii) Public sector's role diluted; (iii) MRTP limit goes; (iv) Free entry to foreign investment and technology; (v) Industrial location policy liberalized; (vi) Abolition of phased manufacturing programme; and (vii) Removal of mandatory convertibility clause.

Assignment of Regulatory Power

The power sector received early attention in the economic reform process, with attempts to attract private participation in the power sector, set forth in a 1991 policy document. In 1997, the central and state governments tried again, with a Common Minimum National Action Plan for Power (CMNAP). The CMNAP recommended corporatization of the SEBs, though within a public ownership framework, and the creation of independent regulatory commissions at the central and state levels. The CMNAP also recommended some specific regulatory approaches, and private entry in the distribution component of the sector. While Andhra Pradesh, Haryana and Orissa had already set up their own State Electricity Regulatory Commissions (SERCs), other states moved after the center passed legislation in 1998 to set up its Central ERC, and to enable the states to create their own SERCs.

Financial Sector Reforms

Structural reforms aim at reallocating real resources in the economy and this process needs to be lubricated by an efficient financial system. India's reform programme therefore included a concerted effort to reform banking and capital market institutions. There has been steady forward movement in these areas.

Banking Sector Reforms

Banking sector reforms were initiated in 1991, the government appointed a committee on the financial system under the chairmanship of M. Narasimham in August 1991. The landmark report, submitted in November 1991, has become the guiding principle of banking sector reform in the 1990s.

The recommendations of first Narasimham Committee Report focused on interest rate liberalization, improvement in prudential norms and standards, strengthening supervision, and increasing competition in the banking sector. In 1997, the United Front government appointed a second Committee on Banking Sector Reforms also under the chairmanship of M. Narasimham to review what had been accomplished and to chart the agenda for a second stage of banking sector reforms. The second Narasimham Committee submitted its report in 1998 and its recommendations are expected to guide banking reforms in the years ahead.

The main objective of banking sector reforms was to promote a diversified, efficient and competitive financial system with the ultimate goal of improving the allocative efficiency of resources through operational flexibility, improved financial viability and institutional strengthening. The reforms have focused on removing financial repression through reductions in statutory pre-emptions, while stepping up prudential regulations at the same time. Furthermore, interest rates on both deposits and lending of banks have been progressively deregulated which are given below: (i) Competition Enhancing Measures, (ii) Measures Enhancing Role of Market Forces, (iii) Prudential Measures, (iv) Institutional and legal Measures, (v) Supervisory Measures, and (vi) Technology Related Measures.

(i) Competition Enhancing Measures

Competition Enhancing Measures, which are: (i) Granting of operational autonomy to public sector banks, reduction of public ownership in public sectors banks by allowing them to raise capital from equity market up to 49 percent of paid-up capital; (ii) Transparent norms for entry of Indian private sector, foreign and joint-venture banks and insurance companies, permission for foreign investment in the financial sector in the form of Foreign Direct Investment (FDI) as well as portfolio investment, permission to banks to diversify product portfolio and business activities; (iii) Roadmap for presence of foreign banks and guidelines for mergers and amalgamation of private sector banks and banks NBFCs; and (iv) Guidelines on ownership and governance in private sector banks.

(ii) Measures Enhancing Role of Market Forces

Measures Enhancing Role of Market Forces, which are: (i) Sharp reduction in pre-emption through reserve requirement, market determined pricing for government securities, disbanding of administered interest rates with a few exceptions and enhanced transparency and disclosure norms to facilitate market discipline; (ii) Introduction of pure inter-bank call money market, auction-based repos-reserve repos for short-term liquidity management, facilitation of improved payments and settlement mechanism; and (iii) Significant advancement in dematerialization and markets for securitised assets are being developed.

(iii) Prudential Measures

Prudential Measures, which are: (i) Introduction and phased implementation of international best practices and norms on risk-weighted capital adequacy requirement, accounting, income recognition, provisioning and expose; (ii) Measures to strengthen risk management through recognition of different components of risk, assignment of risk-weights to various assets classes, norms on connected lending, risk concentration, application of marked-to-marked principle for investment portfolio and limits on deployment of fund in sensitive activities: and (iii) 'Know Your Customer' and 'Anti Money Laundering' guidelines, roadmap for Basel II, introduction of capital charge for market risk, higher graded provisioning for NPAs, guidelines for ownership and governance, securitization and debt restructuring mechanisms norms, etc.

(iv) Institutional and Legal Measures

Institutional and legal Measures, which are: (i) Setting up of Lok Adalats (people's courts), debt recovery tribunals, assets reconstruction companies, settlement advisory committees, corporate debt restructuring mechanism, etc. for quicker recovery/restructuring; (ii) Promulgation of Securitization and Reconstruction of Financial Assets and Enforcement of Securities Interest (SARFAEST) Act, 2002 and its subsequent amendment to ensure creditor rights; (iii) Setting up of Credit Information Bureau of Indian Limited (CIBIL) for information sharing on defaulters as also other borrowers; and (iv) Setting up of Clearing Corporation of India Limited (CCIL) to act as central counter party for facilitating payments and settlement system relating to fixed income securities and money market instruments.

(v) Supervisory Measures

Supervisory Measures, which are: (i) Establishment of the Board of Financial Supervision as the apex supervisory authority for commercial banks, financial institutions and non-banking financial companies; (ii) Introduction of CAMELS supervisory rating system, move towards risk-based supervision, consolidated supervision of financial conglomerates, strengthening of off-site surveillance through control returns; (iii) Recasting of the role of statutory auditors, increased internal control through strengthening of internal audit; and (iv) Strengthening corporate governance, enhanced due diligence on important shareholders, fit and proper tests for directors.

(vi) Technology Related Measures

Technology Related Measures, which are setting up of INFINET as the communication backbone for the financial sector, introduction of Negotiated dealing System (NDS) for screen-based trading in government securities and Real Time Gross Settlement (RTGS) System.

Capital Market Reforms

Major changes have taken place in the capital market in the past several years. In 1991 India's capital market did not have a statutory regulatory framework. The Securities and Exchange Board of India (SEBI), was given statutory powers in 1992 and has since laid down a structure of regulations governing various participants in the capital markets, including rules for insider trading, takeovers, and management of mutual funds. These rules are now in operation and will need to be refined on the basis of experience. The stock exchanges, which were earlier dominated by brokers and lacked effective supervision, are now much better governed. The focus of the new regulations is to ensure investor protection through transparency and full disclosure.

The technology of trading has been modernized. The National Stock Exchange introduced on-line electronic trading in 1994 and the system today allows brokers located in 140 cities and towns all over the country to trade in a single unified market through terminals linked by VSAT to NSE computers. It provides automatic matching of buy and sell orders with price time priority, ensures transparency for investors and assurance of the best price. Competitive pressure has led the Bombay Stock Exchange also to introduce an on-line trading system in 1995, with linkages to brokers all over the country.

The settlement system has also seen major improvement. Earlier, completion of a trade involved physical transfer of share certificates from seller to buyer followed by submission of the certificates to company registrars to effect changes in the register of stockholders. The process was vitiated by long delays, frequent loss of certificates, return of certificates because signatures of the seller on the certificates did not match with signatures on record with registrars, and also the danger of forged certificates. In 1996, a National Depository commenced operations offering investors the facility of holding securities in dematerialized form and settling trades through book entries in the depository, eliminating delays and uncertainties in transfer of ownership. The volume of business done by the Depository has expanded rapidly. In June 1997 only 48 companies with a market capitalization of Rs. 94,000 crore had signed up enabling their securities to be dematerialized. By June 1998 this had increased to 198 companies with a market capitalization of Rs. 2,88,000 crore. The value of securities actually dematerialized increased from Rs. 2518 crore to Rs. 35,000 crore in this twelve-month period.

These changes are slowly putting in place a set of capital market institutions, which can generate confidence among investors and encourage financial intermediation in this area. As with all institutional development, much depends upon how the system actually functions under the new rules and regulations but a good start has been made. The presence of FIIs, which have invested a total of around US $ 9 billion in the stock markets, is an important force, which will push the capital market to come closer to international standards.

Economic Reforms in Agriculture

Even in the backdrop of the slow pace of reforms in the country, policy changes in agriculture were still slower. There were sufficient reasons to take a more cautious approach to economic reforms in this sector. In the first place, distortions in agriculture were not as severe as were evidenced in the highly protected and insulated industrial sector. Aggregate measure of support (ASP) calculated by various scholars, though yielding different results, did not suggest any gross distortion either in positive or in negative terms. A more sensitive indicator, the inter-sectoral terms of trade, although initially adverse to agriculture was gradually improving in favour of agriculture. Reforms in non-farm sectors, and better alignment of Indian currency had a salutary impact on agriculture. Besides, it was recognized that non-price measures, such as development of technology and creation of infrastructure, were more important for agricultural growth than the market oriented measures. In any case, a large section of population in agriculture had very weak linkages with the markets both as producers and as consumers. Those who had such linkages were fairly articulate and would not yield any advantages, which they might be extracting from the system. Government was also extra careful as nothing could be done that might jeopardize Food Security. Finally, agriculture being a state subject, in forging and implementing policies for this sector states had a larger say. Most of the states were dragging their feet in implementing reforms in the non-agricultural sectors. They were more than lukewarm when it came to reforms in agriculture.

Mainly for these reasons no drastic policy changes could take place during the first phase of reforms. Nevertheless, certain irritants and obvious distortions were sought to be removed. The most important among these being the abolition of zonal restrictions on the movement of agricultural commodities, especially food grains. Even after the abolition of zones, occasionally state governments did impose movement restrictions. But, the fact that India was a single market for agricultural commodities was by and large well established. The other direction in which economic reforms got a fillip was in the area of privatization. Private agencies were given larger scope, in the distribution of inputs, provisions of some of services in agricultural extension and in agricultural trade. Also, controls were relaxed for a few commodities, such as non-nitrogenous fertilizers. In line with general trade reforms, there was liberalization of imports as well as exports of agricultural commodities to a certain extent.

Infrastructure

The term 'infrastructure' can include various physical, social and economic indicators, but attention is usually focused on public and quasi-public goods, such as electric power, irrigation, roads and railways, telecommunications and ports. Various aggregate measures of infrastructure are possible. A number of measures have been initiated in the development of infrastructure since 1996.

Part of the Indian economic reform agenda has been to attract foreign direct investment (FDI), especially that which will bring in new technology and improve infrastructure. Statewise data for total FDI approvals for the 'reform decade' 1991-2001 is presented in Table 1.

Table 1: FDI approvals during August 1991- July 2001 in 14 Major States

State's	*FDI Approvals (Rs. Million)*	*1991 Population (Million)*	*FDI per capita (Rs.)*
Bihar	8833.43	86.374	102.27
Rajasthan	25916.69	44.006	588.94
Uttar Pradesh	43304.25	139.112	311.29
Orissa	82289.14	31.660	2599.15
Madhya Pradesh	97709.14	66.181	1476.39
Andhra Pradesh	124701.31	66.508	1874.98
Tamil Nadu	222804.00	55.859	3988.69
Kerala	14360.83	29.098	493.53
Karnataka	208156.32	44.977	4628.06
West Bengal	84234.59	68.078	1237.32
Gujarat	168555.48	41.310	4080.26
Haryana	31947.46	16.464	1940.44
Maharashtra	456286.23	78.937	5780.38
Punjab	19519.22	20.282	962.39
Total	1588618.09	788.846	2013.85

Sources: FDI – Secretariat for Industrial Assistance Newsletter, August 2001; population – http://www.censusindia.net/data.html

Privatization

Privatization is not restricted to the financial sector. With the government owning enterprises in a broad cross-section of industries, the scope of potential privatization is quite sweeping. The political difficulty of this task is highlighted by the absence of any meaningful privatization in a decade of economic reform. Privatization can affect the nature of the demand for credit by reducing politically motivated subsidies, and by reducing overall interest rates through a reduction in government crowding out of private borrowing. Privatization in the financial sector not only can have direct impacts on efficiency and growth, but it can also support the objective of allowing explicit center-state transfers to meet their own objectives more effectively.

Macroeconomic Reforms

Macroeconomic reforms can be divided into following areas, which are: (i). Fiscal policy, (ii). Monetary policy, (iii). Trade Policy, and (iv). Exchange rate, and management.

Fiscal Policy

Fiscal policy refers to a set of policies of government that relate to mobilization of public expenditure to various heads of development and other activities which are not directly related to development such as general and social services. The two objectives of fiscal policy are growth and stability.

Tax Reforms

A tax reform in India was initiated in 1991 by the Chelliah Committee of Tax Reforms (Tax Reforms Committee). The major recommendation of Chelliah Committee of tax reforms is given below: (i). To remove loopholes from the system that lead to evasion; (ii). To simplify and rationalize the tax structure; and (iii). To make the tax structure efficient and transparent from the point of view of revenue collection.

The Finance Minister proposed the setting up of the task forces to recommend measure for simplification and rationalization of direct and indirect taxes under the chairmanship of Dr. Vijay Kelkar in 2002. The prime objectives of the Task Forces of Kelkar Committee are given below: (i). To demystify the process of budget making; (ii). To make budget transparent; and (iii). To facilitate an informed discussion.

Task Force on implementation on Fiscal Responsibility and Management Act, 2003 is the enactment of FRBM Act, 2003 that is a Government constituted a Task Force which is headed by Dr. Vijay Kelkar for drawing up the medium term framework for fiscal policies to achieve the FRBM target. The Task Force was also asked to formulate annual targets indicating the path of adjustment and required policy measures. The Task Force submitted its report in July 2004. Task Force Recommendation a path of fiscal adjustment that is front-loaded and mainly revenue-led, with complementary reform efforts on revenue expenditure and enhanced capital expenditure to counteract the possible contractionary effects on fiscal correction.

The latest most significant measure taken is the introduction of the Fiscal Responsibility and Budget Management Act (FRBM) in 2004, which enjoins the government to eliminate its revenue deficit and reduce its fiscal deficit to 3 per cent of GDP by 2009. Similar acts have been passed by most state governments (23 states so far). So fiscal responsibility has now become part of our legislative commitments. The other most noteworthy development at the federal level is the transformation of state level sales taxes to the Value Added Tax (VAT), which has introduced a large measure of rationality and uniformity in the state tax system. The state sales tax system had also suffered from great complexity in terms of multiplicity of rates and special provisions. A vital feature of this tax reform has been the consultative process among all the states as mediated by the central government, which then resulted in this consensus for massive reform.

Overall, the fiscal reform process spanning both the central and state governments over the last 16 years have been truly wide ranging.

Analysis of level and Composition of Central Tax Revenue in India

The level and composition of central tax revenue as a percentage of gross tax revenue is given in the Table-2. The income tax as a percent of gross tax revenue has increased from 10 percent in 1990-91 to 18 percent in 2006-07. The income tax has shown increasing trends. The corporation tax as a percent of gross tax revenue has also increased from 10 percent in 1990-91 to 30 percent in 2006-07. The customs duties, and union excise duties have declined from 37 and 43 percent to 17 and 27 percent respectively, in the period of time 1990-91 to 2006-07 as a percent of gross tax revenue. The service tax has increasing trends during the period 1995-96 to 2006-07. Service tax has increased from 1 percent in 1995-96 to 8 percent in 2006-07. Tax revenue's for Central Government of India for the period of 1990-91 to 2006-07, and trends of Tax-GDP Ratios in India over period of 1990-91 To 2004-05 are respectively shown in (Appendix Table-1) and (Appendix Table-2).

Table-2: Composition of Central Tax revenue in India: 1990-91 To 2006-07

Year	*Personal Income Tax (In percent of Gross Tax Revenue)*	*Corporation Tax (In percent of Gross Tax Revenue)*	*Customs Duties (In per cent) of Gross Tax Revenue)*	*Union Excise Duties (In per cent of Gross Tax Revenue)*	*Service Tax (In per cent of Gross Tax Revenue)*
1990-91	10	10	37	43	—
1995-96	14	15	33	37	1
2000-01	17	19	26	37	1
2005-06	18	30	14	33	5
2006-07	18	30	17	27	8

Source: Economic & Political Weekly (2006): "Central Government Receipts of India; 1990-91 to 2006-07)", Vol. XL:I No.14, April-8.

State-Wise Percentage Change in Own Tax Revenues in India

The percentage change in own tax revenues from Panchayati Raj Institutions is 47.44, and the percentage change in own tax revenues from Urban Local Bodies is 3.90 over period of time from 1998-99 to 2002-03. While in the same period, the percentage change in total own tax revenues (combined own tax revenues from the Panchayati Raj Institutions and own tax revenues from the Urban Local Bodies) is 8.99. The Gujarat and Orissa are the states of India in which the own tax revenues from Panchayati Raj Institutions, own tax revenues from Urban Local Bodies, and the total own tax revenues or combined own tax revenues from Panchayati Raj Institutions and Urban Local Bodies have the inverse trends or declining trends in the percentage change of own tax revenues. It has shown in (Appendix Table-3).

Criteria and Weightage of the Horizontal Tax Sharing

The following criteria and weightage were adopted for horizontal sharing of taxes by different Finance Commissions as given below: (i). Population; (ii). Per capita income distance; (iii). Index of infrastructure; (iv). Inverse per capita income; (v). Index of backwardness; (vi). Area; (vii). Tax effort; and (viii). Fiscal discipline.

Criteria-wise Weightage in Various Finance Commissions

Table-3. Second Report of Ninth Finance Commission (1990-1995)

Sl. No.	*Indicator*	*Weightage (in Percent)*	
		Income Tax Sharing	*Union Excise Duties Sharing*
1.	Population	25.0	29.94
2.	Per capita Income		
3.	Distance	50.0	40.12
4.	Inverse Per capita Income	12.5	14.97
	Index of Backwardness	12.5	14.97

Note: This criteria of tax sharing is applicable to 90.0 percent of shareable Income Tax and 37.575 percent of Union Excise Duties.

Table-4. Tenth Finance Commission (1995-2000)

Sl.No.	*Indicator*	*Weightage (in Percent)*
1.	Population	20.0
2.	Per capita Income Distance	60.0
3.	Area	5.0
4.	Index of Infrastructure	5.0
5.	Tax Effort	10.0

Note: This criteria of tax sharing is applicable to 100.0 percent of shareable Income Tax and 40.0 percent of Union Excise Duties.

Table-5. Eleventh Finance Commission (2000-05)

Sl.No.	*Indicator*	*Weightage (in Percent)*
1.	Population	10.0
2.	Per capita Income Distance	62.5
3.	Area	7.5
4.	Index of Infrastructure	7.5
5.	Tax Effort	5.0
6.	Fiscal Discipline	7.5

Table-6. Twelfth Finance Commission (2005-2010)

Sl.No.	*Indicator*	*Weightage (in Percent)*
1.	Population	25.0
2.	Per capita Income Distance	50.0
3.	Area	10.0
4.	Tax Effort	7.5
5.	Fiscal Discipline	7.5

Restructuring of Public Finances in the Twelfth Finance Commission, (2005-2010)

Recommendations of the restructuring of the public finances in Twelfth Finance Commission are given below: -

1. The Combined tax-GDP ratio of the centre and states should be increased from 15.6 percent in 2004-05 to

17.6 percent in 2009-10, while primary expenditure should be increased from 22.0 percent in 2004-05 to 23.1 percent in 2009-10, and the capital expenditure should be increased from 5.6 percent in 2004-05 to 6.6 percent in 2009-10.

2. The combined debt-GDP ratio with external debt measured at historical exchange rates should at a minimum, be brought down to 75.0 percent by the end of 2009-10.
3. The system of on lending should be brought to an end over time and the long-term goal for the centre and states for the debt-GDP ratio should be 28.0 percent each.
4. The fiscal debt to GDP-ratio targets for the centre and the states may be fixed at 3.0 percent of GDP each.
5. The centre's interest payment relative to revenue receipt should reach about 28.0 percent by 2009-10. In the case of the states, the level of interest payments relative to revenue receipts should down to about 15 percent by 2009-10.
6. The revenue deficit relative to GDP for the Central and State's Governments, for their combined as well as individual accounts should be brought down to zero by 2008-09.
7. States should follow a recruitment and wage policy, in a manner such that the total salary bill relative to revenue expenditure net of interest payments and pensions does not exceed 35.0 percent.
8. Each state should enact a fiscal responsibility legislation, which should providing for elimination of revenues deficit by 2008-09 and reducing fiscal deficit to 3.0 percent of GSDP or its equivalent.
9. Each state should enact a fiscal responsibility legislation which provide for bringing out annual

reduction targets of revenue and fiscal deficits, bringing out annual statement giving prospects for the state economy and related fiscal strategy, and bringing out special statements along with the budget giving in the detail the number of employees in government, public sector and aided institutions and related salaries.

Monetary Policy Reforms

The basic emphasis of monetary policy since the initiation of reforms has been to reduce market segmentation in the financial sector through increased interlinkages between various segments of the financial market including money, government security and forex market. The key policy development that has enable a more independent monetary policy environment as well as the development of Government securities market was the discontinuation of automatic magnetization of the government's fiscal deficit since April 1997 through an agreement between the Government and the Reserve Bank of India in September 1994. In order to meet the challenges thrown by financial liberalization and the growing complexities of monetary management, the Reserve Bank of India switched from a monetary targeting framework to a multiple indicator approach from 1998-99. Short-term interest rates have emerged as the key indicator of the monetary policy stance. A significant shift is the move towards market-based instruments away from direct instruments of the monetary management. The Reserve Bank of India has put in place a liquidity management framework in which market liquidity is managed through a mix of open market (including repo) operations (OMOs), changes in reserve requirements and standing facilities, reinforced by changes in the policy rates, including the Bank Rate and short term (overnight), policy rate. In order to carry out these market operations effectively, the Reserve Bank has initiated several measures to strengthen the health of its balance sheet.

The process of monetary policy formulation has become relatively more articulate, consultative and participative with external orientation, while the internal work processes have also been re-engineered over the last few years. A recent notable step in this direction is the constitution of Technical Advisory Committee on Monetary Policy comprising external experts to advise the Reserve Bank of India on the stance of monetary policy, which are given below: (i). Objectives of monetary policy reforms; (ii). Instruments of monetary policy reforms; (iii). Developmental measures of monetary policy reforms; and (iv). Institutional measures of monetary policy reforms.

(i) Objectives of Monetary Policy Reforms

- Twin objectives of "maintaining price stability" and "ensuring availability of adequate credit to productive sectors of the economy to support growth" continue to govern the stance of monetary policy, through the relative emphasis on these objectives has varied depending on the importance of maintaining an appropriate balance.
- Reflecting the increasing development of financial market and greater liberalization, use of broad money as an intermediate target has been de-emphasized and a multiple indicator approach has been adopted.
- Emphasis has been put on development of multiple instruments to transmit liquidity and interest rate signals in the short-term in a flexible and bi-directional manner.
- Increase of the interlinkage between various segment of the financial market including money, government security and forex markets.

(ii) Instruments of Monetary Policy Reforms

- Move from direct instruments (such as, administered interest rates, reserve requirement selective credit control) to indirect instruments (such as, open market operations, purchase and repurchase of government securities) for the conduct of monetary policy.

- Introduction of Liquidity Adjustment Facility (LAF), which operates through repo and reserve repo auctions, effectively provide a corridor for short-term interest rate. LAF has emerged as the tool for both liquidity management and also as a signaling devise for interest rate in the overnight market.
- Use of open market operations to deal with overall market liquidity situation especially those emanating from capital flows.
- Introduction of Market Stabilization Scheme (MSS) as an additional instrument to deal with enduring capital inflows without affecting short-term liquidity management role of LAF.

(iii) Developmental Measures of Monetary Policy Reforms

- Discontinuation of automatic magnetization through an agreement between the Government and the Reserve Bank. Rationalization of Treasury Bill market. Introduction of delivery versus payment system and deepening of inter-bank repo market.
- Introduction of Primary Dealers in the government securities market to play the role of market maker.
- Amendment of Securities contracts Regulation Act (SCRA), to create the regulatory framework.
- Deepening of government securities market by making the interest rates in such securities market related. Introduction of auction of government securities. Development of a risk-free credible yield curve in the government securities market as benchmark for related markets.

- Development of pure inter-bank call money market. Non-bank participate in other money market instruments.
- Introduction of automated screen-based trading in government securities through Negotiated Dealing System (NDS). Setting up of risk-free payments and system in government securities through Clearing Corporation of India Limited (CCIL). Phased introduction of Real Time Gross Settlement (RTGS) System.
- Deepening of forex market and increased autonomy of Authorized Dealers.

(iv) Institutional Measures of Monetary Policy Reforms -

- Setting up of Technical Advisory6 Committee on Monetary Policy with outside experts to review macroeconomic and monetary development and advise the Reserve Bank on the stance of monetary policy.
- Creation of a separate Financial Market Department within the RBI.

External Sector Reforms

It was the balance of payment crisis in 1991 that was the key trigger for reforms. Consequently, actions on the external sector have been of the greatest importance. In 1991, the first reform was move an ex ante real devaluation of the exchange rate, and a move of the exchange rate regime from that of a crawling peg towards a market determined one, through somewhat managed.

The trade regime has undergone massive change with the removal of quantitative restrictions along with rationalization of the tariff structure. There has been a massive reduction in the number of tariff rates and the peak rate of tariff has been reduced from around 400 percent to 12.5 percent for nonagricultural products. Tariff reform for agriculture products has been constrained by the intransigence of developed countries in reducing their farm subsidies. Internationally, India has always participated actively in WTO negotiations. More recently, reflecting the hiccup in the achievement of consensus for further global trade reforms, India has also began to participate in a number of regional and bilateral trade agreements that are in the making.

With the change in the exchange rate regime and accomplishment of trade reforms the current account is now open along with limited capital account convertibility. The exchange rate regime focuses on management of volatility without a fixed rate target and the underlying demand and supply conditions determine the exchange rate movements in an orderly way.

Reforms in The Foreign Exchange Market

The foreign exchange market reforms have focused on market development with inbuilt prudential safeguards so that the market would not be destabilized in the process (Reddy, 2002). The move towards a market-based exchange rate regime in 1993 and the subsequent adoption of current account convertibility were the key measures in reforming the Indian foreign exchange market. Banks are increasingly being given greater autonomy to undertake foreign exchange market. In order to deepen the foreign exchange market, a large number of products have been introduced and entry of new players has been allowed in the market. The Foreign Exchange management Act (FEMA) has placed the Foreign Exchange Regulation Act (FERA). The main reason for making FENA that relaxes control on foreign exchange is that India has made currency, i.e. Rupee, convertible on current account. This is to facilitate the external trade and payments and promote the orderly development and maintenance of the foreign exchange market in India. A reform in the foreign exchange market has major recommendations, which are given below: (i). Exchange rate regime; (ii). Institutional framework; (iii). Increase in instruments in the foreign exchange market; and (iv). Liberalization measures.

(i) Exchange Rate Regime

- Evolutions of exchange rate regime form a single-currency fixed-exchange rate system to fixing the value of rupee against a basket of currencies and further to market-determined floating exchange rate regime.
- Adoption of convertibility of rupee for current account transactions with acceptance of Article VIII of the Articles of Agreement of the IMF. De facto full capital account convertibility for non-residents and calibrated liberalization of transactions undertaken for capital account purposes in the case of residents.

(ii) Institutional Framework

- Replacement of the earlier Foreign Exchange Regulation Act (FERA), 1973 by the market friendly Foreign Exchange Management Act (FEMA), 1999. Delegation of considerable power by RBI to Authorized Dealers to release foreign exchange for a variety of purposes.

(iii) Increase in Instruments in the Foreign Exchange Market

- Development of rupee-foreign currency swaps market.
- Introduction of additional hedging instruments, such as, foreign currency-rupee options. Authorized dealers permitted to use innovative products like cross-currency options, interest rate swaps (IRS) and currency swaps, caps/collars and forwards rate agreements (FRAs) in the international forex market.

(iv) Liberalization Measures

- Authorized dealers permitted to initiate trading positions, borrow and invest in overseas market subject to certain specifications and ratification by respective Bank's Boards. Banks are also permitted to fix interest rates on non-resident deposits, subject to certain specifications, use derivate products for assets-liability management and fix overnight open position limits and gap limits in the foreign exchange market, subject to ratification by RBI.
- Permission to various participants in the foreign exchange market, including exporters, Indians investing abroad, FIIs, to avail forward cover into swap transactions without any limit subject to genuine underlying exposure.
- FIIs and NRIs permitted to trade in exchange-traded derivative contracts subject to certain conditions.
- Foreign exchange earners permitted to maintain foreign currency accounts. Residents are permitted to open such accounts within the general limit of US $ 25,000 per year.

Current Economic Situation and Recent Economic Policy Changes

The main objective of the current phase of reforms is to ensure high growth, while making such growth inclusive to reach the benefits of growth to the poor and marginalized sections of our people. Our aim is forge ahead not only with a high rate of economic growth, but also to ensure that the growth process generates more employment, is more equitable, socially just and humane. The Government aims to empower the people, especially the poor, with universal access to education and health, facilitate their full participation in the growth process through gainful employment. Considering the size of the very poor-nearly 250 million – a safety net has been put in place through the National Rural Employment Guarantee Act that will provide one job per family for 100 days in a year.

The Indian economy, on average, has grown at a rate of more than 8 percent during the last three financial years, making it one of the fastest growing economies in the world. This has been accompanied by a benign rate of inflation. The BRICS report identifies India as the only economy that will be capable of maintaining growth rates above 5 percent till the year 2050. India's share of global GDP, in purchasing power parity (PPP) terms, at 5.9 percent in 2005 is fourth highest in the world. In terms of share in world exports, India accounts for 0.9 percent, with the value of exports in US dollar terms placed at US$ 100 billion. However, the robust export growth in excess of 20 percent, during the recent years, points to the fact that the there is still scope for scaling greater heights in the medium term. The poverty level, which was 36 percent in 1993-94, had come down to about 22 percent in 2004-05.

India's foreign exchange reserves are comfortable at US$ 166 billion, and are growing every quarter.

The Indian capital market is deep and robust and allows for the latest market procedures and instruments. The commodity markets are also encouraged, and this is gradually leading to better price discovery.

A liberal policy regime for FDI with gradual opening up of additional sectors has made India comparable to other countries. Except for a small negative list, FDI approvals are now on the automatic route. Being a signatory of MIGA as well as a host of bilateral agreements, repatriation of profits and dividends has no restrictions. Our FDI policy has been both dynamic and interactive and has factored investor perceptions adequately. Safe investment, secured and guaranteed repatriation, and a comparable FDI policy make India one of the most favoured destinations for foreign capital.

The service sector, contributing about 54 percent of GDP, has become an important driver of growth. The country's remarkable progress in developing information and communication technology (ICT) capabilities has resulted in India becoming a global leader in IT-enabled services. Given its young profile, India's working age population can become its biggest source of global competitive advantage. There are many excellent institutions imparting academic and technical education, and quality of India's human resources is constantly being improved. However, in order to exploit this advantage to the fullest, it is essential to ensure access to basic needs. The thrust on social and human development, therefore, is an important plank of the next generation of policy reforms. Such efforts are being complemented by a steep jump in budgetary outlays for social sectors, along with dedicated initiatives for removing poverty and increasing employment.

The Central and State legislatures have worked together in advancing the reform agenda. The finest example is the introduction of the Value Added Tax (VAT) at the level of the States. Besides, introduction of fiscal responsibility legislations at the Centre and in all but five States, as well as definite progress on significant areas like electricity distribution, bear testimony to India's success in carrying forward reforms through broad political consensus.

The Future Challenges

The future challenge is to sustain the momentum of growth and maintain a rate of eight percent per annum in the medium term.

India's GDP in 2005-06 was about US $ 750 billion. The savings rate was 29.1 percent in 2004-05 and presumably higher the next year. The investment rate was 30.1 percent in 2004-05 and presumably higher the following year. Obviously, there have also been productivity gains in these years that have not yet been fully assessed. Given the current state of the economy, to grow the GDP at 8 percent or more requires very large resources for investment. It also requires further gains in productivity, which is possible only if we can make more investments in education and healthcare. The obvious answer is to supplement domestic resources with more foreign capital. The current account deficit was only 0.4 percent in 2004-05 and 1.3 percent in 2005-06, and hence there is ample room to accommodate a large flow of foreign investment without affecting fiscal stability.

Conclusion

The economic reforms process carried out in India in 1991, over the last 16 years has brought forth a burst of new entrepreneurial energies across the board in almost all sectors. India has now recording substantial economic growth in excess of 8 percent. This growth could possibly be constrained by the lack of both quality and quantity of public services supplied by the government of India and its various authorities.

This paper has sought to examine several dimensions of economic reform in India, in the context of the country's federal system and of globalization. In our analysis, we have explicitly recognized that the national government has sub national governments below it, and that all these layers of government simultaneously interact with foreign governments and corporations in a global economy. The present study has examined two groups of reforms, the first involving redrawing of state-market boundaries, including changes in ownership and regulation, and the second concerned with reconfiguring federal institutions themselves.

The benefit of an approach that explicitly takes account of India's federal institutions is that we have been able to identify some areas in which the states may be able to achieve positive reforms acting independently, and other areas where coordination between the Central and the state governments in designing and implementing reform policies may be more appropriate. Furthermore, this study has highlighted the challenges of greater openness to the world economy, and of growing regional disparities. The former requires urgent attention to the financial position of the government in particular, as well as of the financial sector as a whole.

Appendix Table-1
Tax Revenues for Central Government of India: 1990-91 to 2006-07

Finalcial Year	*Gross Tax Revenue (Rs. in Crore)*	*Personal Income Tax (Rs. in Crore)*	*Corporation Tax (Rs. in Crore)*	*Customs Duties (Rs. in Crore)*	*Union Excise Duties (Rs. in Crore)*	*Wealth Tax (Rs. in Crore)*	*Service Tax (Rs. In Crore)*
1990-91	57576	5371	5535	20644	24514	231	0
1991-92	67361	6731	7853	22257	28110	307	0
1992-93	74637	7888	8899	23776	30832	468	0
1993-94	75743	9123	10060	22193	31697	154	0
1994-95	92294	12025	13822	26789	37347	105	407
1995-96	111224	15592	16487	35757	40187	74	862
1996-97	128762	18231	18567	42851	45008	78	1059
1997-98	139221	17097	20016	40193	47962	113	1586
1998-99	143797	20240	24529	40668	53246	162	1957
1999-00	171752	25654	30692	48420	61902	133	2128
2000-01	188603	31764	35696	47542	68526	132	2613
2001-02	187060	32004	36609	40268	72555	135	3302
2002-03	216266	36866	46172	44852	82310	154	4122
2003-04	254348	41387	63562	48629	90774	136	7891
2004-05	304958	49259	82680	57611	99125	145	14200
2005-06	370025*	66239*	110573*	53182*	121533*	265*	17500*
2006-07	442153*	77409*	133010*	77066*	119000*	265*	34500*

*has shown the Budget Estimates and All Other's has shown the Actual Estimates.

Source: Economic and Political Weekly (2006), Vol. XLI No. 14, (Table No.–2, Central Government's Receipts of India: 1990-91 to 2006-07, Page No. 1383.), 8 April.

Appendix Table-2

Levels And Trends in Tax-GDP Ratios in India: 1990-91 To 2004-05

Year	*Central Government Taxes (Gross) (A)*			*States' Government Own Taxes (IB)*			*Total Tax Revenue (All India) (A + B)*		
	Direct Taxes	*Indirect Texes*	*Total Taxes*	*Direct Taxes*	*Indirect Texes*	*Total Taxes*	*Direct Taxes*	*Indirect Texes*	*Total Taxes*
1990-91	1.94	8.19	10.12	0.22	5.08	5.30	2.16	13.27	15.43
1991-92	2.35	7.96	10.31	0.20	5.29	5.49	2.55	13.25	15.80
1992-93	2.42	7.55	9.97	0.17	5.12	5.28	2.59	12.66	15.26
1993-94	2.36	6.45	8.82	0.16	5.21	5.38	2.53	11.67	14.19
1994-95	2.66	6.45	9.11	0.19	5.30	5.49	2.85	11.75	14.60
1995-96	2.83	6.54	9.36	0.19	5.20	5.39	3.01	11.74	14.75
1996-97	2.84	6.64	9.48	0.16	5.05	5.21	3.00	11.69	14.69
1997-98	3.17	5.97	9.14	0.15	5.20	5.35	3.32	11.17	14.49
1998-99	2.68	5.58	8.26	0.14	4.98	5.12	2.82	10.56	13.38
1999-00	2.99	5.88	8.87	0.15	5.16	5.31	3.14	11.03	14.18
2000-01	3.27	5.76	9.03	0.17	5.42	5.59	3.43	11.18	14.61
2001-02	3.05	5.19	8.23	0.17	5.44	5.61	3.22	10.63	13.84
2002-03	3.38	5.38	8.76	0.16	5.54	5.70	3.55	10.92	14.46
2003-04*	3.75	5.49	9.23	0.17	5.72	5.92	3.91	11.24	15.15
2004-05**	4.49	5.73	10.22	0.17	5.81	5.98	4.65	11.55	16.20

Source: Indian Public Statistics: (2004-05), Government of India Ministry of Finance, Department of Economic Affairs, Economic Division.

*has shown Revised Estimates (R.E.), and ** has also shown Budgetary Estimates (B.E.).

Appendix Table-3
State wise Percent Change in Own Tax Revenue in India Over Period of Time: 1998-99 To 2002-03

State / Country	*Percentage Change in Own Tax Revenue of Panchayati Raj Institutions (Rs. in Crore)*	*Percentage Change in own Tax Revenue of Urban Local Bodies (Rs. in Crore)*	*Percentage Change in Own Tax Revenue's of Panchayati Raj Institutions Plus Urban Local Bodies (Total Own Tax Revenue) (Rs. in Crore)*
	1998-99 to 2002-03	1998-99 to 2002-03	1998-99 to 2002=03
India	47.44	3.90	8.99
Andhra Pradesh	19.49	132.45	103.35
Assam	8.02	51.45	36.89
Bihar	0.00	37.94	36.42
Chhattisgarh	8.97	101.63	60.14
Goa	11.62	101.63	60.14
Gujarat	–10.49	–22.40	–22.01
Haryana	19.44	–62.97	–56.72
Himachal Pradesh	245.19	54.35	80.88
Jammu & Kashmir	0.00	–8.55	–8.55
Jharkhand	0.00	126.77	126.77
Karnataka	15.21	–15.57	–12.06
Kerala	39.53	82.02	91.98
Madhya Pradesh	29.81	34.73	33.44
Maharashtra	120.26	–36.56	–20.86
Manipur	0.00	39.10	39.10
Meghalaya	0.00	28.24	28.24
Orissa	–56.25	–71.03	–70.90
Punjab	–26.89	33.75	33.54
Rajasthan	59.21	–76.20	–72.45
Tamil Nadu	41.26	77.50	74.06
Tripura	0.00	83.82	83.82
Uttar Pradesh	16.86	77.85	72.21
Uttaranchal	24.32	74.57	69.74
West Bengal	44.72	127.17	123.68

Source: Twelfth Finance Commission Report, Chapter-8, [Annexure- 8.8 (Para 8.25), & Annexure-8.9, (Para 8.25)], p.- 428-445.

REFERENCES

Ahluwalia, Montek S.; "Indian Economic Reforms an Appraisal", Planning Commission, New Delhi, Undated.

Ahiya, Sandeep, Jaime Allentuck, et. All, (2006); "Economic Reform in India, Task Force Report", Harris School of Public Policy, University of Chicago, January.

Chidambaram, P., (2006); "India's Economic Reforms: Recent Changes and Future Challenges", Stanford University, October – 24.

"Civil Service Analyst", (2005), Vol. II, No. 7, "Economic Special" Economic Reforms p. 115-136, New Delhi.

Economic And Political Weekly (2006), Vol. XLI No. 14, (Table No.–2, Central Government' Receipts of India: 1990-91 to 2006-07, Page No. 1383.), 8 April.

FDI–Secretariat for Industrial Assistance Newsletter, August 2001; population– http://www.censusindia.net/data.html

Government of India, (2004); Report of The Task Force on Implementation of The Fiscal Responsibility and Budget Management Act 2003", Ministry of Finance, July-16.

Indian Public Statistics: (2004-05), Government of India Ministry of Finance, Department of Economic Affairs, Economic Division.

Mohan, Rakesh, (2006); "Financial Sector Reforms and Monetary Policy: The Indian Experience", Conference Paper on Economic Policy in Asia, Stanford Centre for International Development and Stanford Institute for Economic Policy Research, June-2.

Mohan, Rakesh, (2006); "Economic Reforms in India: Where are We and Where do We Go?", Seminar Paper, Institute of South Asia Studies, Singapore, November, 10.

Rao, M. Govinda, (2000); "Tax Reforms in India: Achievements And Challenges", Asia-pace Development Journal, Vol. 7, No. 2, Institute for Social and Economic Change, Bangalore, December.

Rao, M. Govinda, (2005); "Tax system Reforms in India: Achievements and Challenges Ahead", Prepared for the

International Symposium on Tax Policy And Reform in Asian Countries, Hitotsubhashi University, Tokyo, Japan, National Institute of Public Finance And Policy, New Delhi, Jul 1-2.

Rao, M. Govinda, and Kavita Rao, "Trends and Issues in Tax Policy and Reform in India", National Institute of Public Finance and Policy, New Delhi.

Report of Ninth Finance Commission, (1990-1995); Government of India, New Delhi.

Report of Tenth Finance Commission, (1995-2000); Government of India, New Delhi.

Report of Eleventh Finance Commission, (2000-05); Government of India, New Delhi.

Report of Twelfth Finance Commission, (2005-2010); Government of India, New Delhi.

Singh, Nirvikar, and T. N. Srinivasan, (2002); "Indian Federalism, Economic Reform and Globalization", U C Santa Cruze and Yale University, May-20.

"Task Forces on Direct and Indirect Taxes" Website: indiabudget.nic.in. "Genesis of Service Tax in India",

Source: **http://www.servicetax.gov.in/servicetax/overview/ovw.pt-1.htm.**

Vyas, V. S., (2005); "Economic Reforms in Agriculture: The Next Phase", Indian Conference Paper Presented Stanford Centre for International Development, Institute of Development Studies, Jaipur, June 3-4.

2

Experiencing India's Degree of Economic Globalisation, 1993-94 – 2004-05

Manikandan A.D.

I. Introduction

Globalisation is perhaps one of the most important terms in social, political, economical and cultural theories today. Since the 1980s, it has functioned as one of the dominant paradigms for explaining the transformation of political and economic relationships in a world that seems to become increasingly interdependent with the passing of time, with boundaries that once defined national cultures becoming fuzzy (Gikandi, 1995). Since the mid – 1980's, globalisation has been known to be a fashionable term, when it began the issue of public discourse both in the academics and in the non- academics, business media in particular. This has been accompanied by the replacement of two other terms such as 'internationalisation' (as in the increasing interwoveness of national economies through international trade) and 'transnationalisation' (as in the increasing organisation of production on a cross-border basis by multinational organisations). Thus, for instance, "economic globalisation is often perceived as a process in which distinct national economies, and therefore domestic strategies of national economic management are increasingly irrelevant. According to Salawu (2006), "the extent to which an economy is globalised essentially refers to the degree of openness to foreign economic influence in the form of trades, exports or imports of goods and services, economic relations and the multinational investment collaborations with other countries, the larger the index, the higher the degree of economic globalisation". As noticed above, multinational investment collaboration with other countries[2], as one of the major channels through which openness came, however, considerable controversy exists over whether foreign direct investment (FDI) inflows or multinational companies (MNCs) have in fact promoted manufactured exports from developing host economies. It has long been a subject of policy interest and academic debate (Lall et al 1983).

This is not a surprising news that India's increasing integration with the global economy, for example, during the period 1990-2004 the share of exports and imports in gross domestic product (GDP) almost doubled (Srinivasan, 2006) and the rapid rise of foreign direct investment in the post-liberalisation period (the ratio of FDI inflow to GDP is 1.7 per cent (Kumar, 2005), has revived interest in the question. Whether increasing FDI inflows have any significant impact on India's degrees of economic globalisation as compared to the performance of domestic firms for the period of 1993-2004? Most of the recent studies in India have not been given enough attention to this question. Hence, the present study investigates the link between the overall performance of foreign and domestic firms and India's degree of economic globalisation at comparative perspective.

The above objective was achieved using both descriptive statistical analysis and standard econometric tools. The performance analysis has been carried out at aggregate level the industries covered are chemicals and engineering from manufacturing sector, the reason being, more than 60 per cent of total foreign firms came from these industries. The result suggests that FDI leads to the higher level of technological progress through the process of economic globalisation. Thus, policy should be based on two principles. First that, the country "needed highest technological progress" and second that, "it is achieved with the least damage to the Indian economy and ensures the maximum benefits".

The outline of this paper is as follows. Section II gives review of theoretical framework, followed by methodology and data source in section III, Section IV provides the result of the study and finally, Section V concludes the paper with some policy suggestions.

II. Theoretical Framework

According to Markusen (2005), theories of foreign direct investment treated it as a part of theory of capital movements in a factor proportions world. Theory bifurcated into two branches. One could be called the vertical/resource seeking approach, an early example of which is Helpman (1984). This is in fact a natural extension of factor-proportions comparative-advantage models in which activities differ in factor intensities and countries differ in factor-proportions. The alternative is the horizontal or market seeking approach, in which firms exploit firm-specific assets in multiple markets, an early example of which is Markusen (1984). The latter is more a part of non-comparative-advantage theory and, while both approaches are important, does the job of explaining the large volume of intra- industry FDI among high-income countries. For instance, South Korea's motor cars are exported to the United States and American motor cars are exported to South Korea. It does not reflect comparative advantage. On the lines of Heckscher-Ohlin theory a firm irrespective of its ownership, would be exploiting the comparative advantage in the manufacture and exporting of labour-intensive products from a labour surplus country like India, Brazil etc. Given the product, however, the choice of factor-proportion (choice of technology) would vary across the firms under differing perceptions of rigidity in organising the respective factors e.g. labour/capital or policy-induced distortions in the factor market. In the Indian context, the choice of a production technique with higher capital/labour ratio renders some competitive advantage of real cost-efficiency to the exporting firms (Subrahmanian et al. 1994).

The past two decades have been characterised by the growing international integration and a substantial increase in the importance of gross foreign direct investment. Most of these flows have been associated with the higher trades, exports and imports in particular. According to Lopez (2005), 'there are two possible bi-directional links between foreign direct investment and imports. First, if imports are evidence that a market exists for a commodity, FDI might be attracted to the host country to produce their products locally. In other words, a rise in imports in the host economy justifies investment and production by multinationals; thus, imports stimulate foreign inflows. Second, as soon as MNCs establish in the host country, they imports certain types of supplies (basic components and intermediate goods produced by the head quarters/parent firms) to satisfy the quality standards required by the international market, therefore, foreign direct investment firms increase the demand for imports[3]. In addition to this, the facility of Free Trade Zone (FTZ) is more helpful to multinationals to enjoy minimum customs formalities and the duty-free import of raw materials, component parts, machinery and equipment etc. in the production process of them (Driffield, Clarke, and Noor, 2004). In view of this, one can deduce that FDI leads to the higher imports. It could be regarded as any change in foreign direct investment, which leads a country's trade system towards the higher degrees of economic globalisation. The rapid rise of FDI flows in the Indian economy in the 1990s has revived interest in the some pertinent questions.

(i) What is the pattern and trend of India's degree of economic globalisation in the post-reform period from 1993/94 to 2004/05?

(ii) What is the direction of India's degree of economic globalisation whether export-oriented or import-oriented globalisation?

(iii) What is the relationship between industrial development and degree of economic globalisation for the period of 1993/94-2004/05?

(iv) What is the relative contribution of foreign and domestic firms in India's degree of economic globalisation for the period of 1993/94-2004/05?

These are the basic questions this study intended to analyse. The objectives of the study is to show the pattern, trend and direction of India's degree of economic globalisation at the both aggregate and disaggregated level for the period of 1993/93-2004/05, to examine the links between globalisation variables and industrial development at the both aggregate and disaggregated level for the period of 1993/93-2004/05 and to evaluate the relative performance of foreign and domestic firms in India's degree of economic globalisation in the post-reform period from 1993/94 to 2004/05.

III Methodology and Data Source

In order to properly compare and analyse the relationship between the actual performance of foreign and domestic firms and India's degree of economic globalisation, the various measures of economic globalisation were expressed as ratio of gross domestic product or output of the economy. We have looked in to two dimensions of performance viz., trade globalisation performance and technology globalisation performance. For the two groups of firms' average trade and technology globalisation performance ratios were calculated and the difference between the two tested using the test of significance. The study covers the post reform period from 1993/94 to 2004/05.

(a) Selection of Firms

This paper attempts to analyse econometrically the difference of foreign and domestic ownership on India's degree of economic globalisation of 2 industries namely, chemicals and engineering containing the largest number of foreign and domestic companies. Table-1 shows the distribution of foreign and domestic firms in selected industries according to the CMIE "PROWESS" database.

Table-1. Selection of Foreign and Domestic Firms from Chemicals and Engineering Industries

Sl.	*Industries*	*Foreign Firms*	*Domestic Firms*	*Total*
1.	Chemicals	78 (13.15%)	515 (86.85%)	593 (100%)
2.	Engineering	135 (16.32%)	692 (83.68%)	827 (100%)
	Total	213 (15.00%)	1207 (85.00%)	1420 (100%)

Source: "PROWESS" data set published by the Centre for Monitoring Indian Economy (CMIE)

As per the CMIE "PROWESS" database in 2006 there were a total of 1420 companies, of which 1207 (85 per cent of total) firms were identified as domestic firms and 213 firms (1 5 per cent of total) were identified as foreign firms. Industry wise distribution of firms is as follows – Chemicals there were 593 firms, of which 515 (86.85 per cent of total) firms were identified as domestic firms and 78 firms (13.15 per cent of total) were identified as foreign firms. There were 827 firms in engineering, of which 692 firms were identified as domestic firms (83.68 per cent of total firms) and 135 firms were identified as foreign (16 .32 per cent of total firms) (refer Table-1).

(b) Measurement and Definitions of Indicators

(i) Foreign Direct Investment Inflows (FDI inflows): This will be measured by the net inflow of foreign direct investment into the Indian economy for the period of 1991-2004 (refer Table-A1).

(ii) The degrees of economic Globalisation: It is measured by the ratio of traded goods and services, exports or imports to the output of the economy during the period 1993/94-2004/05.

(iii) Export-Gross Domestic Product Ratio (EXGDP): Export–Gross Domestic Product of industry is represented by its trade globalisation ratio. It is the ratio of industry' s exports to gross domestic product of the economy or output of the economy.

(iv) Import-Gross Domestic Product Ratio (IMGDP): Import–Gross Domestic Product of industry is represented by its trade globalisation ratio. It is the ratio of industry' s imports to gross domestic product of the economy or output of the economy.

(v) Net Export-Gross Domestic Product Ratio (NEXGDP): Netexport–Gross Domestic Product of industry is represented by its trade globalisation ratio. It is the ratio of industry' s net exports (net foreign exchange earnings) to gross domestic product of the economy or output of the economy.

Table-2. Measurement and Definitions of Indicators

Sl.	*Dimensions of Performance*	*Performance Indicators and Definitions*
1	Trade Performance	EXGDP = (Exports/GDP*100), IMGDP = (Imports/GDP*100) and NEXGDP = Net Exports/ GDP*100)
2	Technology Performance	ETIGDP = (Embodied Technology Imports/GDP*100) and TIGDP = (Technology Imports/GDP*100)

(*vi*) Technology-Gross Domestic Product Ratio (TIGDP): Technology Import – Gross Domestic Product of industry is represented by its technology globalisation ratio. It is the ratio of total forex spending on technology imports of industry to gross domestic product or output of the economy. The technology imports expenditure includes the expenditure on the import of capital goods(ETIGDP) embodying new technology as well as the imports expenditure on the royalty-payments and know how (disembodied technology) through licensing (refer Table-2).

(c) Hypothesis of the Study

The following five objectives are used to compare the overall performance of foreign and domestic firms in India's degree of economic globalisation for the period of 1991-2004. The main hypotheses are as follows.

(i) There is no significant difference between foreign and domestic firms in terms of EXGDP ratio

(ii) There is no significant difference between foreign and domestic firms in terms of IMGDP ratio

(iii) There is no significant difference between foreign and domestic firms in terms of NEXGDP ratio

Table-3. Dimensions of Performance and Hypothesis of the Study

Sl	*Dimensions of Performance*	*Hypothesis of the Study*
1	Trade Performance & Indicators	Null Hypothesis
	(i) EXGDP	**Ho: μ1 = μ2**
	(ii) IMGDP	**Ho: μ1 = μ2**
	(iii) NEXGDP	**Ho: μ1 = μ2**
2	Technology Performance & Indicators	Null Hypothesis
	(i) ETIGDP	**Ho: μ1 = μ2**
	(ii) TIGDP	**Ho: μ1 = μ2**

(iv) There is no significant difference between foreign and domestic firms in terms of ETIGDP ratio

(v) There is no significant difference between foreign and domestic firms in terms of TIGDP ratio (refer Table-3).

(d) Data Source

The present study entirely relies on secondary data compiled from four main sources. The basic data sources used for the study were collected from Reserve Bank of India Bulletin (RBI Bulletin) published by Reserve Bank of India (RBI) and "PROWESS" electronic database published by the Centre for Monitoring Indian Economy (CMIE). This is supplemented with relevant data from other sources such as International Trade Statistics published by World Trade Organisation and www.keralaplanningboard.org published by Government of Kerala. The data set provided by RBI covers entire industries including, tea, textiles, trading, rubber and rubber products, chemicals and engineering and does not provide information at firm level. Therefore, data at individual firm level has been culled from "PROWESS" electronic database.

IV. Analysis

The Pattern and Trend of the Degrees of Economic Globalisation

India has achieved significant change in the degree of economic globalisation, the degree of export-globalisation, averaging close to 2.0 per cent and the degree of import-globalisation, averaging close to 5.0 per cent per year for nearly one and a half decade. The former is less than the latter. Admittedly in a high measure. All this is the result of the systematic reforms including, reforms of capital market, which associated with the reforms the establishment of National Stock Exchange, broadening the market for government securities, and the introduction of new financial products, initiated by the government after a severe macro economic crisis. The economic liberalisation in general and the trade liberalisation policies in particular have affected the pattern and trend of the degree of globalisation for the period of 1993/04 2004/05. The degree of import-globalisation was left far behind the degree of export globalisation at aggregate level (Graph-1).

Graph-1: The Degrees of Economic Globalisation at the Aggregate Level, 1993/94-2004/05

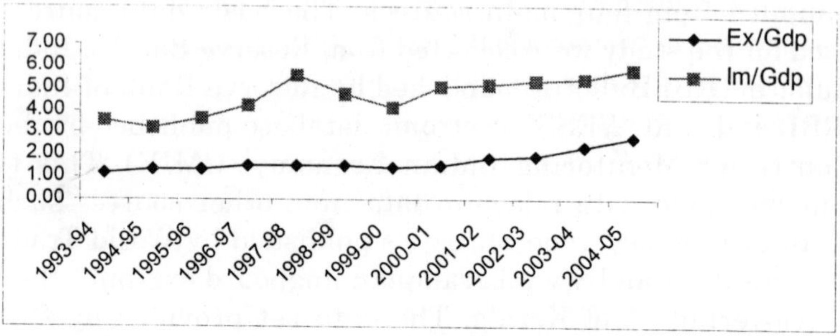

During the 1993/94s, import- globalisation showed a marked increase from 3.5 in 1993/94 to 5.5 per cent in 1997/98. However, after stagnating for a few subsequent years for instance, 4.7 per cent in 1998/99 and 4.1 per cent in 1999-2000 it showed a peaked increase from 5.0 per cent in 2000-01 to 5.8 per cent in 2004-05. While the degree of export-globalisation at the aggregate level showed an unprecedented change from 1.2 per cent to 2.8 per cent over the period 1993/ 94 – 2004/05, averaging close to 1.7 per cent per cent for a nearly one and a half decade.

Let me now turn to the likely impact of the higher degree of economic globalisation of chemicals and engineering industries as compared to aggregated level for the period of 1993/94 – 2004/05 from a disaggregated perspective.

Chemicals industry is one of the key industries in India. The Indian chemicals industry came to be established and developed basically for import substitution rather than for export promotion of the economy. In response to import-substitution stimuli, the period in the 1960s, witnessed an unprecedented growth of production capacity and its product diversification. It has also been observed that the role of foreign collaboration and foreign firms as compared to domestic firms in this process was quite significant (Subrahmanian et al, 1994).

The degree of import-globalisation was left far behind the degree of export-globalisation. However, the degree of export-globalisation in chemicals industry showed a marked rise over the period 1993/94-2004/05. While the degree of import-globalisation in chemicals industry showed a peaked increase from 2.08 per cent in 1994-95 to 3.95 per cent in 1997 – 98. However, after stagnating for a few subsequent years for instance, the degree of import-globalisation showed a marked decrease from 3.95 per cent in 1997-98 to 3.36 per cent in 1998-99 and from 3.36 per cent in 1998-99 to 2.84 per cent in 1999-2000. During the 2000s it showed a peaked increase until 2004-05, averaging close to 4.2 per cent per year in chemicals industry. Although, the degree of export-globalisation in chemicals industry has also remained far below, averaging close to only 1 per cent per year over the period 1993/94 – 2004/05. While the degree of import-globalisation showed significant change, averaging close to 3.5 per cent per year for a nearly one and a half decade. The former is smaller than the latter. Admittedly in a high measure, the reason being, after globalisation the two groups of firms have become a major importer of basic components, raw materials, machinery and equipments etc. (refer Graph-2).

Graph-2. The Degrees of Economic Globalisation in Chemicals Industry, 1993/94-2004/05

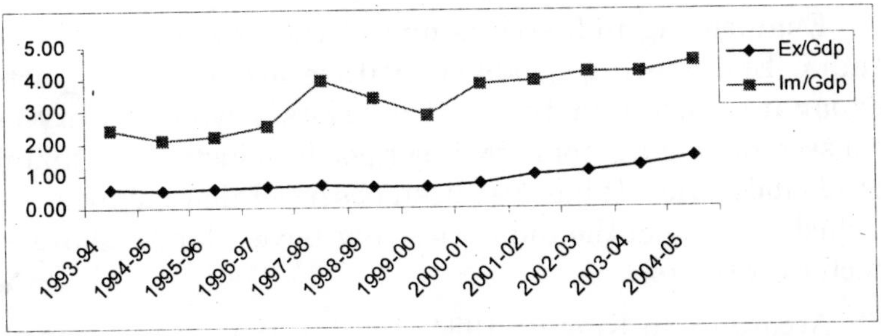

In an analysis of the role of the degree of import-globalisation in explaining the rising importance of the degree of economic globalisation, the present study found that only a part of the increase in the degree of import-globalisation could be attributed to economic globalisation. It is trivially obvious that the degree of import-globalisation at aggregate level and in chemicals industry have been growing very rapidly since 1993/94, averaging close to 4.65 per cent and 3.50 per cent respectively per year over the 1993/94 - 2004/05 period. It is not hardly exciting news that the degree of economic globalisation in general and the degree of import-globalisation in particular have affected by the pattern and trend of the degree of import-globalisation of chemicals industry over the period 1993/94-2004 /05 (refer-Graph-3). In other words, the degree of economic globalisation at the aggregate level has largely influenced by the degrees of export and import globalisation of chemical industry over the period 1993/94-2004/05.

Graph-3. The Degree of Import - Globalisation at the Aggregate Level and in Chemicals Industry, 1993/94-2004/05

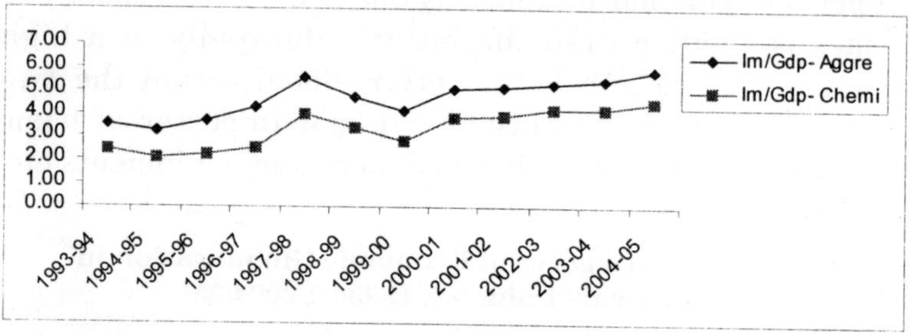

Engineering industry is one of the key industries in India. Engineering goods constitute a dynamic export-expanding sector in India. It consists a wide variety of subsectors ranging from consumer goods industries to capital goods industries. It has also been observed that engineering industry is one of the industries that have a larger share of sectoral FDI stock.

According to Kumar (1994), 'within the manufacturing industry, the new investments were directed to the high technology intensive sectors namely, electrical goods, transport equipment, machinery and machine tools, and metals and metal products sectors which accounted for a large portion of FDI stock'. This shows that engineering industry is one of the leading industries where foreign firms are mainly concentrated (refer-Table-1).

Graph-4. The Degrees of Economic Globalisation in Engineering Industry, 1993/94-2004/05

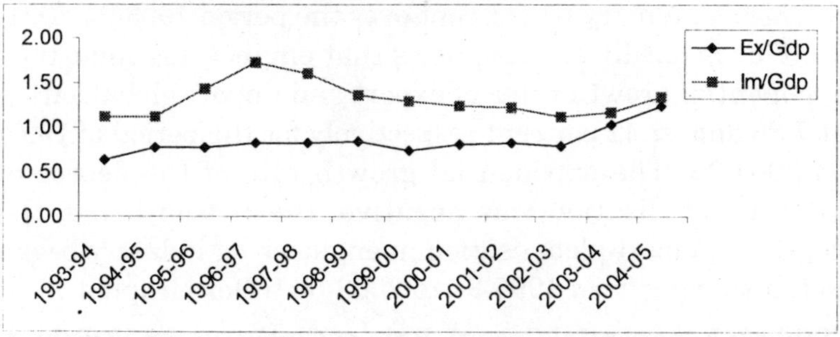

Engineering industry in India has achieved significant progress in the degree of economic globalisation over the period 1993/94-2004/05. The degree of export-globalisation in engineering industry showed a marked increase until 2004-05, averaging close to one per cent per year. While the degree of import-globalisation showed a marked increase over the period 1993/94 –1996/97 on an average of 1.35 per cent per year, and even began to decrease sharply after 1996/97 on an average of 1.30 per cent per year until 2004/05. The degree of import-globalisation is the higher than the degree of export-globalisation in engineering industry. Admittedly in a small measure, averaging close to 1.5 per cent and 1 per cent per year respectively. Interestingly, engineering industry appears to be better than chemicals industry in helping the rising degrees of economic globalisation.

Exponential Growth Rate of Globalisation Variables

The exponential growth rate of globalisation variables namely, exports-globalisation and imports-globalisation have been growing over the period 1993/94 - 2004/05 at aggregate level. The exponential growth rate of export globalisation is 29.2 per cent as compared to the exponential growth rate of import globalisation 60.12 per cent. The latter is the higher than the former. Admittedly in a high measure. While Chemicals industry's exports and imports globalisation again grew fastest at the rate of 20.32 and 64.10 respectively over the period 1993/94-2004/05. The degree of import-globalisation at aggregate level was 60 per cent and that of chemicals industry 64 per cent over the period 1993/94-2004-05. This is hardly exciting news that engineering industry's exponential growth rates of export and import globalisation at 7.38 and –2.42 per cent respectively for the period of 1993/94-2004/05. The exponential growth rate of the degree of import-globalisation was negative, the reason being, the degree of import-globalisation in engineering industry began to fall sharply from 1996-97 to 2003-04 (refer Graph-4).

Table-4: Exponential Growth Rate of Globalisation Variables for the Period of 1993/94 –2004/05 at the Aggregate and Disaggregated Level

Sl.	*Industries*	*Exponential Growth rate of Export (in %)*	*Exponential Growth rate of Import (in %)*
1.	Aggregate Level	29.20 (1420 Firms)	60.12 (1420 Firms)
2.	Domestic Firms	25.13 (1207 Firms)	55.93 (1207 Firms)
3.	Foreign Firms	3.26 (0213 Firms)	2.69 (0213 Firms)
4.	Disaggregated Level – Chemicals	20.32 (0593 Firms)	64.10 (0593 Firms)
5.	Domestic Firms	18.88 (0515 Firms)	61.06 (0515 Firms)
6.	Foreign Firms	1.21 (0078 Firms)	1.87 (0078 Firms)
7.	Disaggregated Level – Engineering	7.38 (0827 Firms)	-2.42 (0827 Firms)
8.	Domestic Firms	5.25 (0692 Firms)	-3.21 (0692 Firms)
9.	Foreign Firms	2.02 (0135 Firms)	0.81 (0135 Firms)

Note: $Y = ab^t$, $\text{Ln } Y = \text{Ln } a + t \text{ Ln } b$

It is now instructive to review the performance of foreign and domestic firms in the case of exponential growth rate of globalisation variables at the both aggregate and disaggrega –gated level over the period 1993/93-2004/05. The general impression that emerged from the study is that domestic firms appear to be performing better than foreign firms in terms of the degree of economic globalisation variables over the period 1993/94-2004/05. For instance, exponential growth rates of the degrees of export and import globalisation were 25.13 and 55.93 per cent respectively for domestic firms, while foreign firm's 3.26 and 2.69 per cent respectively. The former is too higher than the latter. However, the degree of import-globalisation of domestic firms more than two times than its exponentialgrowth of export-globalisation. The conclusion that emerged from the study is that domestic firm appears to be higher import globalising firms as compared to foreign firms since 1993/94. This has also been accompanied by the two greater impacts: (i) the degree of import-globalisation witnessed an unprecedented hike at aggregate level, and (ii) the degree of import-globalisation of domestic firms witnessed a peak in its aggregate level over the period 1993/94-2004/05.

While there was a sharp increase in the exponential growth rate of globalisation variables of domestic firms at the rate of 18.8 and 61 per cent as compared to foreign firm's 1.21 per cent and 1.87 per cent in chemicals industry. However, exponential growth rate of the degree of export and import globalisation variables of domestic firms were 5.25 and –3.2 per cent respectively in engineering industry, while foreign firm's growth rate at 2.02 and 0.81 per cent. The sum and substance of the part on exponential growth rate of the degree of globalisation variables is that the performance of domestic firms appear to be better than foreign firms in the case of growth of globalisation variables (refer Table-4).

Correlation Analysis Between Industrial Development and Globalisation Variables, 1993/94 – 2004/05

In order to compare the relationship between industrial development and the globalisation variables at the both aggregate and disaggregated level for the period of 1993/94-2004/05 we have used the correlation analysis.

Table-5. Correlation Analysis Between Industrial Development and Globalisation Variables, 1993/94 – 2004/05 (Aggregate Level)

Variables	*EXGDP*	*IMGDP*	*ETIGDP*	*DTIGDP*	*TIGDP*	*NEXGDP*	*FEXGDP*	*FIMGDP*
EXGDP	1	0.7660	-0.4207	-0.6372	-0.4753	-0.2554	0.8474	0.2933
IMGDP	0.7660	1	-0.2039	-0.5599	-0.2740	-0.8147	0.8496	0.6579
ETIGDP	-0.4207	-0.2039	1	0.7285	0.9929	-0.0874	-0.1394	0.3871
DTIGDP	-0.6372	-0.5599	0.7285	1	0.8050	0.2529	-0.4161	0.1260
TIGDP	-0.4753	-0.2740	0.9929	0.8050	1	-0.0317	-0.1932	0.3572
NEXGDP	-0.2554	-0.8147	-0.0874	0.2529	-0.0317	1	-0.5286	-0.7509
FEXGDP	0.8474	0.8496	-0.1394	-0.4161	-0.1932	-0.5286	1	0.6361
FIMGDP	0.2933	0.6579	0.3871	0.1260	0.3572	-0.7509	0.6361	1

From Table-5, it could be seen that the correlation between export-globalisation and other globalisation variables namely, import-globalisation and foreign firm's export-globalisa-tion shows a strong positive correlation, which ranges between 0.76 and 0.84. However, the correlation between export and technology globalisation was negative. While there is a weak negative correlation between import and technology globalisation variables whose degree of association is –0.27. Although, there is a strong positive correlation between import globalisation and foreign firm's export and import globalisation variables whose degree of association range between 0.65 and 0.85. There is a weak positive correlation between technology globalisation variables and foreign firm's import globalisation whose degree of correlation range between 0.12 and 0.38. It has been noted that there is a strong positive correlation between technology globalisation and other technology globalisation variables whose degree of relation range 0.72 and 0.99.

Table-6 and 7 presents that the correlation between industrial development and the degree of globalisation variables from a disaggregated perspective during the period 1993/94-2004/05.

Table-6. Correlation Analysis Between Industrial Development and Globalisation Variables, 1993/94 – 2004/05 (Disaggregated Level: Chemicals Industry)

Variables	*EXGDP*	*IMGDP*	*ETIGDP*	*DTIGDP*	*TIGDP*	*NEXGDP*	*FEXGDP*	*FIMGDP*
EXGDP	1	0.8208	-0.3429	-0.6499	-0.4407	-0.5556	0.6568	0.5514
IMGDP	0.8208	1	-0.3876	-0.6003	-0.4664	-0.9289	0.8437	0.6928
ETIGDP	-0.3429	-0.3876	1	0.6156	0.9825	0.3470	-0.3332	-0.1856
DTIGDP	-0.6499	-0.6003	0.6156	1	0.7518	0.4507	-0.3354	-0.1884
TIGDP	-0.4407	-0.4664	0.9825	0.7518	1	0.3970	-0.3582	-0.1999
NEXGDP	-0.5556	-0.9289	0.3470	0.4507	0.3970	1	-0.8185	-0.6733
FEXGDP	0.6568	0.8437	-0.3332	-0.3354	-0.3582	-0.8185	1	0.7550
FIMGDP	0.5514	0.6928	-0.1856	-0.1884	-0.1999	-0.6733	0.7550	1

From Table-6, it could be seen that there is a strong negative correlation between export globalisation and other globalisation variables namely, technology globalisation variables (ETIGDP, DTIGDP, TIGDP) and net foreign exchange earning-globalisation. However, there is a strong positive correlation between export globalisation and foreign firm's the degree of export and import globalisation whose degree of relation range from 0.55 and 65. While there is a very high correlation between import globalisation and foreign firm's export and import globalisation variables whose degree of relation were 0.82, 0.84 and 0.69. It has been observed that there is a weak negative correlation between technology globalisation variables and export and import globalisation in general and foreign firm's export and import globalisation in particular. There is a strong positive correlation among technology variables whose degree of relation range between 0.61 and 0.98. Net export – globalisation has an extremely negative high correlation with import and export globalisa –tion whose degree of association range between –0.55 and –0.92. Foreign firm's import and export globalisation were positively correlated.

Table-7. Correlation Analysis Between Industrial Development and Globalisation Variables, 1993/94 – 2004/05 (Disaggregated Level: Engineering Industry)

Variables	EXGDP	IMGDP	ETIGDP	DTIGDP	TIGDP	NEXGDP	FEXGDP	FIMGDP
EXGDP	1	0.1025	-0.3673	-0.3346	-0.3810	0.5804	0.9433	0.2164
IMGDP	0.1025	1	0.8180	0.3982	0.8193	-0.7501	0.2574	0.8643
ETIGDP	-0.3673	0.8180	1	0.4334	0.9971	-0.9159	-0.1824	0.6414
DTIGDP	-0.3346	0.3982	0.4334	1	0.5006	-0.5659	-0.3374	0.0382
TIGDP	-0.3810	0.8193	0.9971	0.5006	1	-0.9275	-0.2037	0.6193
NEXGDP	0.5804	-0.7501	-0.9159	-0.56592	-0.9275	1	0.4191	-0.5540
FEXGDP	0.9433	0.2574	-0.1824	-0.3374	-0.2037	0.4191	1	0.4539
FIMGDP	0.2164	0.8643	0.6414	0.0382	0.6193	-0.5540	0.4539	1

Table-7 shows the relationship between globalisation ratios and industrial development in engineering industry over the period 1993/94-2004/05. From table-7, it could be seen that the correlation between export-globalisation and other globalisation variables shows that there is a positive correlation, which ranges from 0.10 to 0.94. However, export-globalisa tion is negatively correlated with technology-globalisation variables including, ETIGDP, DTIGDP and TIGDP. Interestingly, study shows that there is a strong positive correlation between export-globalisation and foreign firm's export globalisation.While foreign firm's import globalisation has an extremely weak correlation with export-globalisation.

It has been observed that there is a strong positive correlation between import-globalisati- on and technology globalisation and foreign firm's import globalisation whose degree of association 0.81 and 0.86 respectively. Foreign firm's import globalisation has positive correlation with all other globalisation variables with the sole exception of net export.The degree of technology globalisation has an extremely strong correlation with embodied technology import globalisation whose degree of correlation is 0.99. There is a positive correlation between foreign firm's import globalisation and technology globalisation. It has also been observed that there is a strong positive correlation between foreign firm's import-globalisation and embodied technology import globalisation (refer Table-7).

Test of Significance Results

Let us now discuss the results of the test of significance at the aggregate and disaggregate level for the period of 1993/94-2004/05. To analyse if there is any significant difference in the case of the performance of foreign and domestic firms in the relative contribution into India's degree of economic globalisation we have looked in to the two broad dimen- sions of performance namely, trade globalisation and technology globalisation. There are three indicators have been employed to analyse the trade globalisation namely, EXGDP, IMGDP and NEXGDP. While the dimension of technology-globalisation performance is assessed by measuring ETIGDP and TIGDP ratios (refer Table-2).

Table-8. t-values of Globalisation Variables at the Aggregate Level, 1993/94-2004/05

YEAR	*EXGDP*	*IMGDP*	*ETIGDP*	*TIGDP*	*NEXGDP*
1993-94	0.3181**	0.2222**	-0.4567**	-0.2633**	-0.1940**
1994-95	-0.0708**	0.2863**	-1.5288**	-1.1712**	-0.3585**
1995-96	-0.2386**	0.0195**	-0.4549**	-0.1918**	-0.0702**
1996-97	-0.4604**	-0.0016**	-0.0199**	0.2002**	-0.1005**
1997-98	-0.4190**	0.2615**	-0.7893**	-0.7632**	-0.3202**
1998-99	-0.5482**	0.2644**	0.0527**	-0.0918**	-0.3412**
1999-00	-0.7259**	0.2485**	-0.3437**	-0.2673**	-0.3477**
2000-01	-0.7165**	0.2603**	-1.0885**	-0.7631**	-0.3353**
2001-02	-0.0196**	0.1912**	-1.3493**	-1.4947**	-0.2078**
2002-03	0.3022**	0.4504**	0.3863**	-0.7959**	-0.4283**
2003-04	0.3560**	0.4596**	0.3936**	0.0752**	-0.3844**
2004-05	0.3965**	0.4546**	0.3110**	0.0667**	-0.4081**

Note: Significant at the 5 per cent level

Most of the globalisation variables that are found statistically insignificant at the aggrega-te level over the period 1993/94-2004/05. This tends to suggest that there is no significant statistical difference between foreign and domestic firms in India's degrees of economic globalisation. However, most of the globalisation variables that were found not only – ve but also small t-values. In contrast to this, most of the import globalisation variable was found statistically insignificant but small positive t-values. The conclusion that derived from the study is that there is no significant difference between the two groups of firms.

Table-9 presents the relative contribution of foreign and domestic firms in India's degree of economic globalisation from a disaggregated perspective: Chemicals industry for the period of 1993/94-2004/05. Most of the globalisation variables including, technology and trade globalisation variables were found statistically insignificant at the five per cent level This tends to suggest that there is no significant statistical difference between foreign and domestic firms in India's degrees of economic globalisation in their relative contribution.

Table-9. t-values of Globalisation Variables at the Disaggregated Level- Chemicals Industry, 1993/94-2004/05

YEAR	*EXGDP*	*IMGDP*	*ETIGDP*	*TIGDP*	*NEXGDP*
1993-94	0.1903**	0.1700**	0.9920**	1.3203**	-0.1645**
1994-95	0.2171**	0.2884**	1.0454**	1.0382**	-0.3002**
1995-96	0.0516**	0.1692**	0.4178**	0.5058**	-0.1840**
1996-97	0.0137**	0.2253**	0.7718**	0.6785**	-0.2600**
1997-98	0.1047**	0.3488**	1.2188**	1.1194**	-0.3655**
1998-99	-0.1047**	0.3738**	0.5396**	0.5435**	-0.4090**
1999-00	-0.1128**	0.3859**	0.7558**	0.7743**	-0.4213**
2000-01	-0.0818**	0.3734**	1.1765**	1.0155**	-0.3915**
2001-02	0.2670**	0.2818**	0.9874**	0.3508**	-0.2609**
2002-03	0.3335**	0.4783**	0.9627**	0.1993**	-0.4512**
2003-04	0.6257**	0.5063**	0.3858**	0.3237**	-0.3764**
2004-05	0.8275**	0.5693**	0.4802**	0.4098**	-0.4195**

Note: Significant at the 5 per cent level

It has been observed that most of the globalisation variables were found statistically not only insignificant but also -ve t-values at the aggregate level (with the sole exception of IMGDP variable). In contrast to this, most of the globalisation variables including, trade and technology globalisation variables were found statistically not only insignificant but also +ve small t-values in Chemicals industry. The net export-globalisation variable was found statistically not significant at aggregate level and in chemicals industry. The result suggests from the Table-8 and 9 is that there is no significant difference between foreign and domestic firms in the case of the relative contribution to India's degrees of economic globalisation at aggregate level and in Chemicals industry for the period of 1993-2004.

Table-10 shows the relative performance of foreign and domestic firms in the degree of economic globalisation in India for the period of 1993/94-2004/05 from a disaggregated perspective: Engineering industry. There are few interesting findings can be derived from the result. The most prominent among them being (i) Most of the t-values of IMGDP are found statistically not significant however; t-values were not only negative but also high over the period 1997/98-2004/05. (ii) The most of the technology globalisation variables including, ETIGDP and TIGDP were found statistically insignificant but t-values are –ve and high over the period 1993/94-2004/05. (iii) The net export globalisation variable was found statistically not significant though, t-values were positive as compared to negative t-values at aggregate and in chemicals industry for the period of 1993/94-2004/05.

The conclusion from Table-10 emerged is that there is no significant statistical difference between foreign and domestic firms in the performance of globalisation variables. The conclusion that derived from the study is that there is no significant statistical difference between foreign and domestic firms in the case relative contribution to India's degrees of economic globalisation at the both aggregate and disaggregated level over the 1993/94 – 2004/05 period in India.

Table-10. t-values of Globalisation Variables at the Disaggregated Level – Engineering Industry, 1993/94-2004/05

YEAR	EXGDP	IMGDP	ETIGDP	TIGDP	NEXGDP
1993-94	0.2425**	-0.0375**	-1.3341**	-1.3535**	0.2044**
1994-95	-0.4612**	-0.2579**	-2.2670*	-1.9019**	-0.2056**
1995-96	-0.4635**	-0.8794**	-1.6899**	-1.3432**	0.9062**
1996-97	-0.9132**	-1.0066**	-1.4745**	-1.2367**	0.8262**
1997-98	-1.0182**	-1.3392**	-1.5503**	-1.6512**	1.1705**
1998-99	-0.7926**	-1.4537**	-1.5394**	-1.9041**	1.6419**
1999-00	-1.2716**	-1.5443**	-2.0437*	-2.1665*	1.2727**
2000-01	-1.2392**	-1.8784**	-1.6854**	-1.7326**	1.5066**
2001-02	-1.0061**	-2.1009*	-1.7077**	-1.9535**	1.7321**
2002-03	-0.4347**	-1.3672**	0.0226**	-0.9741**	1.3683**
2003-04	-1.0967**	-1.4133**	-0.1863**	-1.5984**	0.8845**
2004-05	-1.4858**	-2.0943*	-2.5878*	-3.1834*	1.3884**

Note: Significant at the 5 per cent level

Conclusion

This paper has analysed the relative contribution of foreign and domestic firms in India's degrees of economic globalisation for the period of 1993/94–2004/05, the reason being, the rapid rise in the quantity of foreign direct investment flows to the Indian economy in the 1990s. This has also been accompanied by the changes in the sectoral composition of FDI. But also, more importantly, it could be regarded as any change in foreign direct investment, which leads a country's trade system towards the higher degrees of economic globalisation. In other words, the degree of economic globalisation in general and the degrees of import and export globalisation in particular have affected by the pattern and magnitude of FDI flows received by India. There are some findings that derived from the study. The most prominent among them being (i) The degree of economic globalisation came to India primarily in the form of degrees of import globalisation rather than the degrees of export globalisation. The former is higher than the latter. Admittedly in a high measure. (ii) Globalisation has been impacting negatively on industrial development of the Indian economy, the reason being, domestic firms appear to be performing as a high import-oriented globalising firms and it has also been observed that foreign firms appear to be performing as a major importer of technology, which has been impacting positively on industrial development. (iii) The conclusion that derived from the study is that there is no significant statistical difference between foreign and domestic firms in India in the case of globalisation variables over for the period 1993/94-2004/05 at the both aggregate and disaggregated level. The policy recommendation is that government should continue to ensure rationale economic policies that will continually enhance the realization of the much-expected benefits of globalisation through foreign economic influence in the sense that international trade, economic relations with other countries and FDI inflows.

References

Gikandi, S (2002): 'Globalisation and the Claims of Postcoloniality', *South Atlantic Quarterly*, Vol.100 (3), pp. 627-658.

Kumar, N (1994): 'Multinational Enterprises and Industrial Distribution, Characteristics and Performance', Routledge, London.

Kumar, N (2005): 'Liberalisation, Foreign Direct Investment Flows and Development: Indian Experience in the 1990s', *Economic and Political Weekly,* April-2, pp. 1459-1469.

Lall, S and S. Mohammad (1983): 'Foreign Ownership and Export Performance in the Large Corporate Sector of India', *The Journal of Development Studies,* Vol.20 (1), pp. 56-67.

Lopez, P.P (2005): 'Foreign Direct Investment, Exports and Imports in Mexico', *The World Economy*, Vol.28 (8), pp. 1157-1172.

Markusen, J.R., (2005): 'Modelling the Offshoring of White-Collar Services: From Comparative Advantage to the New Theories of Trade and FDI'. NBER and CEPR

Salawu, R.O (2006): 'Globalisation and Industrial Development in Nigeria: An Empirical Investigation', *Indian Journal of Economics,* November-2006, pp. 343- 358.

Srinivasan, T.N (2006): 'China, India and the World Economy', *Economic and Political Weekly,* August-26, pp. 3716-3727.

Subrahmanian, K.K and K.J Joseph (1994): 'Foreign Control and Export Intensity of Firms in Indian Industry', *Working Paper*, Centre for Development Studies, Trivandrum, Kerala.

Appendix

Figure A1: Net Foreign Direct Investment Flows to India for the Period of 1991-2004

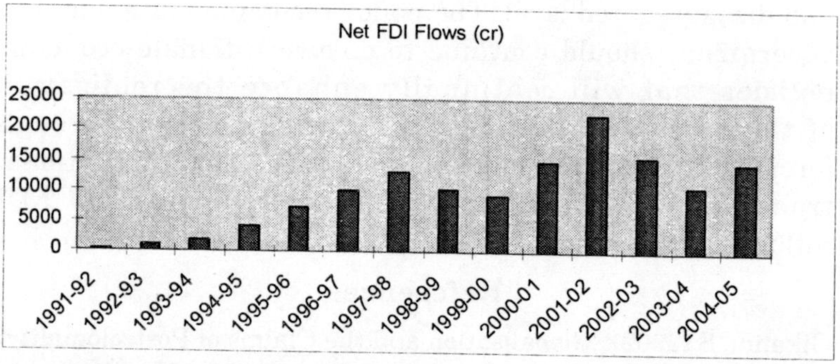

Table-A1: Data used for the Study

Year	*GDP* (Rs. Crore)*	*Aggregate Export (Rs. Crore)*	*Aggregate Import (Rs. Crore)*	*Chemicals Export (Rs. Crore)*	*Chemicals Import (Rs. Crore)*	*Engineering Export (Rs. Crore)*	*Engineering Import (Rs. Crore)*
1993-94	781345	9514.44	27727.38	4579.64	18919.27	4934.80	8808.11
1994-95	917058	12316.98	29463.49	5122.98	19118.89	7194.00	10344.60
1995-96	1073271	14611.91	39176.79	6225.77	23840.68	8386.14	15336.11
1996-97	1243571	18446.29	52625.85	8182.61	31235.36	10263.68	21390.49
1997-98	1390148	21108.24	77123.84	9702.63	54890.34	11405.61	22233.50
1998-99	1598127	24203.48	75498.06	10579.73	53719.28	13623.75	21778.78
1999-00	1761838	24651.84	72738.62	11731.22	50103.46	12920.62	22635.16
2000-01	1902999	29656.20	96313.74	14162.77	72650.71	15493.43	23663.03
2001-02	2081474	38490.35	107070.24	21310.26	81450.21	17180.09	25620.03
2002-03	2254888	44041.34	119538.57	26020.79	94270.04	18020.55	25268.53
2003-04	2519785	58585.34	135729.82	32645.50	106308.87	25939.84	29420.95
2004-05	2838123	78812.66	165919.88	43526.43	127534.95	35286.23	38384.93

Data source: 'PROWESS' published by the Centre for Monitoring Indian Economy (CMIE)

Note: Gross Domestic Product (GDP) at Factor Cost – All India, 1993/94 – 2004/05 (in Current Prices) Base 1993-1994

Table-A2. Data used for the Study

Year	*Chemicals Industry Domestic firm's Export (Rs. Crore)*	*Chemicals Industry Domestic firm's Export (Rs. Crore)*	*Chemicals Industry Foreign firm's Export (Rs. Crore)*	*Chemicals Industry Foreign firm's Export (Rs. Crore)*
1993-94	3939.31	16426.46	640.33	2492.81
1994-95	4419.60	17120.83	703.38	1998.06
1995-96	5221.33	20528.31	1004.44	3312.37
1996-97	6850.88	27113.48	1331.73	4121.88
1997-98	8148.45	50019.69	1554.18	4870.65
1998-99	8708.64	48610.14	1871.09	5109.14
1999-00	9716.29	45218.74	2014.93	4884.72
2000-01	11650.06	66008.55	2512.71	6642.16
2001-02	18234.02	72499.46	3076.24	8950.75
2002-03	22898.01	36875.98	3122.78	7394.06
2003-04	29543.66	97578.43	3101.84	8730.44
2004-05	39881.65	116958.45	3644.78	10576.50

Data source: 'PROWESS' published by the Centre for Monitoring Indian Economy (CMIE)

Table-A3. Data used for the Study

Year	*Chemicals Industry Domestic firm's Export (Rs. Crore)*	*Chemicals Industry Domestic firm's Export (Rs. Crore)*	*Chemicals Industry Foreign firm's Export (Rs. Crore)*	*Chemicals Industry Foreign firm's Export (Rs. Crore)*
1993-94	4010.70	6955.45	924.10	1852.66
1994-95	5496.68	7979.05	1697.32	2365.55
1995-96	6397.71	11273.95	1988.43	4062.16
1996-97	7654.08	15557.83	2609.60	5832.66
1997-98	8443.92	15825.29	2961.69	6408.21
1998-99	10309.14	15387.26	3314.61	6391.52
1999-00	9602.68	16067.60	3317.94	6567.56
2000-01	11466.36	16173.77	4027.07	7489.26
2001-02	12738.55	17553.37	4441.54	8066.66
2002-03	13981.36	18179.40	4039.19	7089.13
2003-04	19616.56	21311.58	6323.28	8109.37
2004-05	26866.85	27660.03	8419.38	10724.90

Data source: 'PROWESS' published by the Centre for Monitoring Indian Economy (CMIE)

1. I heartily thank Prof. A.A Baby for the tremendous encouragement and inspirations throughout the work. Some phrases and ideas have been taken from Salawu, Srinivasan and others. However, I stand alone for the analysis and any errors in the present paper.

* Preliminary draft for presentation. Not to be quoted or reproduced.

ii Mauritius has become second largest source of foreign direct investment, the reason being, agreement of "Double Taxation Avoidance Agreement" signed in 1990 between India and Mauritius.

iii See Lopez (2005) for more details.

3

Wage Inequality in Manufacturing Industries under Neo-Liberal Reform : A Case of West Bengal and Gujarat

Panchanan Das

I. Introduction

The object of this paper is to look at the incidence of wage inequality among distinct types of workers across two-digit manufacturing industries in the registered sector both within and between two states in India, namely West Bengal and Gujarat over the period 1979-80 to 2002-03. The incidence of wage inequality in manufacturing has been a cause of concern because manufacturing activities constitute an important part of all economic activities. Although the extent of inequality is not captured fully by wage disparities alone and, in many cases, inequality in asset distribution may typically be greater than income inequality, wage is the largest single element in income of the working class and its distribution seems roughly to be similar to their income distribution (Williamson, 1982). Thus wage inequality has been widely used as an alternative to income inequality in the literature (Atkinson, 1997). In addition, inequality in educational attainment, in health standards, in access to clean water and sanitation, or access to government services constitute the social face of deprivation cited by the poor themselves. Instead of covering all such dimensions of inequality, this paper is constrained to look at the extent of wage inequality across two-digit industries in the two leading states in the western and eastern parts of the country.

An enormous wage inequality between workers engaged in the organised and the unorganised sectors goes on world over. In India, the unorganised sector is having six times of workforce of the organised sector, while total wage bill in the former is half of the latter[1] . Workers in the unorganised sector are forced to accept even below subsistence wage and they normally suffer from terrible working conditions with practically no income or social security. Workers in the organised sector, on the other hand, are able to enjoy relatively higher wages, better working conditions and above all, most secure jobs anywhere in the developing world. They are supposed a privileged group who often have a much higher standard of living than common masses, including peasants and agricultural labourers and even many of the service sector workers (Bagchi, 1972). Thus the incidence of wage inequality of the workers in total manufacturing seems to be much higher than what actually shows in the registered sector.

A few number of studies captured some aspects of wage inequality in Indian manufacturing. Using Employment and Unemployment surveys 1993-94 and 1999-2000, Glinskaya et al (2005) investigated wage differentials between the public and private sectors in India, and found, by applying their own methodologies, that the public sector premium ranges between 62% and 102% over the private-formal sector. Golbraith et al. (2004) estimated Theil indices of pay, without specifying whether it covers total wages or total emoluments, in the ASI sector in India covering 1973 to 1997 and observed a rising trend in pay inequality among workers in this sector during the post-liberalisation period. In this paper we look at different aspects of wage inequality separately for unskilled and skilled workers defined below in registered manufacturing industries located in West Bengal and Gujarat over the period 1979-80 to 2002-03.

The analysis of this paper proceeds as follows. Section 2 discusses the data source and methodological issues in measuring wage inequality. Different aspects of wage inequality for workers engaging roughly similar kind of work in manufacturing are addressed in section 3. Section 4 finds relationship between wage and productivity growth in manufacturing. Causality, if any, between them is examined by applying vector error correction method. Section 5 offers concluding remarks.

II. MEASURING WAGE INEQUALITY

2.1 Data and variables

The data from the Annual Survey of Industries (ASI) published by Central Statistical Organisation (CSO), Government of India has been used in estimating wage inequality separately for ordinary workers and other employees in manufacturing across different industry groups. In annexure IV of the ASI, workers are defined to include all persons engaged directly or indirectly in the production process. Employees, on the other hand, include all workers defined above and other persons engaged in supervisory and managerial activities. We treat the former group in employees as unskilled labour and the latter group as skilled labour. Thus figures for skilled labour can be obtained by subtracting the number of workers from total employees engaged in a factory. ASI also provides data for wages and total emoluments corresponding to pay for workers and employees defined in it. Thus pay for a skilled worker is obtained by subtracting wages from total emoluments given in the ASI. Money wages are deflated by cost of living index numbers for industrial workers provided by the Labour Bureau, Ministry of Labour, Government of India, to have real wages. There are, however, some well-known inherent problems in constructing cost of living index numbers (Bagchi, 1972) and we have to bear some limitations of it.

2.2 Methodology

In this study we have used Theil index as a measure of wage inequality. This index is a member of generalised entropy (GE) measures of inequality. GE is a class of inequality measures having the following formula:

$$GE(\alpha) = \frac{1}{\alpha^2 - \alpha}\left\{\frac{1}{N}\sum_i\sum_j\left(\frac{X_{ij}}{\mu}\right)^{\alpha} - 1\right\}. \qquad ...(1)$$

where a is a parameter representing the weight given at different points of the wage distribution. The most commonly used values of a are 0, 1 and 2. A value of $\alpha = 0$ gives more weight to wage differences in the lower tail, $\alpha = 1$ applies equal weights across the distribution, while a value of $\alpha = 2$ gives proportionately more weight to the gaps in the upper tail. Theil index of inequality is the GE measure with parameter $\alpha = 1$. By applying L-Hostital's rule, at $\alpha = 1$, Theil index takes the following form:

$$T = \frac{1}{N}\sum_i\sum_j \frac{X_{ij}}{\mu}\ln\left(\frac{X_{ij}}{\mu}\right) \qquad ...(2)$$

where X_{ij} is the real wage of person in industry i in state j, m is the mean wage and N is the total number of persons. It gives equal weights across the distribution. The Theil inequality index defined in equation (2) is just a weighted geometric mean of relative wages. Under perfect equality the value of index equals zero. There is, however, no upper limit for this inequality index; it depends on the size of the population.

Theil index obeys the following principles:

Pigou-Dalton principle: the transfer of income from someone lower in the income distribution to someone higher in the income distribution, holding everyone else's income constant, should increase the numerical value of an inequality index.

Principle of Symmetry: any permutation of the *n*-vector of individual incomes will result in the same measure of inequality.

Principle of Homogeneity: a proportionate change in everyone's income will not change the inequality index.

Theil index also allows us to decompose the total change in wage inequality into the change within groups and the change between groups, provided that members of the population are classified into mutually exclusive and exhaustive groups.

$$T = T^b{}_g + T^w{}_g$$

For aggregative data $T^b{}_g$ can be used as a lower bound for Theil's T Statistic in the population:

$$T_g^b = \sum_i \sum_j \frac{X_{ij}}{X} \log \left(\frac{X_{ij}/X}{N_{ij}/N} \right) \qquad ...(3)$$

where i indexes the industry groups and j indexes state, X_{ij} and N_{ij} represent wage and number of workers in industry i and in state j, X and N give the total number of workers and total wage respectively. Theil index defined in equation (2) measures between-group inequality. Between-group inequality is computed by assuming each group member receives the mean group wage.

Within-group inequality is defined as a weighted sum of inequality within each of the subgroups where the weights are relative wages:

$$T_g^w = \sum_i \left(\frac{X_i}{X} \right) T_i \qquad ...(4)$$

T_i is the Theil index of group i.

The basic advantage of using Theil index is that it gives meaningful result even for a distribution with limited information (Golbraith et al. 2004). The decomposition of this index into between and within components, however, is not linked to individual earnings functions in a rigorous manner. Thus, although this decomposition is mathematically correct and seems intuitive and appealing for descriptive purposes, it does not provide an unambiguous basis for evaluating the partial effects of individual factors on total income inequality. Therefore, this decomposition cannot tell us which factor is more dominant in determining the level of income inequality (Adelman et al, 1984).

III. Wage Inequality in Manufacturing : Estimating Theil Index

The widening wage gap between skilled and unskilled workers in industries particularly in the developing world is well documented. The uptrend in wage differential between them is a consequence of disproportional movement of their pay even in real terms and the rate of disproportion is incredibly high in a fast growing region. The rate of increase of wage rate for the supervisory class is far above the rate for the workers in such region particularly in the 1990s and afterwards (Das, unpublished document). The increase in wage rate for workers in many cases, however, is mainly due to make up for the rise in the cost of living. In most cases employers as oligopsonists are in a position to exploit the workers and some compensation for increases in cost of living has been made not through the normal way but after costly negotiations between workers' union and the employers (Bagchi, 1972).

In this section we have estimated wage inequality not between skilled and unskilled workers but between workers engaged in roughly similar kind of work in the organised manufacturing sector in West Bengal and Gujarat. In estimating different components of Theil index we have applied the methodology used in Galbraith et al. (2004)[2] to the ASI data by taking into account the pay for unskilled and skilled workers separately. In our exercise the elementary unit is two-digit manufacturing industry in West Bengal and Gujarat. We have taken 15 two-digit manufacturing industries in the factory sector located in these two states over the period 1979-80 to 2002-03. Thus our data set consists of 30 elementary units for every year within the reference period. As mentioned above, total Theil index is a resultant of index for 'within' group and index for 'between' group. These sub indices may be industry specific or region specific.

3.1 Overall Inequality

Figure 1 displays Theil index (total) of wage for unskilled and skilled workers across 15 two-digit industries in two states in India over the period 1979-80 to 2002-03. Wage inequality among unskilled workers is found to be substantially higher than inequality among skilled workers in almost every year. While the values of total Theil index in our study are not exactly the same as portrayed in Galbraith et al. (2004) owing to the differences not only in composition of elementary units but in the reference period as well, the pattern of overall inequality shown in Figure 1 roughly be similar to the type exposed in them. Although there has been no particular trend in estimated total Theil values over the past couple of decades, wage inequality particularly for skilled workers declined in the 1980s and increased sharply in the 1990s. For unskilled workers also we observe a similar type of change in inequality during the same period but relatively at a lower rate. Thus wage inequality for manufacturing workers of both kinds in the two states together has started to rise after 1990-91.

Figure 1. Theil index of wages: West Bengal and Gujarat

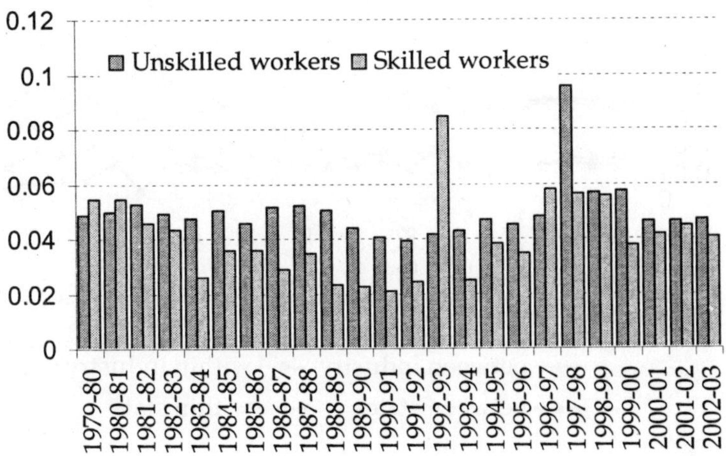

3.2 Components of inequality

One can analyse the pattern of overall wage inequality displayed in Figure 1 by decomposing total Theil values into 'within' and 'between' components. To examine wage disparity between the two states we have used the estimated Theil indices across industries within-state and the indices between-state. Similarly, inequality across industries is captured by analysing Theil indices between states within-industry and inequality between-industry. Figures 2a and 2b present such aspects of inequality for unskilled and skilled labour respectively over 1979-80 to 2002-03. The estimated results reveal that the wage inequality between industries is more prominent than inequality between states for either type of workers in registered manufacturing. Inequality between industries contributes much more to overall wage inequality displayed in Figure 1 than do increases in regional inequality.

Figure 2a Wage inequality (Theil index) for unskilled workers

Figure 2b Wage inequality (Theil index) for skilled workers

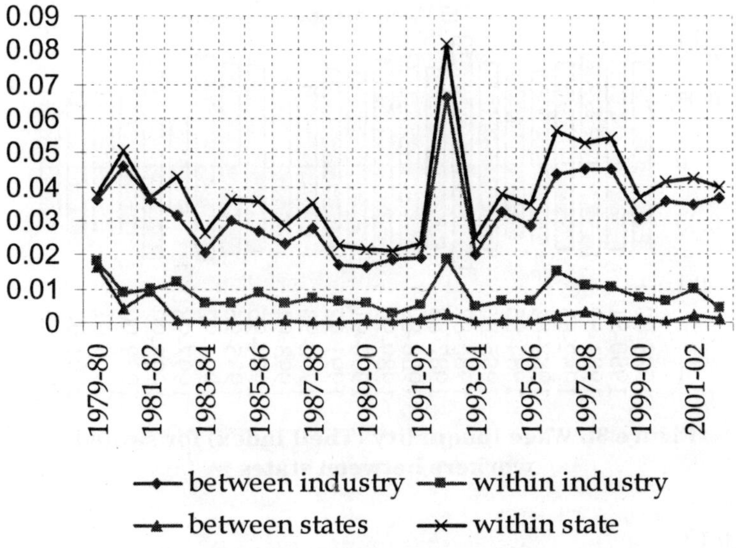

3.3 Contribution of individual state to overall inequality

The components of Theil index between states as shown in Figures 3a and 3b reveal that the wage per capita for workers doing roughly similar jobs in registered manufacturing are very much different in different states in our study. Theil index for unskilled workers in West Bengal is positive, while that in Gujarat is found to be negative all through (Figure 3a), implying that wage rate for unskilled workers is much higher in the former than in the latter.

For skilled workers, on the other hand, Theil values in West Bengal were positive in the 1980s and turned to be negative thereafter and the reverse is observed in Gujarat (Figure 3b). Thus payment for skilled workers was higher in West Bengal in the 1980s and was much higher in the

Figure 3a Wage inequality (Theil index) for unskilled workers between states

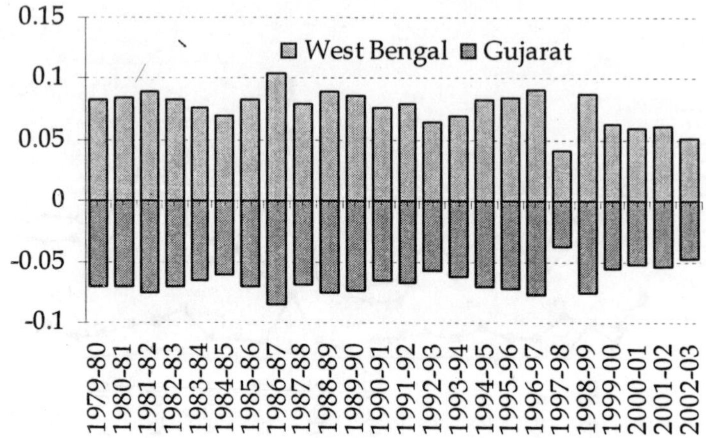

Figure 3b Wage inequality (Theil index) for skilled workers between states

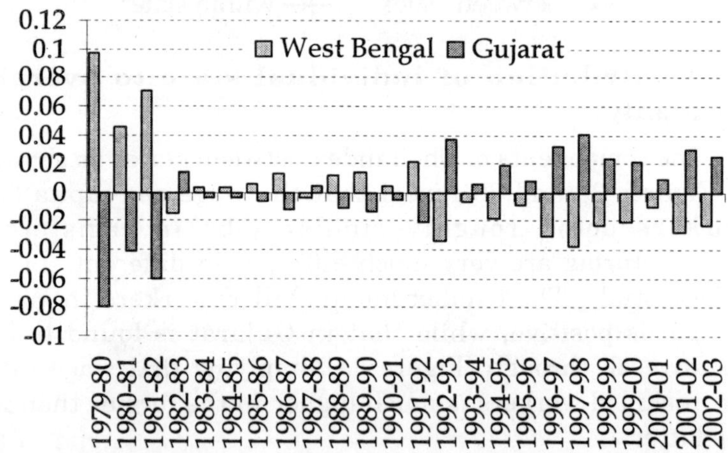

early 1980s, while the rate of pay for them was better in Gujarat in the 1990s. By comparing the Figures 3a and 3b one can observe that the wage differential between the states is much higher for unskilled workers than the regional variation of wage for skilled workers.

What have been suggested by the Theil index between the states shown above are confirmed by the actual time path of real wage rates in the ASI sector for both types of workers as observed between West Bengal and Gujarat (Figures 4 and 5). There has been a persistent wage difference between the states even for workers engaging roughly in the similar kind of jog in manufacturing. Real wage per worker of either type in registered industries in West Bengal has been significantly higher compared to Gujarat till the early 1990s. The higher incidence of casualisation of labour in Gujarat than in West Bengal (Bagchi and Das, 2005) is largely attributable to relatively lower wages in the former.

Figure 4. Movement of real wage rate in total registered industries: unskilled workers, 1970-71 to 2002-03

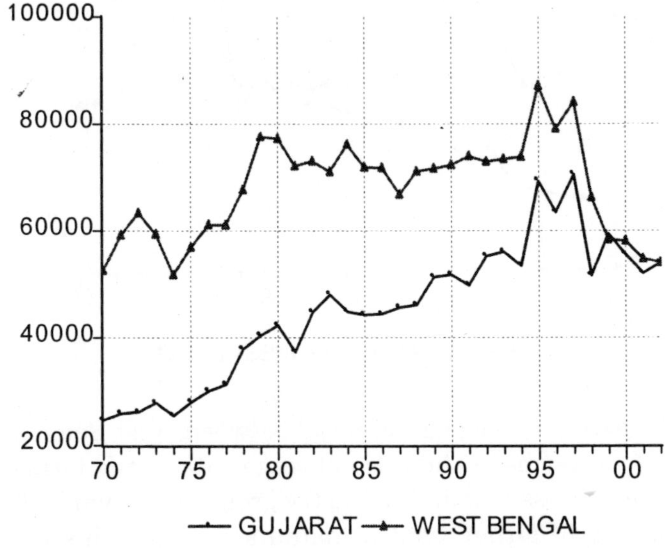

The wage per unskilled worker in West Bengal industries had been falling in the first half of the 1980 followed by an uptrend in the 1970s, it had stagnated between the late 1980s and mid 1990s, and thereafter it began to crash down.

There has also been no particular time trend in wage per capita for skilled workers in registered industries in the state. On the other hand, wage rate for both types of workers in Gujarat industries had moved up with some fluctuations till the mid 1990s and started to fall drastically there after. Managers and supervisors in manufacturing enjoyed much more pay in this state compared to West Bengal under neo-liberal reform.

Figure 5 Movement of real wage rate in total registered industries: skilled workers, 1970-71 to 2002-03

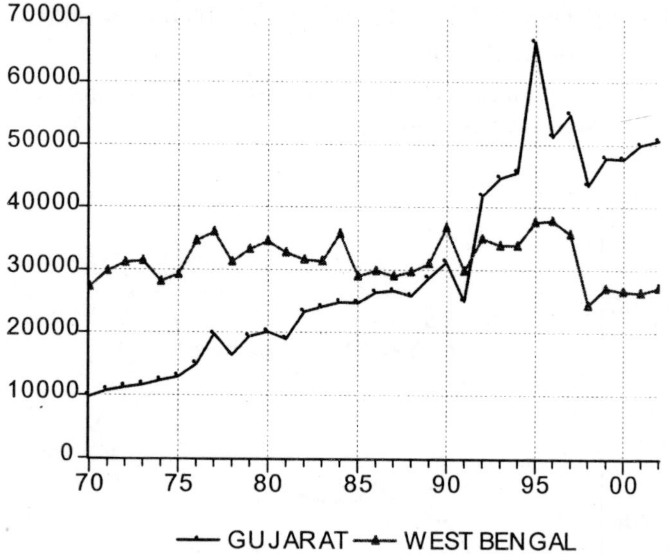

The extent of wage differential between West Bengal and Gujarat, in terms of the ratio of wage rate in the former to the latter, across two-digit industry groups is shown in Table 1. Workers of either type in manufacturing industries in West Bengal received much higher wages in almost every industry group in the ASI sector and indeed in some industries like basic metals, leather and beverages, the wage rate had been double or even three times more compared to those in Gujarat during the period 1979 to 1990. In West

Bengal the wage rate, particularly for unskilled workers, continued to be higher in the 1990s, but the wage gap between the two states has fallen during this period. Pay for skilled labour had also been higher in almost every industry group in West Bengal compared to Gujarat in the 1980s. In the following decade, however, the differences in wage rate between the states has declined in every industry group, and in some industries skilled workers are paid more in Gujarat than in West Bengal.

Table 1 Wage ratio between West Bengal and Gujarat: across two-digit industries

	Workers		*Other employees*	
	1979-1990	*1991-2002*	*1979-1990*	*1991-2002*
Food products	1.11	0.70	1.01	0.75
Beverages, tobacco	3.63	1.44	2.73	1.32
Textiles	1.08	1.38	0.95	1.09
Textile products	1.67	1.24	1.05	0.95
Wood, furniture	0.99	0.91	1.02	0.87
Paper, printing	1.33	1.23	1.19	1.16
Leather	2.13	1.60	2.11	1.09
Chemicals	1.10	1.05	0.86	0.69
Rubber, petroleum	1.63	1.52	1.12	0.94
Non-metallic products	1.79	1.49	1.22	0.97
Basic metals	2.16	2.08	1.47	1.32
Metal products	1.56	1.32	1.10	1.20
Machinery	1.66	1.45	1.28	1.09
Transport equipment	1.59	2.08	1.23	1.30
Other manufacturing	2.94	1.61	1.69	1.38

Source: Annual Survey of Industries, Various issues, CSO, Government of India.

Note: Figures shown in the Table are calculated as the ratio of wage rate in West Bengal to that in Gujarat.

The dissimilarity in wage rates between the states mentioned above may be a result of the substantial differences not only in composition of industry and technology used, but in the attitude of distinct state governments towards their working people and bargaining power of workers as well. The relatively higher wages for manufacturing workers in West Bengal may partly be owing to the strong bargaining power of labour union in the state.

3.4 Contribution of Different Industries to Inequality

We have already noted that inequality across industries within a region has been more dominating than inequality between states. Figures 6a and 6b display Theil indices of wages in different manufacturing industry groups in the states for unskilled and skilled workers respectively over time. Wage inequality for ordinary workers is mainly concentrated in chemicals, basic metals, and transport equipment industries paying more than average wages, and in food products and non metallic product industries with wages lower than the average level. While the incidence of wage inequality in transport equipment industries has declined, that in basic metal and chemical industries goes up markedly in the 1990s.

Figure 6a Wage inequality (Theil index) for unskilled workers between industries

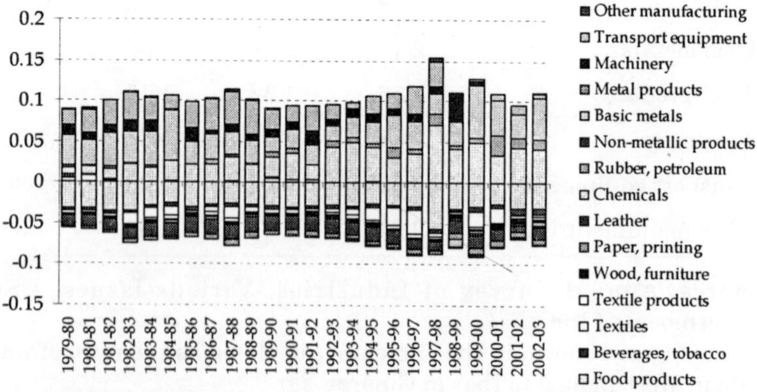

Figure 6b Wage inequality (Theil index) for skilled workers between industries

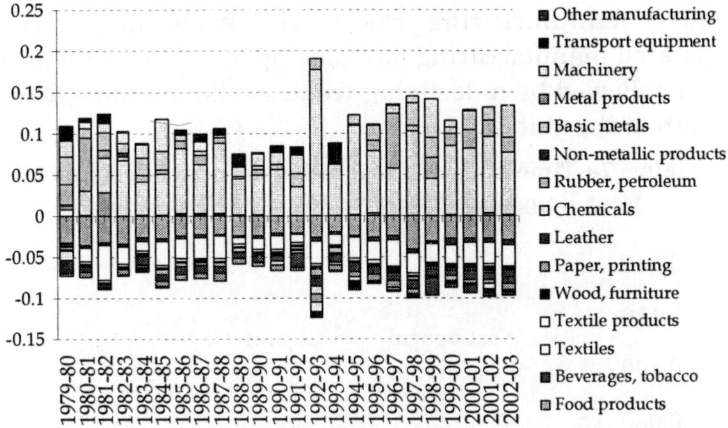

Wage inequality for skilled workers has also been much higher in chemical industries where wage rates are relatively higher than the rate in other industries. Among the low wage industries, inequality has been persistent in food products and textiles. In many industries, particularly in petroleum and basic metal industries, wage inequality for skilled workers has increased in the post-reform period.

3.5 Temporal Pattern of Wage Inequality

By comparing different components of Theil index of wages for two different types of workers we have shown that inequality across industries has been significant in the manufacturing sector of the two states in our study. Figures 7a and 7b display the differences in the incidence of wage inequality across two-digit industry groups over time as observed between West Bengal and Gujarat for unskilled and skilled workers respectively. Wage inequality for ordinary workers as for skilled workers had been lower in the former compared to the latter till the late 1990s. A sharp rise in over all wage inequality among ordinary workers in manufacturing in the year 1997-98 shown in Figure 1 was accounted for by the steep rise of inequality among them in

West Bengal (Figure 7a). On the other hand a steep rise in overall pay inequality for skilled workers in 1992-93 was caused by an exceptional rise of Theil value for them in Gujarat manufacturing (Figure 7b). Wage inequality in registered manufacturing has gone up at a rapid rate in the 1990s followed by a declining trend in the previous decade in both of the states.

Figure 7a Time path of Theil index across industries in West Bengal and Gujarat for unskilled labour

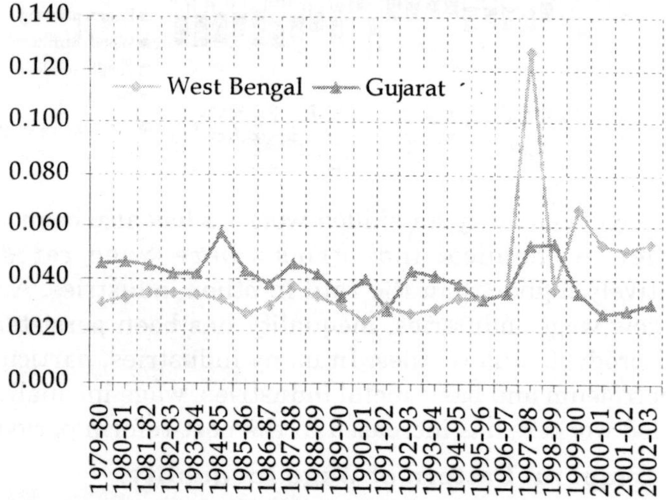

The persistent wage differential of the type described above is partly an outcome of government policies as well as the way of fixing wage rates. Wages in a country without well developed labour market like ours are not usually determined by market conditions but by the institutional arrangement of wage settlement. In the organized sector in India, both public and private, wages are set through a collective bargaining process. Workers' unions and the management of each organization take part in this process. Moreover, in many cases, pay structure and other benefits of workers in this sector are settled periodically by the Pay Commission of the Government of India on some normative

Figure 7b Time path of Theil index across industries in West Bengal and Gujarat for skilled labour

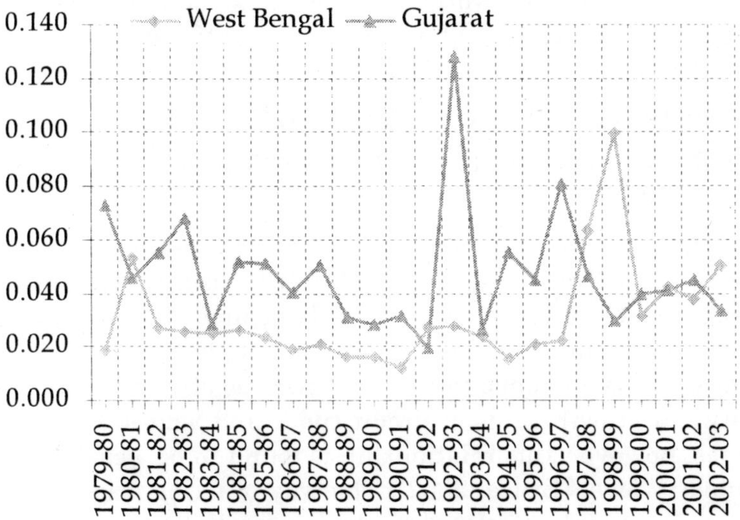

considerations. Apparently, this way of fixing pay hardly takes into account productivity and other economic factors and wages in many cases may rise disproportionately. We will discuss the issue in detail in the next section. In the unorganized sector, where labour is vulnerable to exploitation due to illiteracy and having no effective bargaining power, minimum wage rates are fixed by the government under the provisions of the Minimum Wages Act, 1948. In 1996 the national minimum wage was fixed at Rs. 35.00 per day and was raised to Rs. 45.00 in 1999 and further to Rs. 66.00 in 2004. It may be thought that the fixation of pay through government initiatives is more likely to maintain uniformity in wage structure across the regions. But the government in different states has failed to uphold homogeneity in actual pay due to some political or other reasons. While in West Bengal the lowest and the highest rates of minimum wages are fixed at Rs.62 and Rs.204 respectively, the rates were much lower in Gujarat (Rs.50 and Rs. 99) and many other industrially advanced states

(Annual Report 2004-05, Ministry of Labour, GOI). Thus remarkable pay differentials between different types of workers or between workers doing the same kind of job in different areas persist in the sub continent and it is attributable, at least partly, to the institutional factors.

IV. WAGE AND PRODUCTIVITY GROWTH

4.1 Relationship between Growth Rates of Wage and Productivity

In the text book economic theory, workers' contributions to output will rise as labour productivity rises causing more demand for workers. If wages are determined by supply and demand, an increase in demand will imply an increase in wages. Thus economic theory predicts a positive relationship between growth rates of productivity and wages. In many cases, however, this relationship is found to be weak at the industry level (Bruce, 2002). The way of fixing wages even in organized manufacturing industries in India could hardly reconcile the positive relation between productivity and wage.

Thus the extent to which the productivity gains are shared by the workers is an empirical question. While the productivity gains at least in industrially advanced regions in the reform period are by now well-documented, little work has considered how those gains actually pass to the workers. The empirical relation between growth rates of wage and productivity can be explored by allowing for causality and cointegration between the two within a VAR framework. Table 2 gives the estimated results of this relationship for West Bengal and Gujarat manufacturing by utilising data for total industries recorded in the ASI over 1970-71 to 2002-03.

As shown in Table 2, wage growth and productivity growth are significantly cointrgrated implying long run relationship between them in both of the states. The cointegration coefficient gives a rough idea about wage elasticity with respect to productivity. The estimated values of this wage elasticity vary between the states: the high growth state of Gujarat registers low value of elasticity. Although wage growth and productivity growth are cointegrated, the estimated figures reveal a short run disequilibrium relationship between them. Empirical evidence in our study reveals virtually no causal connection between wages and productivity growth in manufacturing industries not only in West Bengal but in industrially advanced state of Gujarat as well.

Table 2 Relation between wage growth and productivity growth in registered manufacturing: VAR estimation

West Bengal:

$$Dg_{yt} = -0.355u_{t-1} + 0.047Dg_{yt-1} - 0.087Dg_{xt-1}$$

(-1.817) (0.211) (-1.217)

$$Dg_{xt} = 2.567u_{t-1} - 0.875Dg_{yt-1} + 0.283Dg_{xt-1}$$

(5.622) (-1.664) (1.682)

$$u_{t-1} = (g_y - 0.586g_x - 0.035)_{t-1}$$

(-4.182) (-2.212)

Gujarat:

$$Dg_{yt} = -0.812u_{t-1} - 0.302Dg_{yt-1} - 0.145Dg_{xt-1}$$

(-3.117) (-1.795) (-1.836)

$$Dg_{xt} = 2.234u_{t-1} - 1.118Dg_{yt-1} - 0.090Dg_{xt-1}$$

(3.079) (-2.381) (-0.411)

$$u_{t-1} = (g_y - 0.455g_x - 0.036)_{t-1}$$

(-3.448) (-1.847)

Source: As for Table 1

Note: Dg_{yt} and Dg_{xt} represent change in wage growth and productivity growth respectively in time t. Figures in parentheses give t values.

Labour productivity in manufacturing grows at a faster proportional rate compared to wage rate in either of the state, but the mismatch is found to be very high in Gujarat particularly in the 1990s. Estimated figures of growth rates of wage and labour productivity across two digit industry groups in West Bengal and Gujarat over different policy regimes are shown in Tables 3 and 4 respectively. In West Bengal growth rates of real wages ranges between -2.7 percent in beverages and tobacco industries to 2.9 percent in petroleum products and in Gujarat it lies between -0.7 percent in transport equipment to 4.4 percent in beverages and tobacco industries over the period 1979-80 to 2002-03. There has been a severe deterioration in the growth of real wage in almost every industry in either of the state in the deregulation phase; indeed the actual real wage per worker in many industries has declined in this period. Food products industries in West Bengal suffered from the record fall in wage followed by textile products in the deregulation phase compared to the earlier regime. Although Jute Textiles in this state are not so seriously affected in terms of wage fall, Cotton textiles in Gujarat have been badly affected in the reform period relative to the controlled regime. There has, however, been a great contrast in the pattern of change of labour productivity between these two states. Labour productivity in a large number of industries in West Bengal has fallen, while in almost all industries in Gujarat it had jumped up in the reform period, compared to the earlier period. Thus the disparity in wage growth and productivity growth has significantly been higher in Gujarat than in West Bengal.

Table 3 Wage and productivity growth across two-digit industries in West Bengal

Industry groups	*Real Wage*			*Productivity*		
	1979-2002	*1979-1985*	*1986-2002*	*1979-2002*	*1979-1985*	*1986-2002*
Food products	0.1***	6.4	-1.9**	2.6*	18.4	-0.4***
Beverages, tobacco	-2.7	0.4***	-4.2	3.5***	-26.7***	-2.2***
Textiles	1.9	0.7***	1.2	3.0	-4.6	3.0
Textile products	1.7	4.5	0.1***	3.3*	16.8***	2.7***
Wood, furniture	0.8*	0.9	0.0***	-1.5	-0.4***	-4.2
Paper, printing	1.1	-1.8	0.9	4.5	-1.1***	6.7

Industry groups	*Real Wage*			*Productivity*		
	1979-2002	*1979-1985*	*1986-2002*	*1979-2002*	*1979-1985*	*1986-2002*
Leather	0.2***	-0.8***	0.5***	5.0	7.2*	8.9
Chemicals	1.5	2.2	0.5***	8.6	1.6***	10.5
Rubber, petroleum	2.9	1.4	2.2	1.1***	0.7***	-4.9***
Non-metallic products	1.2	2.0*	0.5	5.3	1.5	7.6
Basic metals	1.6	1.3***	1.9	3.3	2.6***	7.2
Metal products	0.8	-0.1***	1.3	3.6	1.0***	3.8
Machinery	1.1	1.0***	0.5	3.5	3.7***	2.8
Transport equipment	1.6	3.2	0.4***	2.1	4.4	1.0***
Other manufacturing	-0.6***	0.5***	-2.5*	4.9	31.4*	5.2**
Adjusted R-squared	0.9995	0.9999	0.9998	0.9976	0.9997	0.9981
Durbin-Watson stat	1.5457	2.2219	1.9959	1.8131	2.4052	2.1231

Source: As for Table 1

Note: * significant at 5% level,

** significant at 10% level,

*** insignificant, and the rest are significant at 1% level.

Table 4 Wage and productivity growth across two-digit industries in Gujarat

Industry groups	*Real Wage*			*Productivity*		
	1979-2002	*1979-1985*	*1986-2002*	*1979-2002*	*1979-1985*	*1986-2002*
Food products	4.0	6.1	2.2	6.2	7.3**	4.6
Beverages, tobacco	4.4	5.8**	4.5	7.4	-1.0***	10.5
Textiles	0.0***	1.8***	-0.8*	3.1	2.9**	2.9
Textile products	4.3	5.5	3.5	4.7	14.0	4.0
Wood, furniture	2.0	3.4	2.8	1.0***	8.1	-0.8***
Paper, printing	1.8	3.8	0.5***	4.5	3.0***	5.4
Leather	2.6	4.8	2.5	7.9	15.6	10.9
Chemicals	1.9	5.1	1.1	8.0	10.8	7.6
Rubber, petroleum	3.3	1.2***	3.6	7.7	3.6***	8.2
Non-metallic products	2.8	0.9***	3.4	9.3	3.9***	10.7

Industry groups	Real Wage			Productivity		
	1979-2002	1979-1985	1986-2002	1979-2002	1979-1985	1986-2002
Basic metals	1.9	2.5	2.1	7.8	-3.2***	9.4
Metal products	2.0	2.5	1.2***	3.2	0.0***	3.2
Machinery	2.2	4.7	1.3	5.3	8.3	3.9
Transport equipment	-0.7***	-2.4**	-1.5***	4.5	-2.2***	5.5
Other manufacturing	4.3	0.7***	5.2	7.9	9.6**	6.7
Adjusted R-squared	0.9969	0.9998	0.9990	0.9978	0.9998	0.9982
Durbin-Watson stat	1.5128	2.2588	1.8203	1.9116	2.7110	2.1340

Source: As for Table 1
Note: * significant at 5% level,
** significant at 10% level,
*** insignificant, and the rest are significant at 1% level.

In many cases the disparity between wage and productivity growth is highly caused by working conditions rather than the differences in intensity of work done even by the hard workers (ILO, 2004-05). A poor worker in a less developed region performing strenuous work long hours under bad working conditions with little access to technology, education, or other factors may have low productivity compared to a worker in a relatively developed region working relatively fewer hours. Thus, a worker of the former type will receive low pay in spite of supplying intensive work even if wage is fixed following the productivity rule as cited in the elementary text books[3] .

Disproportional growth of productivity and wage rate may be the cause of added vulnerabilities and insecurities among the working class. It may be attributed to continuing absolute poverty and rising inequality that are compounded further by social inequality. This is partly because higher proportional rate of productivity growth through labour-saving innovation creates massive loss of employment for ordinary workers relative to skilled workers over time. The temporal change in workers' share in total employees in registered manufacturing activities over the past three decades shows a serious dislocation of ordinary workers compared with skilled workers in the states (Figure 8). The share has been falling in either of the state but at a faster rate in Gujarat where productivity growth has been significantly high. In West Bengal, the share had fallen at a much lower rate in the 1980s and, it started to rise in the post-reform period.

Figure 8 Share (in fraction) of workers in total employees in registered manufacturing industries: West Bengal and Gujarat

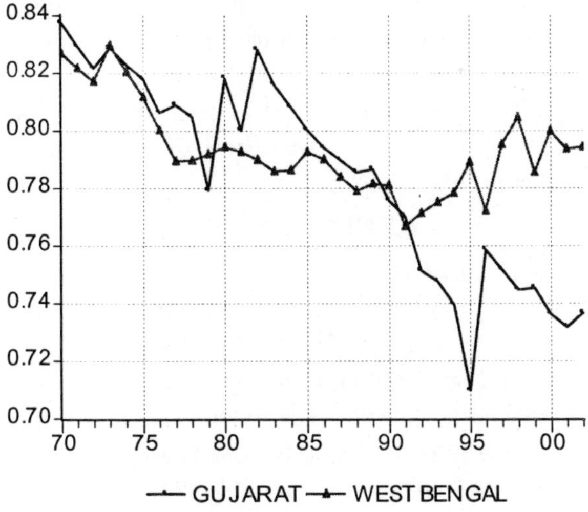

V. Conclusion

In this study wage inequality among unskilled workers is found to be substantially higher than inequality among skilled workers in almost every year. Wage inequality among workers engaged in similar type of job in manufacturing in the registered sector in West Bengal and Gujarat has been growing in the 1990s. While inequality across industry groups has been more prominent than inequality between states, we observe substantial wage differential between the states. Real wage per worker of either type in registered industries in West Bengal has been significantly higher compared to Gujarat till the early 1990s. Moreover, wage inequality for ordinary workers as for skilled workers had been lower in the former compared to the latter in the late 1990s.

Although wage growth and productivity growth are cointegrated, the estimated figures reveal a short run disequilibrium relationship between them in either of the state. Labour productivity in manufacturing grows at a faster proportional rate compared to wage rate, but the mismatch is found to be very high in Gujarat particularly in the 1990s and it may be the cause of added vulnerabilities and insecurities among the working class. Inequality in income and consumption is largely attributable to human suffering and social unrest. The higher the inequality measure, the greater the number of marginalised as observed in Gujarat.

REFERENCES

Adelman, I. and Levy, A. 1984, Decomposing Theil's Index of Income Inequality into Between and Within Components, *Review of Income and Wealth,* 30, pp. 119-121.

Alesina, A. and D. Rodrik, 1994, Distributive Politics and Economic Growth, *Quarterly Journal of Economics*, 109, pp. 465-489.

Atkinson, Anthony. 1997. Bringing Income Distribution in from the Cold, *Economic Journal*, 107, pp. 297-321.

Bagchi A K. 2004. Nanny States for Capital and Social Darwinism for the Workers, *The Indian Journal of Labour Economics*, 47 (1), pp. 69-79.

- 2004. Demographic Regimes and Social Reproduction of Labour, *Economic and Political Weekly*, 39 (30), pp. 3367-77.

- 1998. Studies on the Economy of West Bengal since Independence, *Economic and Political Weekly,* 33 (November 21), pp. 2973-78.

Bagchi, A.K. 1972, *Private Investment in India 1900-1939*, Cambridge University Press, London.

Bagchi A. K., P. Das and S. Chattopadhyay, 2005, Growth and Structural Change in the Economy of Gujarat (1970-71 to 2000-01), *Economic and Political Weekly*, 40 (28), pp. 3039-47.

Bagchi A.K. and P. Das. 2005. Changing Pattern of Employment under Neo-liberal Reforms: A Comparative Study of West Bengal and Gujarat, *The Indian Journal of Labour Economics*, 48 (4), pp. 945 – 958.

Bound, John, and George Johnson. 1992, Changes in the structure of wages in the 1980s: An evaluation of alternative explanations. *American Economic Review,* 83 (June), pp. 371–92.

Bruce, Christopher. 2002. The Connection between Labour Productivity and Wages, *Economica*, 7 (2), Abstract version.

Das P. 2005. Economic Reform, Output Growth and Structural Change – A Comparative Study of West Bengal and Gujarat, *Paper presented at the Annual Conference of The Indian Econometric Society* on January 20-22, 2005

- 2006. Growth and Structural Change in West Bengal: 1960-61 to 2000-01, *Paper presented at the Symposium on Development Economics in Mumbai University* on February 21-22, 2006.

Engle R. F. and C. W. Granger. 1987. Cointegration and Error Correction: Representation, Estimation and Testing, *Econometrica,* 55 (2), pp. 251-276.

Galbraith, James. 2005, Global Inequality and Global Policy, *Journal of Catholic Social Thought*, 2 (1), pp. 125-151.

Galbraith, J., D. Roy Chowdhury and S. Srivastava. 2004, Pay Inequality in the Indian Manufacturing Sector, 1979-98, *University of Texas Inequality Project Working Paper No. 28.*

Glinskaya, Elena and Michael Lokshin. 2005, WAGE DIFFERENTIALS BETWEEN THE PUBLIC AND PRIVATE SECTORS IN INDIA, *World Bank Policy Research Working Paper 3574*, April 2005.

Government of India (1995): *Index Number of Wholesale Prices*, (various issues), Ministry of Industry, New Delhi.

-*Annual Survey of Industries*, Various issues, Central Statistical Organisation

- *National Accounts Statistics*, 1950-51 to 2002-03, Central Statistical Organisation

- *Annual Report* 2004-05, Ministry of Labour

ILO. 2004-05, World Employment Report

Kaldor, N. 1956, Alternative Theories of Distribution, *Review of Economic Studies*, 23, pp. 83-100.

Katz, Lawrence, and Kevin M. Murphy. 1992. Changes in relative wages, 1963–1987: Supply and demand factors, *Quarterly Journal of Economics,* 107 (February), pp. 35–78.

Keynes, J.M. 1936, The General Theory of Employment Interest and Money, MacMillan, London.

Levy, Frank, and Richard J. Murnane. 1992. U.S. earnings and earnings inequality: A review of recent trends and proposed explanations, *Journal of Economic Literature,* 30 (September), pp. 1333–81.

Nickell, S. and R. Layard. 1999. Labor Market Institutions and Economic Performance, *Handbook of Labour Economics*. (eds) O. Ashenfelter and D.Card. Amsterdam, Elsevier. C, pp. 3029-3084.

Pavcnik, N., Blom, A., Goldberg, P. and Schady, N. 2004. Trade Liberalization and Industry Wage Structure: Evidence from Brazil, *World Bank Economic Review*, 18 (3), pp. 319-44.

Perotti, R., 1996, Growth, Income Distribution, and Democracy: What the Data Say, *Journal of Economic Growth,* 1, pp. 149-187.

Persson, T. and G. Tabellini, 1994, Is Inequality harmful for Growth? Theory and Evidence, *American Economic Review*, 84(3), pp. 600-621

1. As per NSS 56th round (2000-2001), total number of workers and total wage bill are nearly 3.7 crores and Rs. 1512338 lakh respectively at the national level, while the respective figures recorded in the ASI are 61.3 lakh and Rs.2767074 lakh in 2000-01.
2. In calculating Theil index we have used the software developed by Galbraith in Excel_Macro format in the work of the University of Texas Inequality Project.
3. Productivity rule of wage determination is supposed to give proper justice for labour under perfectly competitive market, but is subject to monopolistic and monopsonistic exploitation in other conditions.

4

An Empirical Analysis of Wage Inequality in a Group along with Performance : A Case of a Chhattishgarh Firm

Vandana Kashyap
Dr. (Smt.) Radha Pandey
Dr. Amarkant Pandey
Sumbit Kumar Mishra

I. Introduction

Empirical research in this area has been limited in large part due to a lack of relevant micro data since many surveys are of households or individuals (not necessarily those working at the same company) and few are organized at the firm level. However, professional Group in A Firm provide a rich source of data on employee salaries and team performance for persons who work together. Therefore, this paper uses data from A farm from 1988 to 2005 to estimate the effect of wage inequality on team performance. We use A firm's data for three main reasons: data on salaries are readily available, measures of team productivity are commonly collected, and it is reasonable to expect that players have good knowledge of their co-workers' salaries in this institutional setting.

The next section outlines the conceptual framework. Section III develops the empirical specification and describes the data. Section IV reports the empirical results and section V concludes.

II. Conceptual Framework

The effect of wage inequality on group performance is theoretically ambiguous. Greater wage disparity among workers in the same workgroup (i.e., on the same team) can motivate those nearer the bottom of the pay distribution to work hard for the future reward of a higher salary. This demonstration effect is mitigated if the low-paid worker does not see the high-paid person as a reasonable role model, whose performance could never be achieved. Alternatively, greater wage disparity among workers could cause dissension and hurt "team morale" or "team chemistry," thus hindering group success and lowering group performance. This requires knowledge of one's relative standing within the group, which is often not the case for a traditional office environment where salary might be considered a taboo subject among employees or employers might have wage secrecy policies. However, we assume that professional Team Members in a Group are aware of their relative pay given that their salaries are published in newspapers and magazines, discussed on television and radio, and often the subject of public scrutiny.

Can there be too much inequality, such that it begins to cause resentment by the lower-paid and hurt the productivity of all workers, especially where firm output depends on teamwork? Akerlof and Yellen (1990) argue that workers proportionately withdraw effort as their actual wage falls short of their fair wage (which they term the fair wage-effort hypothesis). They posit that a "fair wage" is a function of the wages received by other members of the same firm, the same team in our case, as well as market conditions, so that workers in low demand will perceive a lower fair wage than workers in high demand. Kahneman, Knetsch, and Thaler (1986) studied common beliefs about fairness and concluded that market forces do have some influence on what people consider fair.

Levine (1991) and Ramaswamy and Rowthorn (1991) more directly tie intra Group inequality to its effect on team performance, but with different implications. The latter paper formalized a critique of the Solow (1979) condition by Akerlof and Yellen (1986). The critique was that for a production function in which labor and effort are multiplicative, shirking reduces the efficiency of labor's own input, but does not have other consequences. Ramaswamy and Rowthorn (1991) formally relax the multiplicative assumption and analyze a production function in which effort is not necessarily labor-augmenting. They show, as Akerlof and Yellen (1986) informally predicted, that this reduces the elasticity of effort with respect to the wage, which is most relevant for production processes characterized by high complementarity between workers, such as professional baseball. They argue that heterogeneous labor creates a damage potential for workers. Players with strong damage potential are likely to receive higher wages to lessen their desire to lower team output; those with less damage potential would receive lower wages as they do not have to be appeased. This suggests that greater salary inequality has a non-negative impact on team performance.

In contrast, Levine (1991) argues that a lower-variance wage distribution increases worker cohesiveness and raises firm output. Conversely, greater wage inequality hurts team cohesiveness and lowers firm output. He suggests that compressed wage distributions can foster cooperation for reasons such as bonuses being based on group output thereby aligning the financial interests of group members. Also, limited differences in wages and status can foster trust and facilitate participation in group efforts to achieve the group's goals. In the end, the overall effect of greater wage disparity on team outcomes is an empirical issue and we test these competing hypotheses using professional Group data.

Some social scientists estimated the effect of wage inequality on team performance using firm's data.

Specifically, they find a negative and significant effect of wage disparity, as measured by the Herfindahl-Hirschman index (HHI), on team winning percentage. However, the only control variables are total team salary and a time trend. There are no variables indicating team productivity, such as offensive and defensive statistics, which have been shown to have substantial explanatory power for team performance (Zimbalist, 1992).

We make two substantive changes to the model estimated by these social scientists. First, we include ERA, errors, and OPS as covariates. Second, we investigate the robustness of the conclusion that increases in wage inequality lower team winning percentage to the measure of inequality. Therefore, in addition to the HHI, we use the Gini coefficient, and four generalized entropy inequality measures to capture the extent of dispersion in intrateam salaries.

III. Empirical Specification and Data

Replicating These social scientist's view, we first estimate a panel model of the following form where is the highest percentage of team attaining job in time period and is team 's total salary in year in rupees and is intended to capture team productivity. is a measure of team 's intrateam wage inequality at time. As indicated, we use six different measures of inequality which differ in their sensitivity to income differences in different parts of a team's wage distribution. These are HHI, Gini, and four from the generalized entropy class of inequality measures . In terms of the error structure, captures unobserved heterogeneity across teams, represents unobserved time effects which are modeled as time dummies, and are idiosyncratic disturbances.

We argue that total team salary is an imperfect measure of a team's productivity. Therefore, we also estimate the following model which is the same as equation (1) except for the inclusion of and exclusion of total team salary, . The vector includes controls for time-varying, team-level characteristics, which more accurately reflect a team's productivity. These are the offensive production statistic (OPS), errors (E), and earned run average (ERA), respectively capturing offensive, defensive, and pitching ability. OPS equals on-base percentage plus slugging percentage. E is the total number of errors committed by a team. And ERA is the average number of earned runs allowed per nine innings.

The inequality measures are defined as follows. The Generalized Entropy (GE) class of inequality measures is given by, where indexes individuals 1 to n, is income of person, are frequency weights, and is mean income. In addition, and. The larger is the more sensitive is to differences in income nearer the top of the overall distribution, and conversely, the more negative is, the more sensitive the inequality measure is to income differences at the bottom of the distribution.

The Gini coefficient is a common measure of income inequality for countries, ranging from 0 (perfect equality) to 1 (perfect inequality). Mathmatically, one formula is where is the Lorenz curve, giving the proportional of total team payroll that is received by the lowest 100u% of recipients. The Gini coefficient is then equal to the area between a given Lorenz curve and the Lorenz curve for a team on which everyone receives the same income, expressed as a proportion of the area under the curve for the equal distribution of income. The Herfindahl-Hirschman index is typically used to measure the concentration of production in an industry and equals the sum of the squares of the market shares for each firm. Using MLB data, , where is the number of players on a team and is the share of total team salary accruing to player. HHI gives greater weight to players with larger salaries.

Table 1 contains descriptive statistics for the sample. The data cover the 1988 through 2005 seasons. Average team salary is just over 33 '00 rupees . Mean HHI is 828, above the median of 781. Values below 600 or above 1000 occur for approximately 10 percent of the observations. In 2002, the HHI ranged from 620 for Oakland to 1496 for Tampa Bay. The mean Gini coefficient is .54. In 2002, the Gini ranged from .419 to .675 (again for Raipur and Bhilai).

Table 1. Descriptive Statistics

Variable	*Obs*	*Mean*	*Std. Dev.*	*Min*	*Max*
Winning Pct (*1000)	498	499.84	69.089	327	716
Salary (/100k)	493	333.50	223.83	42.63309	1259.291
HHI	493	828.12	220.88	420.7219	2158.32
GE(-1)	493	1.1921	0.513	0.15675	3.1047
GE(0)	493	0.6427	0.199	0.13529	1.17675
GE(1)	493	0.5492	0.188	0.13054	1.24132
GE(2)	493	0.7011	0.377	0.1401	2.95331
Gini	493	0.5456	0.084	0.28575	0.72808
OPS	498	740.74	43.16	638	854
Errors	498	117.44	20.01	57	181
ERA	498	4.224	0.589	2.91	6.38
Time	540	9.5	5.192	1	18

We expect a positive coefficients for total team salary since greater resources, for example, among large-market teams, enables better Team players to be hired for industry . For the more direct measures of team productivity, higher OPS, fewer errors, and a lower ERA should increase winning percentage, ceteris paribus. As mentioned, the effect of greater intrateam wage inequality on team performance is theoretically ambiguous. A non-negative coefficient would be consistent with the damage potential theory, while a negative coefficient would support the team cohesiveness model.

IV. Empirical Results

Table 2 reports estimates for equation (1), corrected for group-wise heteroskedasticity and autocorrelation. Table 2A (in the appendix) reports results from models with the same variables, but in log-log form. As expected, higher salaries are significantly associated with higher winning percentages. An extra '00s Rupees adds between 1.06 and 1.76 tenths of a percentage point, on average. Columns (1) through (6) differ only in the measure of intrateam salary inequality. The main result from Table 2 is that all six inequality measures are significantly negative. Thus, when we control for team productivity using total salary, higher inequality does appear to have a negative effect on winning, in support of the team cohesiveness hypothesis. This conclusion is robust to the log-log specification.

Table 2. Panel Regression Estimates of the Effect of Inequality on Team Performance

	Dependent variable: Winning percentage (*1000)					
	(1)	(2)	(3)	(4)	(5)	(6)
Team salary ('00s)	0.109	0.176	0.147	0.119	0.106	0.133
	(4.70)***	(7.59)***	(7.12)***	(5.36)***	(4.46)***	(6.16)***
HHI	-0.039					
	(2.72)***					
GE -1		-21.332				
		(2.73)***				
GE0			-49.873			
			(2.80)***			
GE1				-57.941		
				(3.08)***		
GE2					-29.757	
					(3.21)***	
Gini						-85.473
						(2.03)**
Time	-3.420	-5.025	-3.986	-3.012	-2.815	-3.831
	(3.17)***	(5.51)***	(4.04)***	(2.70)***	(2.47)**	(3.52)***
Constant	527.046	514.923	521.227	520.372	511.567	538.764
	(44.76)***	(61.03)***	(52.12)***	(55.58)***	(68.10)***	(26.82)***
Observations	493	493	493	493	493	493
Number of ID	30	30	30	30	30	30
Absolute value of z statistics in parentheses						
* significant at 10%; ** significant at 5%; *** significant at 1%						

Table 3 replaces total salary as the measure of team productivity with three indicators of team productivity, OPS, errors, ERA. We feel this more directly captures a team's ability than salary expenditure.

Table 3. Panel Regression Estimates of the Effect of Inequality on Team Performance

Dependent variable: Winning percentage (*1000)						
	(1)	(2)	(3)	(4)	(5)	(6)
OPS (*1000)	1.245	1.244	1.248	1.246	1.245	1.246
	(37.45)***	(37.89)***	(37.93)***	(37.42)***	(37.32)***	(37.61)***
Errors	-0.418	-0.410	-0.414	-0.418	-0.417	-0.418
	(6.18)***	(6.05)***	(6.12)***	(6.18)***	(6.17)***	(6.17)***
ERA	-95.277	-95.473	-95.820	-95.513	-95.393	-95.646
	(37.64)***	(39.55)***	(39.26)***	(37.93)***	(37.36)***	(38.80)***
HHI	-0.004					
	(0.71)					
GE -1		4.004				
		(1.28)				
GE0			3.192			
			(0.40)			
GE1				-2.804		
				(0.35)		
GE2					-1.735	
					(0.47)	
Gini						-2.890
						(0.16)
Time	-0.777	-1.025	-0.882	-0.765	-0.771	-0.787
	(2.61)***	(3.10)***	(2.61)***	(2.36)**	(2.51)**	(2.34)**
Constant	39.369	34.514	34.798	37.785	37.287	38.093
	(1.52)	(1.36)	(1.35)	(1.46)	(1.46)	(1.39)
Observations	493	493	493	493	493	493
Number of ID	30	30	30	30	30	30
Absolute value of z statistics in parentheses						
* significant at 10%; ** significant at 5%; *** significant at 1%						

The team productivity measures have the expected signs and are statistically significant at the 1 percent level. However, Table 3 shows that none of the inequality measures are significant, in contrast to the previous results. The inequality measures which capture differences in the upper part of the distribution have negative (and insignificant) point estimates, while those which emphasize differences near the bottom of the distribution have positive (and insignificant) point estimates. Table 3A (in the appendix) again uses log-log functional form and shows that 5 of the 6 inequality measures are still insignificant. The lone exception is the coefficient of HHI, which is significantly negative at the 5 percent level. Though significant, the magnitude of this HHI effect is such that it would require a doubling of inequality to reduce team winning percentage by just 2.4 percentage points (from .500 to .476). A more reasonable increase in inequality of 10%, lowers winning percentage by just .24 percent – not a major impact. Thus, we tell a cautionary tale in which greater inequality is not an important factor in Firm team performance.

V. Conclusion

Using data from Firm for the period 1988 through 2005, we find that, in general, there is no consistent effect of intrateam salary inequality on team performance. Using six measures of inequality and two functional forms, only the HHI measure of wage inequality is ever significant (negatively), and even then the magnitude of the effect is such that it would require a doubling of inequality to reduce team winning percentage by just 2.4 percentage points (from .500 to .476). A more reasonable increase in inequality of 10%, lowers winning percentage by just .24 percent. Thus, we interpret this near unanimous lack of significant performance effects from greater inequality as evidence against the team cohesiveness theory, and in favor of the damage potential hypothesis.

REFERENCES

Akerlof, George and Janet Yellen (1990), "The Fair Wage-Effort Hypothesis and Unemployment," *Quarterly Journal of Economics*, vol. 105, no. 2, May.

Akerlof, George and Janet Yellen (1986), *Efficiency Wage Models of the Labor Market,* Cambridge University Press.

Depken, II, Craig A. (2000), "Wage disparity and team productivity: evidence from major league baseball," *Economics Letters*, 67, pp. 87-92.

Kahneman, Daniel, Jack Knetsch, and Richard Thaler (1986), "Fairness as a Constraint on Profit Seeking: Entitlements in the Market," *American Economic Review*, vol. 76, September, pp. 728-41.

Katz, Lawrence A. and David Autor (1999), "Changes in Wage Structure and Earnings Inequality," in Ashenfelter and Card, editors, *Handbook of Labor Economics,* volume 3A, Amsterdam, North Holland.

Ramaswamy, Ramana and Robert E. Rowthorn (1991), "Efficiency Wages and Wage Dispersion," *Economica*, New Series, vol. 58, no. 232, pp. 501-14.

Solow, R. M. (1979), "Another possible source of wage stickiness," *Journal of Macroeconomics*, vol. 1, pp. 79-82.

Zimbalist, Andrew (1992), "Salaries and Performance: Beyond the Scully Model," chapter 7 in *Diamonds Are Forever: The Business of Baseball,* Paul M. Sommers, editor, Washington, D.C.: Brookings Institution.

Appendix

Table 2A. Panel Regression Estimates of the Effect of Inequality on Team Performance

Dependent variable: ln(Winning percentage)						
	(1)	(2)	(3)	(4)	(5)	(6)
Ln(salary)	0.080	0.131	0.117	0.099	0.087	0.103
	(4.47)***	(6.47)***	(6.78)***	(5.91)***	(5.03)***	(6.18)***
Ln(hhi)	-0.080					
	(2.92)***					
Ln(ge –1)		-0.045				
		(2.62)***				
Ln(ge0)			-0.063			
			(3.13)***			
Ln(ge1)				-0.062		
				(3.35)***		
Ln(ge2)					-0.046	
					(3.33)***	
Ln(gini)						-0.119
						(2.88)***
Time	-0.008	-0.013	-0.011	-0.008	-0.007	-0.009
	(3.14)***	(5.54)***	(4.64)***	(3.47)***	(2.85)***	(3.95)***
Constant	5.447	4.081	4.276	4.560	4.771	4.459
	(13.70)***	(12.37)***	(15.16)***	(17.11)***	(17.50)***	(16.47)***
Observations	493	493	493	493	493	493
Number of ID	30	30	30	30	30	30
Absolute value of z statistics in parentheses						
* significant at 10%; ** significant at 5%; *** significant at 1%						

Table 3A. Panel Regression Estimates of the Effect of Inequality on Team Performance

Dependent variable: ln (Winning percentage)						
	(1)	(2)	(3)	(4)	(5)	(6)
Ln(OPS)	1.880	1.890	1.897	1.893	1.887	1.896
	(37.65)***	(38.30)***	(38.22)***	(37.58)***	(37.28)***	(37.82)***
Ln(Errors)	-0.102	-0.097	-0.099	-0.100	-0.101	-0.100
	(6.64)***	(6.29)***	(6.39)***	(6.52)***	(6.57)***	(6.47)***
Ln(ERA)	-0.825	-0.836	-0.839	-0.837	-0.833	-0.839
	(38.80)***	(41.47)***	(41.39)***	(40.30)***	(39.51)***	(40.88)***
Ln(HHI)	-0.024					
	(2.22)**					
Ln(ge−1)		0.009				
		(1.50)				
Ln(ge0)			0.007			
			(0.76)			
Ln(ge1)				-0.001		
				(0.18)		
Ln(ge2)					-0.005	
					(0.81)	
Ln(gini)						0.005
						(0.27)
Time	-0.001	-0.002	-0.002	-0.002	-0.001	-0.002
	(2.47)**	(3.39)***	(2.93)***	(2.44)**	(2.24)**	(2.67)***
Constant	-4.374	-4.607	-4.636	-4.613	-4.580	-4.629
	(12.03)***	(13.49)***	(13.49)***	(13.30)***	(13.16)***	(13.40)***
Observations	493	493	493	493	493	493
Number of ID	30	30	30	30	30	30
Absolute value of z statistics in parentheses						
* significant at 10%; ** significant at 5%; *** significant at 1%						

5

Governing Poverty in India : Magnitude and Dimension

Satya Bhan Yadav

Introduction

Poverty alleviation has been an important goal of development policy in India since independence. To provide a minimum standard of living for all within a reasonable period has been the implicit or explicit objective of all policies and programmes during planning period. Poverty reduction schemes targeted at the poor are supplementing market forces and generic growth strategies in India. Attempts have been made to attain higher rate of growth by raising the purchasing power of the rural and urban poor with the endowment of land and non-land assests as well as through employment generation programmes. This paper has four parts - first part comprises with general introduction. Part - II incorporates the magnitude of poverty estimates given by Planning Commission and individual scholars. Part - III includes policies and programmes started by the Government of India & finally, suggestions and conclusions regarding poverty reduction have been elaborated in part-IV.

Part–II

Poverty Estimates

Poverty in India along with other developing economies is not only a economic phenomenon but also a social one. According to Estimates by Planning Commission, the proportion of the people below poverty line remained more than 50 per cent till the mid – 1970's without any significant change. Planning Commission reveals that poverty ratio declined perceptively in the late 1970's and 1980's from 51 per cent in 1977-78 to 39 per cent in 1987-88. However, after 1987-88 the NSS which began providing annual estimates of mean consumption shows no significant trend in poverty or inequality in rural areas, and therefore in the incidence of poverty. While in urban areas, poverty has declined largely because of an increase in per capita real cousumption by the people on goods & services. However, till the 1980's overall poverty incidence in India has not changed significantly which led to the initiation of immediate requirement of poverty alleviation programmes. Consequently, the Government of India had to give top priority to the poverty reduction schemes & programmes first ever in the Vth Five Year Plan.

The intensity of poverty has also declined considerably both in rural and urban areas since 1990s or the 'great year' 1991 when economic reforms were started in India. According to the 55th Round of NSS, nearly 260 million Indians (193 million in rural and 67 million in urban) remained below the poverty line in 1999-2000. Poverty incidence shows large variations across states. In 1993-94 rural poverty incidence varied from about 2 percent in Punjab to 58 percent in Bihar. The NSS data also show that 40 percent of the rural poor were living in Bihar, Orissa, Madhya Pradesh and West Bengal. It also reveals that the rate of poverty reduction in these states found to be much slower than those of others. The 55th Round of NSS also presents that the percentage of rural poor of backward states such as Bihar, Orissa, MP and UP rose from 53 per cent in 1993-94 to 61 per cent in 1999. Interestingly, some of the better - off states such as Maharashtra, West Bengal and Gujarat had a relatively higher share in rural poverty while the urban poor were concentrated in Uttar Pradesh, West Bengal, Maharashtra, Madhya Pradesh and Andhra Pradesh where all India urban poverty rose from 56 per cent in 1993-94 to 60 per cent in 1999-2001.

The latest 61st round of the National Sample Survey conducted in 2004-05 estimates all-India poverty in 2004-05 (as defined by proportion of population with per capita consumption below official poverty lines calculated as per the methodology of the 1993 expert group) was 28.7 per cent in rural areas, 25.9 per cent in urban areas, and 27.9 per cent overall. The good news is that poverty is indeed lower now than before the economic "reforms' of 1991. According to the 61st round of NSS poverty has declined between 1993-94 and 2004-05 in rural areas of all states as well as in most urban areas except Orissa and Uttarakhand. Nonetheless, the main conclusion must be that the 61st round results confirm that actual poverty reduction after 1993-94 has been much less than the earlier official assessment of 55th round.

As against the earlier official claim that the rural poverty ratio had declined from 37 per cent in 1993 to 27 per cent in 1999-2000, the 61st round places this at nearly 29 per cent in 2004-05. Similarly, urban poverty is now placed at nearly 26 per cent in 2004-05 against 33 per cent in 1993-94 claimed earlier from official 55th round data.

Poverty, on the other hand, is disproportionately high among weaker sections of the society such as Scheduled Caste, Scheduled Tribe, Minorities and Backward Classes. According to the NSS, these sections accounted for more than 81 per cent of the rural poor in 1999-2000. Estimates show that the percentage of Scheduled Tribes among the rural poor has increased from 14.8 in 1993-94 to 17.5 in 1999-2000. While the percentage of poor among the STs declined from 50 in 1993-94 to 44.2 in 1999-2000. Four states namely Bihar, Madhya Pradesh, Maharashtra and Gujarat together accounted for 75.5 percent of the poor among STs in 1999-2000. As far as Scheduled Castes are concerned, more than 58 percent of the poor in rural areas were concentrated in UP, West Bengal and Bihar. As per the survey, the incidence of poverty among Scheduled Caste was high in Uttar Pradesh, Madhya Pradesh and Bihar both in urban and rural areas.

Independent scholars have also conducted various studies parallel to Planning Commission and other governmental agencies. The late 1960's witnessed a spurt of interest among economists in the study of poverty in India. Some eminent scholars such as Dandekar and Rath (1974), Srinivasan (1974), Vaidyanathan (1986), Minhas (1988) had conducted various studies with regard to poverty, its nature, dimensions & remedials. There are large and obvious differences in scope, aim, design and method of estimating poverty by NSS and those of independent scholars. However, the different sources using different methods, give different estimates are confusing. But greater attention must be paid to assessing the purposes, concepts and methods underlying data sets, their reliability and suitability for generating reasonably and comparable estimates of poverty.

Emerging Scenario

On the basis of the above analysis we may draw some conclusions. First, some states like Bihar, Orissa, Madhya Pradesh, Uttar Pradesh and Assam remained laggards in poverty alleveation. Rajasthan is the only state which could perform well in poverty reduction among all these states. It is worth mentioning that the above mentioned all states were called 'BIMARU'. Second, poverty has declined considerably over the last three decades but the magnitude and features arising due to poverty reduction show different trends. The states which were having high agricultural growth rate could manage efficiently with regard to poverty alleviation while other low agricultural productivity states remained slow in implementing the programmes & schemes of poverty reduction. Third, rural poverty as well as urban poverty have shown declining trend after the initiation of new economic reforms in the last decade of 20th century. Fourth, across weaker sections of the society including SCs,

STs and OBCs have been benefited through the policies and programmes implemented by the Central & State Government. It is also noteworthy that the decline seems to be greater among the very poor compared with the poor across social groups. One more important aspect to be discussed here is that the rural - urban divide is widening especially after new economic policies and reforms were undertaken since 1991. The average per capita household expenditure in rural India increased slightly over 1.5 per cent from 1970 to 1989 and thereafter during 1990s it showed deceleration. While, the per capita expenditure growth in urban has accelerated over the period thereby widening the existing rural - urban disparity. Most of the surveys and studies by the NSS and other independent scholars reveal that the rate of decline in urban poverty has been faster that that of rural poverty.

Table: Percentage of Poor and Very Poor in Rural and Urban Areas

Item	*Poverty Ratios*			*Changes in Poverty (Per Annum Changes as Percentage of Base Year)*	*(In Per Cent)*
	1983	*1993-94*	*2004-05*	*1983-94*	*1993-05*
Rural					
Poor	45.76	37.26	29.18	-1.77	-1.97
Very Poor	25.52	15.38	9.64	-3.80	-3.38
Urban					
Poor	42.27	32.56	36.02	-2.18	-1.81
Very Poor	22.45	16.00	12.00	-2.72	-2.25
All					
Poor	44.93	36.02	28.27	-1.89	-1.94
Very Poor	24.79	15.54	10.32	-3.55	-3.09

Source: Estimated from published data of NSS 43rd, 50th and 61 rounds of consumer Expenditure Surveys.

Part–III

In order to eradicate poverty the Government both centre and states along with the NGOs have made serious attempts especialy during the last three decades. However, for the first time poverty alleviation was the main thrust of the Vth Five Year Plan since planning era started in India. It has been a very crucial issue for ruling political party and the government to drive compaign against poverty. In other words, that basic needs and minimum living standards figure so prominently not only in rhetoric of all political parties, but also in the sizeable public resources committed for this purpose is a reflection of both moral and political compulsions. The evolution of policies and programmes can be categorised here as under:

(a) Various poverty alleviation and employment generation programmes such IRDP, NREP, TRYSEM, JRY, SGRY, DWACRA, NRY were started to provide productive employment and to enable people to earn extra income than agriculture.

(b) To provide better access to minimum standard of education, health, transport and safe drinking water to rural and urban deprived classes a series of programmes/schemes were initiated by the Government with the help of non - governmental agencies.

(c) Certain steps were taken to bridge up the gap between haves and haven'ts. Reservation for SC and ST was made constitutional in educational institutions, local bodies and government jobs in order to bring them to the mainstream of development. Educational fee concessions and scholarships were provided to the students of weaker sections of the society. For OBC these provisions were made in the last decade. However, reservation for OBC in higher educational institutes is still under consideration.

(d) Various social welfare programmes and schemes were started for disabled, aged, widows, pregnant and divorced to help them to avail minimum needs.

(e) The Public Distributain System (PDS) was launched and amended subsequently in order to provide subsidised ration and other essential commodities to the poor people in rural and urban India at reasonable prices. For instance in Kerala, Tamil Nadu and West Bengal have a strong distribution network to reach the supplies where they are most needed and there it has proved to be a poverty alleviation measure.

(f) Special areas like hills, desert, drought prone areas were paid full attention through special programmes include DDP, DPAP and hill development programmes.

All the programmes and policies were aimed at providing better living conditions to the rural and urban poor. These programmes were implemented and funded by the both central and state governments. Even some of the international donation agencies have also come forward to provide funds for combating against poverty, inequality and diseases. As indicated earlier that these policies and programmes have sizeable impact on the poverty. Over the years, the functioning of these programmes and their impact on the poor has attracted a great deal of attention. The structure, content and funding of these programmes remained mostly in the hands of the central government. Typically each programme is administered by a separate agency each with its own line hierarchy and operating independently. These features taken together with the rigidity of central guidelines, make of fragmentation and duplication of schemes.

Part–IV

It is very interesting that poverty has been a core issue even after six decades of independence. Even today, every government and the political parties, give top priority to the poverty alleviation programmes. Sometimes they promise to the people to provide wheat, rice and *Sarees* at cheaper prices in their manifesto during the election. Tamil Nadu may be said the best laboratory for such experiences. The picture that is emerging in the various states of India shows different patterns partly due to differences in the on set of demographic transition and partly due to differences in rates of transition. Population is termed as the main cause of increasing poverty. India has been facing a major demographic transition in the last few decades and would likely to continue for a few more decades. Demographic transition is change from a stable population with high mortality and fertility to a stable population with low mortality and fertility and this brings about a perceptible change in the age structure of the population. This is happening in India and the transitions would put several million elderly persons in the grip of poverty and deprivation. Though, the population pyramid of India in transition resembles that of the world as a whole, the pyramid of Kerala is approaching the shape of the developed world and that of Uttar Pradesh resembles the group of less developed countries. Population pyramids of other states lie in between these two typologies of transition.

Social indicators such as education, health, roads, electricity, safe drinking water and communication facilities to the most of rural poor have immensely helped them to overcome poverty since 1991. However, during 1970s and 1980s these infrastructural facilities were out of the reach of the poor people in rural areas. During the last two decade, many programmes and schemes were initiated for rural development. Pradhan Mantri Gram Sadak Yogna has been proved to be a historic milestone in rural road construction. Every village of 500 population were taken into consideration for rural road connectivity under this schemes. National Rural Health Mission including Pulse Polio Eradication Compaign has provided health & safety cover to urban and rural Children to the great extent. Large number of people have been benefited by these programmes. Mid-Day Meal Scheme is another most important scheme for rural children especially hill, desert and drought prone areas. Sarva Shiksha Abhiyan is making significant contribution to the remote and far distant places. All those programmes have generated the capacity to live with sustainable livelihood and dignity to the weaker and deprived sections of the society. The social movements and increasing awareness among the *dalits* and minorities especially Uttar Pradesh, Bihar, Madhya Pradesh, Kerala and North Eastern states provide interesting insights into possible scenario of escape from poverty en block.

As far as the outlays on targeted poverty alleviation programmes are concerned, it have increased rapidly during the planning period. Prior to 1970, outlays were limited to special schemes for nutrition of Scheduled Castes and Tribes social welfare and backward areas and rural works programmes during the Fourth Plan (1969-74) which provided Rs. 6 billion or less than 4 per cent of public sector outlay. During the Eighth Plan (1992-97), the outlay on a vastly larger and more varied poverty alleviation programme amounted to Rs. 460 billion which is nearly 11 per cent of the total public sector outlay. Over the years there is the need and immense scope for improving the efficacy of poverty alleviation programmes by more funding, better targeting, reducing waste and corruption and creating institutional conditions for greater accountability. To sum up, the focus should be on rationalising the approach, organisation and priorities of the poverty alleviation programmes rather than on cutting back the outlays. The Central Government as well as the State Governments should make joint efforts to combat poverty and inequality.

REFERENCES

Ahluwalia, MS (1978): "Rural Poverty and Agricultural Performance in India", *Journal of Development Studies*, Apiril 14, pp. 298-323.

Datta, K.L. and Savitha Sharma (2000): *Facets of Indian Poverty*, Concept Publishing Company, New Delhi.

Dreze, Jean (2000), " Poverty: Beyond Headcount Ratio," The Hindu, Sept. 9

Government of India: Planning Commission reports and NSS surveys.

Government of India: Economic surveys- 2001-02, 2002-03, 2003-04, 2005-06

Kapila, Uma (ed.) **(2006):** "Indian Economy since Indipendence, Academic foundation, New Delhi.

6

Poverty Reduction : Changing Role of District Poverty Reduction Agency

N.L. Narasimha Reddy
N.V. Shivaiah
V.J. Mani Kumar
S. Narasimha Rao[1]

1. Introduction

The concern of the state for poverty reduction goes back to the beginning of the planned economic development (1951)[2]. In the early 1980s a *District Rural Development Agency* (DRDA) was created. The motive behind establishing DRDA was to perform specialist role at the district level for poverty governance. DRDA was also entrusted with the responsibility of implementing special programmes[3] from time to time. A number of other institutions have also been working at the district level for improving the well-being of ST, SC, BC and minority communities.

The approach to poverty reduction has evolved over the past 50 years in response to the deepening understanding of the complexity of development. As a result People's empowerment approaches have gained importance in rural development, which resulted in more inclusive definitions of poverty. There has been considerable shift in poverty alleviation programmes with the emergence of Self-help Groups (SHGs).

Consequently, a new thinking has emerged on schemes relating to self-employment and credit delivery system for the poor. This change in thinking is largely reflected by the introduction of Swarnajayanti Gram Swarojgar Yojana (SGSY) to promote self-employment among women and men and enabling them to cross the poverty line. DRDA has moved away from individual beneficiaries of providing subsidies by linking bank credit to group based approach to facilitate self-help movement. It is now involved in new ways of implementation – 'DRDA is expected to play a different role in the promotion of SHG-bank linkage programme. It has to facilitate simultaneously the process of formation and strengthening of groups, and building relations between SHG and local banks'.

Accompanying this change of perspective is a better understanding of the implication of institutional arrangements (at district, state and national levels) for achieving the ends of greater service, scale and sustainability. At the district level, the DRDA has been playing an important role in the promotion of self-help movement. There are also a range of institutions involved in experience generation, capacity building and service delivery in the promotion of self-help groups. In fact with the graduation of the movement, institutions are now expected to equip to deal with new generation of needs (e.g., livelihood promotion).

Andhra Pradesh is a leading State in the promotion of self-help group movement in India. The State has also benefited from the experience generated by special projects such as UNDP in selected districts. Based on this experience, the state initiated a State wide programme, namely District Poverty Initiatives programme (DPIP)[4] , with a separate institutional set up. This almost forced DRDA into an insignificant position. Subsequently, there was a realization for converging the DPIP and DRDA. This resulted in bringing DPIP and DRDA under the single Project Director.

In the above background, Poverty Learning Foundation (PLF) has undertaken a study[5] in Rangareddy district of Andhra Pradesh (AP) to understand the changing role of

DRDA in the promotion of poverty reduction strategies at the district level. This paper has three parts. First part examines changing priorities in poverty and governance. The second part, in brief, provides on district planning for managing change. And the final part on role clarity exercise to perform new or evolving role.

2. Poverty and Governance

As discussed above, several institutions have been working at the district level for promoting micro-finance activities as part of poverty reduction. This naturally demanded a change in DRDA functions and operations. There was no doubt that DRDA had made considerable progress in its new role. In the process, its functional relations with line departments and banks had also been evolving. It had to further modify to the demanding conditions in response to special projects.

DRDA had to work through line functionaries and at mandal level MPDO provided important link[6]. MPDO continued to perform all other rural development functions, while the role in facilitation of SHG movement had come down. Two aspects were important: (a) SHG, VO and Mandal samakya had emerged and taken over certain roles; and (b) Integration of *Velugu* and DRDA[7] had created many opportunities for making available appropriate number of staff and suitable machinery in the promotion of micro-finance (Table 1).

The emergence of SHG and their institutions has resulted in creating community level structures for decentralized management of micro-finance activities in poverty reduction. For example, Chevella local bank has been finding it easier to provide bulk loans to Mandal Samakya, which was formed in 2000, than directly delivering SHG-bank linkages. Similarly, DRDA also receives application and process support to groups under SGSY through Mandal Samakya. In the words of one senior official - People's organizations were not there in the past. This is

Table 1. Organizational Structures of DRDA, Velugu and Community levels

	DRDA	*VELUGU*	*Community*
District	PD	PD, APD, and DPM	
Cluster (A group of mandals)	4 APOs	APM	
Mandal	MPDO (EO-RD), EO-DWCRA	CC and Master book keepers	MS
Cluster of villages	Community organizer	CA, Village book keepers	VO and SHG

a new chapter in the development. This provides opportunity for sustainable development[8]. Different departments are now taking interest in them:

- For getting information (e.g., mother and child health)
- For creation of awareness and mobilization of people (i.e., children's enrolment in schools, immunization, family planning)
- For the implementation of development programmes

Stakeholders have considered the following as key aspects in relation to managing change in the district.

Planning: An important concern that emerged was lack of process to assess and translate the poverty needs into plans at the district level. The interventions tended to be very generic across the sample mandals. The high intensity of problems in Peddemul demanded for disaggregated view on the needs, strategies and resource allocations.

Poverty reduction should be defined in the larger context. There was a need for change in our thinking that poverty reduces only with financial assistance.

The plans by various institutions seemed to be

mechanically prepared based on information flow and priorities set by functionaries

Banks provided very routine information in preparation of the credit plan

There was no way for DRDA and others to come together in preparing the plans. It came to light that trainings were provided without concerning what the other had done and as a result same member was covered by two institutions at different points of time. There was no information to monitor these and bring converge.

The planning across institutions was quite inadequate to deal with the issues identified by the people.

The resource mobilized at MDO/MPP level was also used without concerning about the priorities.

Targeting: The process of identification of the people for government support under anti-poverty programmes has undergone change with the emergence of SHGs at the centre stage. Two aspects are important in this context: (a) change from conventional mode of identification camps to participatory identification of the poor; and (b) the process of delivering support has also undergone change from individual beneficiary approach to group based approach.

The above have brought in changes in the roles of different actors in the identifying and supporting anti poverty programmes. In the view of the officials met during the study – 'SHGs and their networks were assigned with roles of addressing poverty issues. All the development actors looked at them for different development functions'. However, the following emerged as major concerns from the voices of different stakeholders:

- MPDO role in the identification of individual beneficiaries (for DRDA/SC, BC Corporation, etc support) was confined to forwarding applications accepted by the bankers. Occasionally, MPDO also included application received by his office or during his/her field visit. As there was no mechanism to identify and target the poor, the households outside the groups were deprived of opportunity of accessing their entitlements.

- Bankers had no mandate in the changed conditions to support the poor under anti-poverty programmes and thus engage in giving approvals to those approaches and pursue the bank manager. MPDO would have to naturally consider these applications as s/he has to fulfil her target.
- There was disagreement among stakeholders on poverty data prepared in villages under VELUGU, though it was supposed to form the basis for targeting the poor. The MPPs, in sample mandals, had felt that the data would not valid as it had many inconsistencies. They suggested that such processes should be facilitated by well trained and competent people in future.
- SHGs and their networks were identifying and supporting groups with micro-finance to reduce poverty. In most of the sample villages, a large number of poor had not organized into SHG. Consequently, they were deprived of opportunities of accessing developmental support. SHG networks were supporting groups based on performance. While this was important, there was no initiative to guide groups which were not performing well. So, the groups consisting of the poor had been left out of SHG-bank linkage and/or Mandal Samakya support.
- All the above raises the following questions: What is the way out for the poor? What role one expects from SHGs and their institutions and development institutions?

Enhancing Capabilities: Functionaries are constantly learning to perform their roles in tune with changes in programmes. But there is a need to emphasize the creating specialist roles among functionaries as per the emerging needs in the program. In so far as capacity development is concerned, two things are important: (a) Human resources and their capabilities in DRDA; and (b) system for meeting the demands of training at the district level.

As stated above, different institutions in the district have been operating in isolation with each other. As a result, they end up targeting same person or duplicate efforts. Given the expanding need for capacity building in view of SHG movement as well as emerging focus on livelihood promotion, there is a felt need to strategize use of resources available in the district for attaining better results. So, it is essential to focus on the following:

- Convergence of resource allocated for capacity building at the district levels taking into consideration plans of SHG and other institutions.
- A system is needed for assessment of capacity development needs; and constant up-gradation of training material and modules taking new development and latest perspectives.
- The capacities and resources available within the district are to be properly channelled. There is a need to create environment for collaboration and networking than competing in order to create combined impact. The district has though gained from the initiative of CARE (AP), it did institutionalize a system for feeding such learning into larger process.
- There is also need for DRDA to create change institutions for influencing the training courses and agendas of other institutions.
- Support systems have not been developed to optimize the benefits by seeking support of resource organizations, rating institutions and NBFCs.

Monitoring: The participatory approaches and CBO based development initiatives have brought importance to monitoring. This means that monitoring should be our integral part of planning, implementation and capacity building. A separate functional responsibility should also be built in the organization. And, there should be pro-active measures on the part of DRDA to facilitate monitoring roles among staff and other intuitions associated with the process. The current situation is as follows:

- At present, different institutions involved in SHG promotions have been playing a very limited role. Even though Mandal Samakya provides financial support to "A Grade' groups, it is not involved in proper monitoring roles.
- While there is emphasis on grading of groups for linkages with banks, there is no process for monitoring the implementation of grading.
- There is a need for facilitating self-monitoring monitoring at various levels as a back up support to QPA and decentralize monitoring responsibilities.
- There is also need for a system to monitor poverty in the district and help in decision making on poverty.

3. Change Management

Traditional development theory holds that function of development is capital investment (channelling official development assistance). Without denying the importance of financial resources, at least as essential is the development of local organizations through which people define and pursue their individual and collective interests within the guiding framework of national policy. The organizations must, in turn, be supported by institutional structures and policies that create the necessary social and political space for them to function in their members' interest.

Entitlements of the Poor: There is no doubt that group approach has brought in several gains. The Stakeholders regarded group approach as a sustainable model for effective and productive socio-economic development. Other gains of group approach as identified by them are as follows:

- provides for micro-credit requirements of the poor
- strengthens poverty alleviation programmes; and
- creates employment for self-enterprises and empowers people, particularly women.

At the same time, micro-policy environment is not sensitive to the needs of the poor and marginal households. Though identification of the poor is now done with people's participation, stakeholders report cornering of resources by informed people (mostly group leaders) in the absence of quality check on the process. Thus, the poor are deprived of opportunities and government entitlements.

In one sample village, as much as 67 per cent of the households had not been organized into SHGs, due to migration. Perhaps there was need for a separate strategy in such cases. This reminds us of the importance of other strategies in poverty reduction. Probably, one needs to explore ways of supporting members outside the groups or contextually develop a special package for delivering credit facilities to the poor.

Micro-Finance: When examining the DRDA, it is important to understand the implications of the decision of the government to become actively involved in micro-enterprise development through credit programmes or other enterprise development services. While it expands the scope for banks and private micro-finance providers, there is a limited effort in micro-production, services and training areas. Therefore, following points should be taken note of while implementing the micro-finance programmes:

- Recognizing the heterogeneity of the poor should lead to more innovation of experimentation, which deepens the downward reach of financial services

- Recognizing that there is still a large unsatisfied demand for financial services among the bankable poor.

Different Tiers of SHGs: Micro-finance sector should focus on strengthening the primary unit (i.e., SHG) if the movement should sustain in the long run. Other tiers of SHG (VO, Mandal Samakya) may have to evolve to provide or facilitate various services needed by the groups; and functional support of the banking sector as well as development institutions.

Functions of SHG Institutions: The prevailing environment is in favour of giving most functional responsibilities to the institutions of SHGs. But, at the same time, no one is concerned with the kind of needs the groups would have to perform such roles. Further, there is no clarity on the role to be played by various institutions in the context of the role assigned to SHGs. To properly institutionalize the decentralized management, various actors need engage in role delineation process.

SHG-Bank Linkage: Recent growth of SHG-Bank linkage model and its ready acceptance and success in terms of outreach, advocates a focus on the formal banking sector as a provider of micro-finance. The success of the SHG-bank linkage banking model reduces the need for other micro-finance service providers. It is important that the NGO should engage in innovation and generation of future ideas in poverty reduction.

Deepening the Credit: Women are also depending on NBFC, moneylenders and others for meeting their credit needs. It is time that efforts are made to deepen the credit to enable them to take up viable livelihood activities of certain scale. For example, MACS (Chevella) supported 100 members with bore-wells.

Being Well-Informed: Groups have gained knowledge on government programmes and various institutions. As a result, groups are demanding different institutions for sharing information. While this may facilitate transparency, several people in the village take to reactive mode in the absence of proper information. In addition, the information is reaching only a few in the village. All these will have harmful effect on the process of development. Thus, there is a need for a plan for reorienting the people on programmes, actors and functions through trainings and capacity building courses.

Going Beyond Micro-Finance: Economic decentralization needs a quantum jump from access to financial services to wealth creation at member and household levels.

- Members expressed the need for SHGs to look for opportunities beyond members as next generation strategy in SHG building. So, capacity building plans should go beyond members to address the needs of young women and women.
- DRDA should aim at creating services providers, networks and markets for facilitating growth of small business, employment and local economy.
- Micro-finance will need to be grounded on business strategies. Some service providers may be placed with VO and Mandal Samakya. For example, BASIX though focus on credit, promotes business strategies to deepen the credit.
- Mechanisms are required to meet the demands of the members for legal and health services.

Pilots and Special Projects: The district has gained experience from the initiative of CARE (AP) in Chevella. Stakeholders have acknowledged the contribution of the project in experience building on micro-finance, particularly facilitating Mandal Samakya. At the time of the study, CARE was working out on modalities with DRDA to transfer all the groups. These groups had started joining Mandal

Samakya facilitated by the DRDA. This brings for discussion the following issues:

- Pilot projects of this kind are always important in experience generation
- Government should develop a mechanism to handle such projects after facilitating the institution withdrawal
- A proper understanding on integration is needed. In case this is meant almost disintegration of other institution, ways are to be found to sustain.
- Creating higher order institutions also mean long term commitment to handhold and developing management skills.
- It is worthwhile to explore options, in such cases for linking Samakyas with banks to position as sub-unit of the bank.

Velugu as a special project has been contributing to the systemic learning in DRDA. DRDA needs to use this to prepare itself bringing reform in organisation and management process of poverty reduction in the district.

- Understanding poverty governance needs to assign functional roles and responsibilities to different actors; and providing skills and competencies accordingly.
- Estimating the work load at different institutional points and the need for special services to plan for human resources and capacities.
- Acquiring competencies required for dealing with the need emerging from VELUGU intervention simultaneously after the project period.

Capacity Development: SHGs have put in the place learning process among women. Members are willing to taking up new ideas with exposure to experiences generated by enterprising women. Groups have expressed limitations faced by several members due to skills and competencies. It is time for different institutions in the district to jointly prepare and implement capacity building plans. There is a need to pool human, financial and technical resources available in the district to create an impact.

Challenges before DRDA: Responding to the above challenges will place DRDA in a role that demands new competence. It also means reorientation to people-centered development approaches, acquiring capacities to address many of the issues involved and providing the necessary leadership. DRDA must undertake a re-examination of its roles and commit itself to developing new managerial and technical capabilities. There are different challenges before DRDA, but the important ones are:

- while it is necessary to effectively use SHG as an instrument of poverty reduction, it should not shy away from its larger role in facilitation of the district level poverty reduction strategy;
- to be involved in understanding the diverse and complementary strengths and limitations of the different actors in their quest to improving the well-being of the poor;
- to build the growing partnership with people, actors with similar agenda and service providers and develop capacity building support systems in the promotion of savings and credit and beyond i.e., livelihood promotion and enterprise development and to facilitate linkages and relations between each other;
- to build on experiences generated by different institutions; and channel the combined strength of a range of other actors involved in this process; and
- to understand disaggregated needs of poverty reduction vis-à-vis micro-finance. The focus on micro-finance should not blur the vision of overall poverty reduction priorities.

4. Developing action Plans for Managing Change

Based on the above understanding, different stakeholders were involved preparation of action plans. The methodology included:

- Facilitated reviews and consultation meetings at different levels to draw inputs for the planning.
- Consultations were held with SHG, VO and MS members to map major concerns and emerging priorities.
- Discussions were also held with key functionaries of DRDA-IKP.
- In preparing this plan, different documents were consulted. Some of the important documents referred were process-monitoring report, field planning documents, etc.

Action plans were developed for capacity building, livelihoods, etc. A sample output from this process is given below:

Table- 2

Key action areas	*Proposed plan*
Proposed Strategy	• Prioritizing & targeting of training needs based on categorization • Development of need based modules • Modules for new and old groups • ToT for CRPs on new modules • Monitoring system on trainings • Redefining the roles of the staff
Core Activities in 2005-06	1. Identification and training of CRPs 2. Procuring training material 3. Preparation of training calendar 4. Identification and training bookkeepers

Key action areas	*Proposed plan*
	5. Development of training modules (with external support)
	6. Sector specific trainings to the staff & community
Critical Resources for Implementing activities	• Providing support and infrastruc ture material for training
	• Training for existing MVTC and DWCRA buildings
	• Budget for trainings & material
	• Developing TOTs with the support of external resource persons
	• Strengthening monitoring system
OPERATIONAL PLAN	• Community self monitoring at VO level, MS level
	• Project monitoring systems
	• Building information systems
	• Facilitating role for various functionaries on monitoring.
	• Preparation of training resource persons to take up task

5. Facilitating roles for managing change

As a sequel a two-day workshop was also organized on 'Role Clarity' for different functionaries in order to translate the action plan into action. The process involved in facilitating understanding on evolving roles in step-by-step process, which included:

- Core Responsibilities
- Expected role to discharge the responsibilities
- Functions involved in performing the role
- Any other functionary performing similar role
- If so what are the functions that distinguish from the other actor

- Can you redefine the identity of the position with respect to core objective of the program
- Dependent and independent functions to be performed by the DRDA and IKP staff in view of the new roles.

A sample output indicating restructuring process from the above process is given below:

Plan for restructuring DRDA-IKP

Table- 3

Functionary	*Proposed Action*
APDs	Rather than functional responsibility, territorial responsibility may be fixed
DPM % APOs	70% functional
	30% territorial
	Wherever functional convergence is possible efforts should be made by bifurcating the function
	(ex. EGM (APO) / DPM (LH)
EO – DWCRA	Positioning them in appropriate place and cadre
DRP	Positioning them as CCs or MTCs
CO/s	Identify them as VBKs through VOs and call them as VBKs only

6. To sum up

The primary outcome of this action-research was developing three-stage process for facilitating change management in poverty reduction. PLF is further working on this to build on and develop a comprehensive methodology for facilitating change as part of poverty and governance at micro-level, which is a missing link as of now.

References

1. The authors are associated with Poverty Learning Foundation (PLF), Secunderabad. PLF is involved in research and action in poverty reduction.

2. In the first five-year plan, emphasis was on increasing food production. It was realized that the 'more food campaign' did not achieve the desired results as people's participation aspect had been neglected. This led to the launching of the Community Development Programme in 1952. During fourth and fifth plan periods, the overall rural development strategy consisted of special programmes for under-previliged target groups and backward areas. Consistent with the national policy to increase employment opportunity and income levels of families below the poverty line the Integrated Rural Development Programme (IRDP) was launched during the year 1978-79. Under IRDP a number of sub schemes came into existence such as TRYSEM, DWCRA, CITRA etc., to meet the specialist needs and target groups. For example, DWCRA came into existence to improve women's participation. In late 1990s the focus shifted from shifted from individual beneficiary approach to group approach which resulted in the design of SGRY.

3. The special development programmes can be grouped under two categories, mainly beneficiary oriented programmes and area development programmes.

4. It is known as Velugu. The name is subsequently changed as Indira Kranthi Patham

5. The study was supported by CARE-India. DRDA-IKP and Poverty Learning Foundation has jointly carried out a study in two mandals, which are representative of two extreme scenarios in the district. The study has brought out the need for separate strategy for backward Mandals.

6. MPDO office is working as the nodal agency of rural development at the mandal level. MPDO as E.O for Rural Development is monitoring the individual loans, the revolving fund provided to the SHGs and SGSY loans.

7. It is effort DRDA is his role which was earlier the responsibility of DRDA is now being played by the Velugu staff. In this context, since Velugu is not permanent, it is crucial to address the following for a futuristic framework.

8. Even in the case of UNDP, this did not happen. (One participant felt differently and stated his experiences in this regard.

7

Governance and The Scenario of Health in India : A Critical Analysis

Akshayakumar Panigrahi

Introduction

Health has always been a major concern of people through the ages irrespective of place and time. Almost everywhere it is considered as one of the essential requirements for the overall well being, irrespective of developed and developing countries. If we look into the history it is found that, in the early civilizations of Harappa and Mohenjodaro which when excavated revealed well planned cities with baths and drainage systems. It implies that even in the beginning of the civilization they are concerned about taking care of health.

Health is a broad concept. It is not only always free from diseases but also it looks into the over all well being. Whose health it is? Who should be held responsible for the over all health in a place? Is it an individual affair or a community involved in it or that of the State? At the micro level it is defined as individual health which is the responsibility of the person concerned whereas at macro level it is defined as the over all health of the people irrespective of caste, class, rich or poor. In this paper it is discussed about the over all health status in India since independence. So the first part of the paper is looking into the overall role of state for the sake of health from broader aspects, followed by the scenario in India which includes the role of state, constitutional provision, role of central and state government. In the second part the paper discussed the historical analysis of achievement of health since pre independence. Basically it examines the rate of fertility, mortality, infant mortality rate and achievement in family planning since 1950 to 2000. For the analysis the paper utilizes the data from the available secondary sources. Especially from census of India, Ministry of Health and Family Welfare, Indiastat.com and United Nations publications.

Who is responsible for the overall health in a place especially in a geographical coverage? Lack of clarity about the state's role, whether in the changing economic scenario or in health, has had a range of negative consequences. First there has been a gross mismatch between available resources and states' goals, which has inevitably led to the erosion of accountability and morale, as well as the inadequate monitoring of performance. Second, there has been a lack of prioritization, contributing to the misallocation of limited resources in response to political and other pressures. Finally, state interventions have been stretched to areas best left to the private sector, resulting in financial and human resources being spread too thinly for impact.

What do you mean by Governance?

Governance is nothing but a process in which the state should follow certain rules and regulation for running a system under control. It may be political, social, economic or any other else. It is a broad term and its meaning differ to different persons with different purpose. It involves the nature of interaction between defined institutions which includes the constitution, the legislation, the executive and the judiciary and those civil societies with cultural values, social norms, traditions or structures that have important influences on this interaction process. According to World Bank (2001) governance is defined as the power of the state in managing a country's social and economic resources with accountability, rule of law, transparency and citizen participation. Gray (2001) defines 'governance' as the relationships of authority and function through which policies and practices are affected and rights and obligations are established and regulated. In the similar manner Rhodes (1997) defines it as self organizing, inter organizational networks characterized by interdependence, resource exchange, rules of the game and significant autonomy from the State. According to the UNDP (1997) it is the exercise of political, economic and administrative authority to manage a nation's affairs. In short, from the above definitions it is clear that governance is a broad concept which includes almost all the things into together and control from different dimensions. But in this paper, we use the term 'governance' as the role of state and its intervention for the development of health of the people, with special reference to India. We are looking into the constitutional provisions and the role of state in the improvement of health of the people. With this objective an attempt is made to look into the historical involvement of government and achievement in health by taking some of the important health indicators as mentioned above.

Role of State

The State's role has been actively debated, particularly in the context of arguments that excessive state intervention has stifled private initiative, creating a burgeoning bureaucracy and fiscal imbalances.

According to the recommendation of the WDR (World Development Report) 1993, the state should intervene in some specific areas such as immunization, school based health services, information and selected services for family planning and nutrition, and AIDS prevention. Apart from this, some special packages were introduced on the basis of their cost effectiveness which includes services to ensure pregnancy related care (prenatal, childbirth, postpartum), family planning services, tuberculosis control, the control of

STDs and care for common childhood illness (diarrhoeal diseases, acute respiratory infections, measles, malaria and acute malnutrition). Whereas WDR 2000 describes government role as stewardship, listing three basic tasks as formulating health policy – defining vision and direction, exerting influence-approaches to regulation and collecting and using intelligence.

Despite the lack of unanimity over the state's role in health care, there seems to be agreement that universal access and equity in a poor country are dependent on the state's provision, or financial support, of basic health care for the poor. Protecting the vulnerable is considered a core function of the state and publicly financed health care is an important tool in poverty alleviation. But what services should the state provide or support and how?

In over all it is said that the state intervention on health is only on the basis of cost considerations has a serious moral, ethical and equity implications. The WHO Director General Dr Brundtland says: 'Health systems are not just concerned with improving people's health but with protecting them against the financial costs of illness. The challenge facing governments in low income countries is to reduce the regressive burden of out of pocket payment for health by expanding prepayment schemes, which spread financial risk and reduce the specter of catastrophic health care expenditures.

In sum the essential functions of the state in health are as follows. Stewardship functions:

- Formulating health policy, defining its vision and direction
- Regulating and framing laws, setting standards and enforcing them
- Monitoring the main determinants of health and demographic indicators and evaluating the impact of health related interventions

- Collecting and using health intelligence for epidemiological surveillance and policy formulation
- Guiding and overseeing the health system for universal access, equity, and consumer satisfaction.
- Mobilizing resources and facilitating a health finance framework that ensures fairness and financial risk protection.
- Planning and encouraging the development of human resources for health
- Mobilizing public opinion and promoting popular participation in pubic health activities.

Constitutional Provisions on Health in India

The Indian constitution does not list health as a fundamental right. But Article 47 reads as the state has to raise the nutrition level and improve public health as in the Directive Principle of State Policy. Whereas Article 21 which provides the fundamental right for protecting the life and liberty can be interpreted as inclusive of the right to health, implying state obligation to protect citizens from medical negligence. The only obligation is that for the sake of welfare state and over all development purpose, state is interfering to develop the health infrastructure as well as other required things. Thus the state emerged as the main provider of health care.

With this motto the constitutional provision divides the role of state and centre for taking care the health of the people in a macro level. The constitution places public health and sanitation, hospitals and dispensaries in the state list, where as medical education, drugs, family planning, the control of the spread of communicable diseases from one state to another, mental health and the medical professions are in the concurrent list and in the central jurisdiction (the union list) on national importance in medical education and research. Apart from this the centre has played a dominant role in all aspects of health, mainly because of its financial clout in a centrally planned economy.

Health Scenario at the Time of Independence in India

At the time of Independence, an attempt is made to set up the National Planning Committee by the Indian National Congress and a sub committee on health is formed under the chairmanship of Col. S.S. Sokhey to assess the health situation and the health services in the country. In 1943 an initiative had been taken for a comprehensive nationwide health survey under the chairmanship of Sir Joseph Bhore and the committee popularly known as the Bhore Committee to analyze the over all health scenario in India especially the rate of mortality. The Bhore Committee revealed that a high level of mortality rate is among infants and mothers in the reproductive age group. In spite of this, the large number of deaths caused by communicable diseases was also extremely high. A severe shortage of health personnel, hospitals and dispensaries aggravated the problem.

The committee pointed out that deaths could be prevented by better sanitary facilities, safe drinking water, proper diet and medical facilities. The survey indicated that malaria, cholera, small pox and plague were taking a high annual toll. The National Planning Committee on Health in 1948 noted that above all, poverty was the root cause of most diseases and the short life span of 27 years.

Health Scenario in India at the Post Independence Period

It was the time when there were extremely high fertility and mortality due to certain multiple reasons. So at that time the first priority was to reduce the death rate which was the major concern and caused by the major communicable diseases like small pox, malaria, plague and cholera. Probably due to this reason the more important recommendation of Bhore committee was to control the mortality rate especially by the control of the four major communicable diseases of pre Independence India, namely small pox, malaria, plague and cholera. In the recent past there is substantial improvement for eradicating the above concerned diseases.

The percentage of funds allocated in the five year plans for health have been grossly inadequate and nowhere commensurate to the recommendations of the Bhore Committee. The allocation for the first two decades after independence, though modest, saw the growth of health infrastructure and manpower to reach health to the tillers of the soil. The later plans, though much larger focused more on the urban based curative infrastructure like medical colleges, hospitals and the training of doctors even though the rural PHC (Public Health Cetres) suffered due to the unwillingness of such city trained doctors to serve in the rural areas and provide leadership to the rural health team of the PHC.

The heart of an over centralized system, viz. the Ministry of Health and Family Welfare based in Delhi, developed plans which encouraged, urban development of medical services through the majority of the population. In 1973 the Minimum Needs Programme was introduced and it produced multi purpose workers chiefly to achieve targets of the family planning programme and control resurgent malaria under the grab of health care for the villages. Since then there are a lot of initiatives had been taken to improve the health of the people in India by implementing health based welfare programmes with specific programmes for child, women, poor and needy persons.

Present Health Scenario in India

The following section discusses the comparative aspects of indicators of health in a historical prospective. Especially it looks into the progress which has taken place over a period of time. For that reason the paper looks into the trend of population, decadal population growth, crude birth rate, crude death rate, infant mortality rate, achievement in the family planning, life expectancy at birth etc.

Trend of Population in India

Chart 1 indicates the trend of population since 1901 to 2001. From the following figure it clearly indicates that over this period continuously the population is increasing except in 1901 to 1941. The reason was due to the high birth rate and high death rate which are almost equal in this period. It clearly indicates that at the time of independence there was high trend of mortality because of communicable diseases and epidemics. But over the period since independence Government of India had taken a lot of measures to reduce the high mortality.

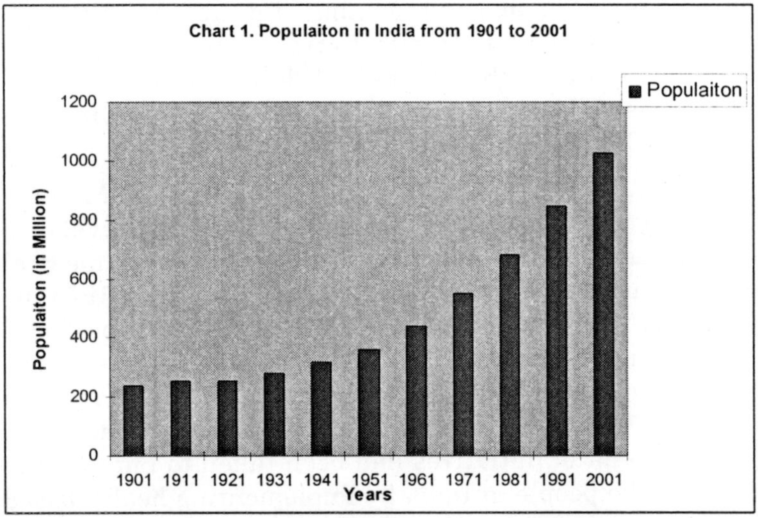

It is not enough if we look into only the trend of population over the period. It is logical to see the decadal growth rate of population over the period, which will give more appropriate picture to examine the over all achievement in health sector in India.

Decadal Population Growth Rate in India

Chart 2 indicates the decadal population growth rate in India since 1901 to 2001. From the chart it is clearly shown that up to 1950 the decadal growth rate was almost 12 per cent where as afterwards it increases drastically. In the period 1971 to 1991 the decadal growth rate was almost 23 per cent. But in the period 1991 to 2001 the decadal growth rate is slightly declining and it is expected to reduce further in future. This paper discusses about only the rate of mortality and fertility as the important factors of growth of population and these variables are directly indicative of the over all development of health scenario. Though the level of migration is one of the factors for population growth but it is in no way linked to the health status. It is assumed that emigration and immigration balanced each other.

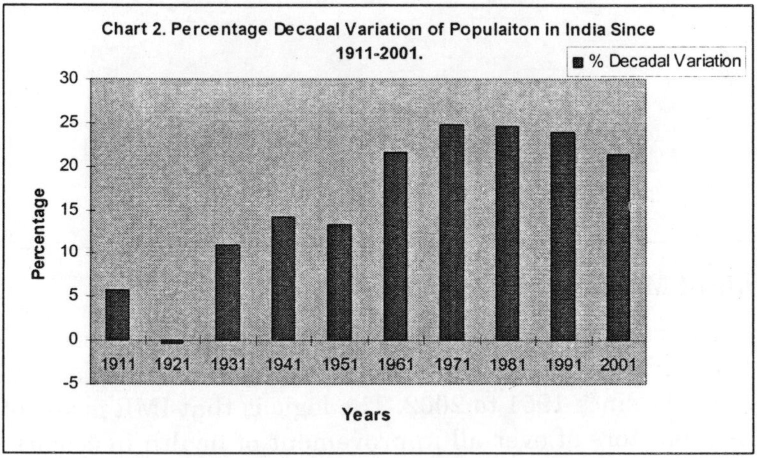

Apart from the trend of population and decadal growth rate it is interesting to see the level of crude birth rate and death rate over the period, as these are directly linked to the improvement of health. So the following section will discuss about CBR and CDR over the period 1991 to 2001.

Fertility and Mortality Rate in India

Chart 3 shows the trends of CBR (Crude Birth Rate) and CDR (Crude Death Rate) from 1911 to 2001. From the chart it is clearly shown that up to 1951 there was no difference in CBR and CDR. Afterwards from 1961 to 1991 there is a drastic decline of CDR in comparison to CBR. Though both the trend lines are decreasing, the rate is little higher in the case of CDR in comparison to CBR. After 1991, both the trend lines tend to decline and the rate is almost closer to each other, that is why the decadal growth rate is decreasing.

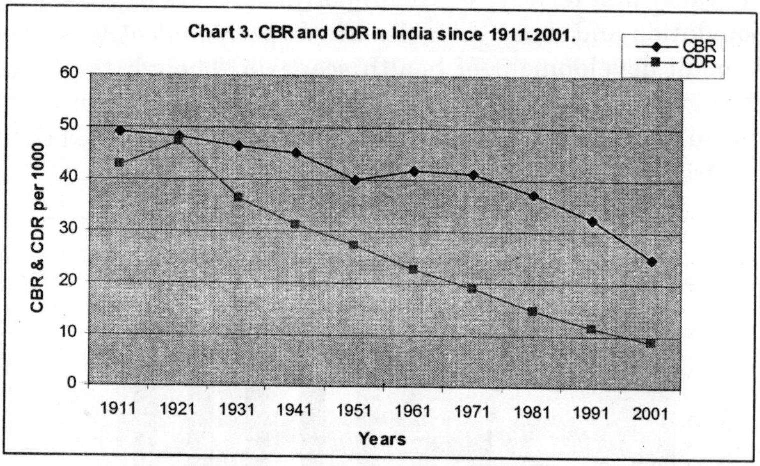

Infant Mortality Rate in India

Apart from this an attempt is made to look into the infant mortality rate (IMR) by taking sex and place of residence since 1951 to 2002. The logic is that IMR is one of the indicators of over all improvement of health in a place. It is interesting to see the trend of IMR which will give the clear picture of over all development of health in India over a period of time. Chart 4 presents the trends of IMR since 1951 to 2002 according to sex of the infant. From the chart it is clearly shown that in 1951 the total IMR was almost 145 children per 1000 live births, whereas there is little deviation according to sex, as around 150/1000 deaths for male infants in comparison to 140/1000 deaths for female infants. Since 1961 the IMR is decreasing over the period but there is little variation in the rate of decline. In 2002 the IMR in India reached at around 60/1000 which is almost half in comparison to 1951.

Similarly an attempt is made to look into the IMR in accordance with the place of residence (rural vs. urban) over the period 1971 to 2002. Chart 5 clearly indicates that there is a clear difference in IMR according to the place of residence. Although both the trend lines show a decline over the period, still there is little variation. From the chart it is

Chart 4. IMR by Sex in India since 1951 to 2002.

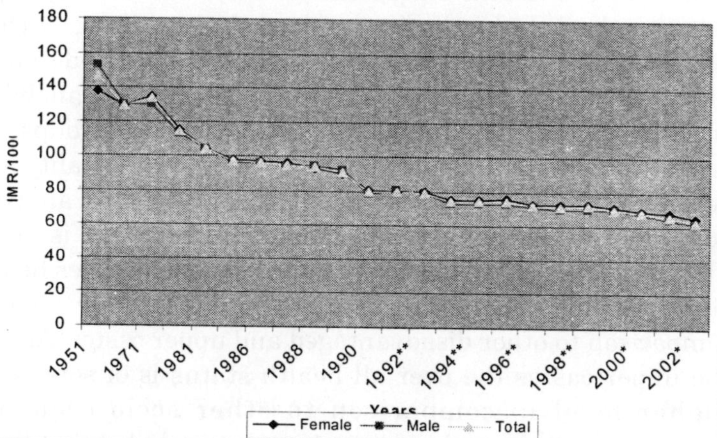

Chart 5. IMR by Place of Residence in India since 1971 to 2003

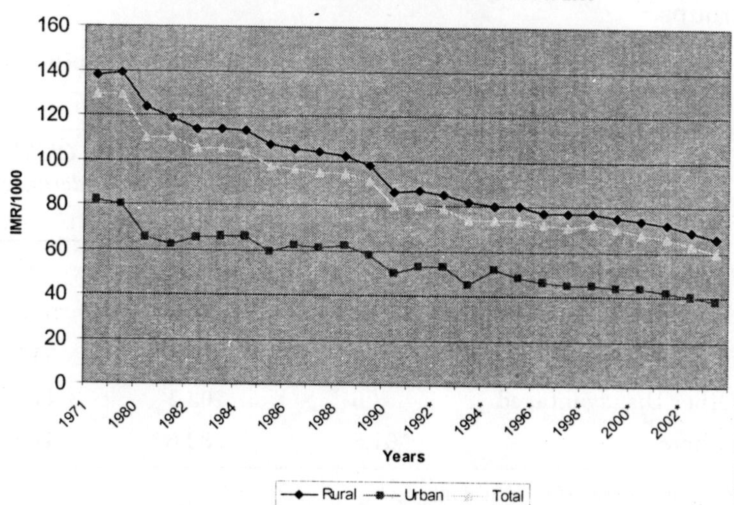

clearly shown that in rural India, IMR was almost 140/1000 deaths where as it is only 80/1000 in the case of urban India in 1971. In 2002 IMR reached around 70/1000 in rural India and 40/1000 in urban India. Over all it is concluded that though there is difference in IMR in rural and urban India but over the period the rate is decreasing.

Apart from the above analysis, an attempt is made to look in to the health status among socio economic groups. Here scheduled castes, scheduled tribes, other disadvantaged and upper castes (others) are considered as socio economic groups for the analysis. Due to unavailability of all the information among the socio economic groups, we are confined to only infant mortality; under 5 mortality and percentage of children underweight are taken into analysis only for the period 1999-2000. From the table-1 it is found that among the scheduled castes and scheduled tribes health status of infant and children are comparatively poor in comparison to other disadvantaged and upper castes. Among the upper castes the over all health status is of somewhat higher level in comparison to other socio economic groups. From this analysis it is strongly concluded that there is disparity in health status among the socio economic groups.

Table-1. Differentials in Health Status Among Socio-Economic Groups (1999-2000)

Indicator	*Infant Mortality / 1000*	*Under 5 Mortality / 1000*	*% Children Underweight*
India	70	94.9	47
Scheduled Castes	83	119.3	53.5
Scheduled Tribes	84.2	126.6	55.9
Other Disadvantaged	76	103.1	47.3
Others	61.8	82.6	41.1

Sources: www.indiastat.com

Not only the CBR, CDR and IMR are important for measuring the improvement of health status in a place, but also the life expectancy is also equally important. In order to see the over all improvement in health, it is important to see the life expectancy at birth over a long period of time. The following table-2 presents the life expectancy according to sex and total population over a period of time from 1950 to 2050. From the analysis it is found that the life expectancy is increased over this period. In 1950 it was only 38.7 years where as in 2000 it became 64.2 years. Apart from that, it is interesting to see the differential level of life expectancy by sex. During the period before 1975, the life expectancy among the males was somewhat higher in comparison to females but afterwards the life expectancy among the females exceeded from that of males. It is projected that the life expectancy will be 71.6 and 75.4 years by the year 2025 and 2050 respectively.

Table-2. Life Expectancy at Birth since 1950-2050

Years	*Life Expectancy (yrs) at Birth*		
	Female	*Male*	*Total*
1950	38.0	39.0	38.7
1975	52.4	53.3	52.9
2000	64.9	63.6	64.2
2025	73.4	69.9	71.6
2050	77.4	73.5	75.4

Sources: United Nations, 2002.

India and the Countries in the World

From the above analysis it is not enough to strongly conclude anything about the improvement of heath status in India without comparing with the over all status of health from the other nearby countries. With this objective an attempt is made to look in to the overall demographic and health status of the selected countries from Asia. Table-3 presents the total population, average annual growth rate, total fertility rate, IMR and life expectancy at birth for both sexes of the selected countries from Asia. It is interesting to see that in countries like China, Japan, Republic of Korea and Thailand, the average annual growth rate is less than 1 per cent. Whereas Sri Lanka and Australia reached at 1 per cent and other few countries including India, Indonesia, Myanmar, Singapore, Vietnam, Bangladesh and Iran reached at above 1 per cent but less than 2 per cent of average annual population growth. Similarly in China, Japan, Korea, Singapore, Thailand and Australia the total fertility is less than 1 child per woman. Whereas in other countries including India, the total fertility rate is more than 2 children per woman. Apart from this it is interesting to see the level of infant mortality rate. It is found that in Japan, Singapore and Australia the IMR is only around 5/1000 live births. Whereas in countries like India, Pakistan, Nepal, Bangladesh and Afghanistan the IMR is much more than 70/1000 live births. Similarly there is huge difference in life expectancy at birth as well as by sex. From the table it is clear that in Japan, China, Korea, Singapore, Thailand, Australia and Sri Lanka the average life expectancy is around 75 years whereas in India and other nearby countries life expectancy is around 65 years. Though from the over all analysis it is found that there is substantial improvement of health status in India over the period but in comparison to other countries the performance is not satisfactory. It is interesting to see that there is a variation in the achievement in the health scenario within the countries in Asia.

Achievements in Family Planning in India

Apart from the above analysis it is interesting to see the achievement in family planning which is one of the indirect estimates of health status. In this paper we used achievements in sterilization, IUD insertion, CC users, OP users and CPR (Couple Protection Rate) since 1993-94 to 2005-06. From the table-4 it becomes clear that the number

Table-3. Demographic Estimates for Selected Countries 1999-2000

Country	*Mid-2000 Population (Millions)*	*Average Annual Growth Rate (%)*	*Total Fertility Rate (Per women)*	*Infant Mortality Rate (per 1000 live births)*	*Life Expectancy at birth (years)*	
					Male	*Female*
China	**1277.6**	**0.9**	**1.8**	41	**67.9**	**72**
DPR Korea	24	1.6	2.1	22	68.9	75.1
Japan	126.7	**0.2**	**1.4**	**4**	**76.8**	**82.9**
Republic of Korea	45.9	**0.8**	**1.7**	**10**	**68.8**	**76**
Indonesia	212.1	1.4	2.6	48	63.3	67
Malaysia	22.2	2	3.2	**11**	69.9	74.3
Myanmar	45.6	1.2	2.4	79	58.5	61.8
Philippines	76	2.1	3.6	36	66.5	70.2
Singapore	3.6	1.4	**1.7**	**5**	**74.9**	**79.3**
Thailand	61.4	**0.9**	**1.7**	29	65.8	**72**
Vietnam	79.8	1.6	2.6	38	64.9	69.6
Afghanistan	22.7	2.9	6.9	152	45	46
Bangladesh	129.2	1.7	3.1	79	58.1	58.2
India	**1013.7**	**1.6**	**3.1**	**72**	**62.3**	**62.9**
Iran	67.7	1.7	2.8	35	**68.5**	**70**
Nepal	23.9	2.4	4.5	83	57.6	57.1
Pakistan	156.5	2.8	5	74	62.9	65.1
Sri Lanka	18.6	**1**	2.1	**18**	**70.9**	**75.4**
Australia	18.9	**1**	**1.8**	**6**	75.5	81.1
More Developed Rgn.	1188	**0.3**	**1.6**	**9**	**71.1**	**78.7**
Less Developed Rgn.	4867.1	**1.6**	**3**	**63**	**61.8**	**65**
World	**6055**	**1.3**	**2.7**	**57**	**63.3**	**67.6**

Sources: www.indiastat.com

of sterilization is decreasing over the period. In 1993-94 the number of sterilization was 4.5 millions whereas over the period it decreased and reached at 1.522 millions in 2005-06. It means that the number of sterilization cases is

Table-4. Year wise Family Planning Achievements (1993-94 to 2005-06)

(Figures in Millions)

Family Planning Methods/Items	*1993-94*	*1994-95*	*1995-96*	*1996-97*	*1997-98***	*1998-99***	*1999-2000***	*2001-02*	*2002-03*	*2003-04*	*2004-05*	*2005-06*
Sterilization* Achievements	4.5	4.58	4.42	3.87	4.24	4.21	4.59	1.773	2.9	3.05	1.518	1.522
IUD Insertion Achievements	6.02	6.7	6.86	5.68	6.17	6.08	6.19	3.21	4.15	4.26	2.65	2.76
CC Users Achievements	17.28	17.71	17.3	17.21	16.8	17.31	18.36	11.68	15.42	16.33	15.53	18.16
OP Users Achievements	4.3	4.87	5.09	5.25	6.39	6.94	7.86	6.79	7.64	8.24	7.18	7.24
CPR (%)	45.4 (31.3.94)	45.8 (31.3.95)	46.5 (31.3.96)	45.4 (31.3.97)	45.4 (31.3.98)	44 (31.3.99)	46.2 (31.3.00)					

Sources: www.indiastat.com

decreasing in India over the period because of the availability of alternative modern technologies to avoid the risk of pregnancies. Similarly the number of IUD insertion is also decreasing over the period. But it is interesting to see that the number of CC users and OP users is slightly increasing over the period. There is almost no change in CPR over the period which is almost 45 per cent throughout the period. From the above analysis it is strongly concluded that in the present days there are a number of modern technologies available with plenty of alternative options to avoid the risk of pregnancy. Therefore, the demand for traditional methods for family planning is reduced over the period. It clearly indicates the achievement of family planning in India.

Discussion

Apart from the above discussion an attempt is made to look into the achievements under "Health for All by the Year 2000" programme in India. From the table-5 it is clear that there is a drastic decline in CBR, CDR, IMR and TFR in 2000 in comparison to 1950. Within these fifty years there was a lot of improvement in the reduction of mortality rate. Simultaneously, the couple protection rate and the life expectancy at birth have also increased drastically over these fifty years.

Table-5. Achievements under "Health for All by the Year 2000" Programme in India

Indicators	*Past Level*	*Current Level*
Crude Birth Rate (Per thousand population)	40.8 (1951)	25.8 (2000)
Crude Death Rate (Per thousand population)	25.1 (1951)	8.5 (2000)
Infant Mortality Rate (Per thousand Live Births)	146 (1951-61)	68 (2000)
Maternal Mortality Ratio (Per 100000 Live Births)	437 (1992-93)	407 (1998)

Indicators	*Past Level*	*Current Level*
Total Fertility Rate (Per Woman)	6.0 (1951)	3.2 (1999)
Couple Protection Rate (%)	10.4 (1970-71)	48.6 (2000)
Life Expectancy at Birth (In Years)	(1950-1951)	(2001-2006)
Male	37.1	63.87
Female	36.1	66.91
Immunization Status (% Coverage)	1985-86	2001-2002
For Pregnant Women		
TT	40	85.6
For Infants		
BCG	29	100.4
Measles	44	90.8
DPT	41	95.4
Polio	36	96

Sources: www.indiastat.com

It is interesting to see the coverage of immunization status from 1985-86 to 2001-02. From the table-5 it is clearly evident that the coverage of TT for pregnant women was only 40 per cent in 1985-86 whereas it increased to 85.6 per cent in 2001-02. Similarly over this period the coverage of BCG, Measles, DPT and Polio for infants is approaching 100 percent. It clearly indicates the over all achievement of health status of infants and pregnant women in India.

Conclusion

From the above discussion it is clearly shown that there is drastic improvement of over all health status among the infants, children, and women especially pregnant women in India. Similarly, the life expectancy at birth, immunization coverage and the availability of health care facilities are also increasing over this period. All these achievements are only after the independence and within the frame work of five year plans. Since 1950 the Government of India has implemented various policies with the aim of improving the health status of the common people, especially that of the targeted sections like women under the age-group 18-44 years, infants, children as well as socio economic groups like scheduled tribes, scheduled castes and the poor. Really it is a great achievement for the over all development of a country and it is possible only by the intervention of government policies.

References

Anita, N.H., et al. (2000) Health and Medical Care: A People's Movement. Foundation for Research in Community Health, Pune.

Gray, A.G. (2001) Theories and Practices of Clinical Governance, ESRC Seminar on Evaluating Clinical Governance, Stockport Health Authority.

Narayana, K.V. (1997) Health and Development: Intersectoral Linkages in India, Rawat Publications, Jaipur and New Delhi.

Rhodes, R. A. W. (1997) Understanding Governance: Policy Networks, Governance, Reflexivity and Accountability, Open University Press, Buckingham.

Som, Chandra Vanu (2002) Governance in 21st Century: Does Clinical Governance Provide A Way Forwards Better Governance in Health Service Organizations? *The Administrator,* Vol. 45, pp. 180-98.

UNDP, (1997) Good Governance for Sustainable Human Development: A UNDP Policy Document, New York, Vol. 6, No. 1, pp. 34-39.

United Nations, (2002) World Population Ageing 1950-2050. Department of Economic and Social Affairs Population Division. ST/ESA/SER.A/207. New York.

World Bank, (2001) Governance the Critical Factor, The World Bank, Washington, DC.

8

Forest and Its Sustainability in Arunachal Pradesh

Ram Krishna Mandal

The phenomenal increase in population of both human beings and animals in the last century and fast growing industrialization and urbanization in the last few centuries have overstrained the nature which are getting degraded much faster than before. With the advent of high yielding varieties, augmentation of irrigation facilities, increased use of fertilizers, adoption of improved agronomic practices, concerted efforts of researchers, planners, government and above all the farming community, green revolution was brought about in the mid 1960's. This led to a quantum jump in food grain production from 51 Mt in 1950-51 to a record figure of 203 Mt in 1998-99. With the adoption of intensive agriculture to meet the varied growing demands for food, fuel, fibre and cattle fodder, natural resources have been put under intense pressure resulting in fast degradation and lowering of production efficiency.

On the other side, the demographic pressure is rapidly mounting on the natural resources. The present population of over 1000 million, accounting for about 18 percent of the world's population, is estimated to become 1.4 billion by 2025 and 1.7 billion by 2050 AD, needing annually about 380 Mt and 480 Mt food grains respectively. This scenario along with the increasing industrialization and urbanization will place tremendous pressure on the shrinking natural resources. Unless corrective measures are taken, this will make the damage to the environment and the very resource base irreversible. However, we still have the capacity to produce enough food to meet the basic requirement of the burgeoning population, but the moot question is whether, we can do so while maintaining our natural resources and preserving the bio diversity at the same time.

Common property resources imply local commons like village pond and tanks, pastures and threshing grounds, watershed, river beds, sources of fuel woods, medicinal herbs, bamboo, resin, gum, etc. Local commons are open only to those having historical rights, kinship ties, community membership, etc.

A series of policy interventions along with market focus are likely to be unleashed in the wake of opening up and globalization. This will alter the land use and tenurial system (directed to institutionalization of modern private property) with serious environmental and social consequences to both private and communal property resources. By passing the transitional task of creating an environment for the evolution of co-operation based new 'Common Property Resources Management (CPRM)' institutions may further aggravate the already prevailing unquiet environment of India's North-East.

The Seven North-Eastern States have a geographical area of 2.55 lakhs sq.kms and a population of 384.95 lakhs out of which 325.23 lakhs of population live in rural areas of this region. Thus, 84.5% of population lives in rural areas. This region is rich in forest and bio-diversity. 64.3% of its geographical area is covered under forest. The region is also recognized as hydro-power house to feed at least one-third of the requirement of power in India. The area is rich in mineral resources and maximum of these are yet to be tapped. Under the given condition, the area is rich in natural resources. But over 40% of rural population lives under poverty in the region. The development in the region can be achieved only after eradication of poverty from North

Eastern Region. Arunachal Pradesh is one of the seven States of North East Region. As per the State forest report 1999, published by the Forest Survey of India; forest cover of Arunachal Pradesh is 68,951 sq.km, accounting 82.21 percent of its total geographical area. The recorded forest area of the state is 51540 sq km, which is about 61.5 % of its total geographical area. Thus, the state is fortunate to have such high percentage of its area under valuable forest cover against the national percentage of 23.28. Again, out of its area, 70% constitutes broad and narrow valleys, 10 percent foothills and flat areas and 20% snow clad peak areas. The agricultural operations are confined to only 5 percent of its total geographical area, out of which 62 % to 65 % are under shifting cultivation (jhum).

Arunachal Pradesh has a peculiar characteristic of its transitionality in its environmental conditions and socio economic parameters due to its situation on the globe. It is situated near the tropic of cancer, lying between $26^0$28'N and $29^0$30'N latitude and between $91^0$30'E and $97^0$30'E longitude. The area falls in the climatic transition between torrid and temperate zones of the Northern Hemisphere. It is greener than the other parts of the world situated on the same latitudes where the dry deserts of the Thar, the Syrian and Nafud deserts of Arabian sub-continents of South west Asia, the eastern deserts of Egypt and the Nubian and Libyan deserts of the Great Sahara are lying. The regional setting has great political importance as it is considered to be "Frontier Area" bounded by China, Myanmar, Bhutan, as the nearest neighbours along with State boundaries of Assam and Nagaland.

Arunachal Pradesh is the largest state of the North-Eastern Region covering an area of 83,743 sq.km. with just above 10 lakhs of population (2001census). Socio-culturally, the state incorporates an extremely diverse population of local tribes and sub tribes, which have been scheduled by the Government (SC/ST Order Amendment Act, 1967), and non tribal comprising of people from almost all the Indian States with diverse cultural/religious composition. What is interesting about the majority of population is that the tribal groups numbering about 110 major ethnic segments have developed their pattern of life in total isolation from any comparable societies of the world that we observe today, each independent of the other woven like a gigantic mosaic of diverse socio-cultural identity.

The dependence of human activities on natural resources is not only recognized but well acknowledged also. Surprisingly, mainstream economists especially a group of engineer cum neoclassical economists rarely pays attention to the importance of natural resources or environmental resources. Arunachal Pradesh is very rich in terms of natural resources and sustainable use of these resources may make sure sustainable development. These natural resources may be classified as open access or common property resources depending upon property rights and the rights and responsibilities for harvesting and conservation.

As per 2001 census, the population of Arunachal Pradesh is 1097968 out of which 40% of its population is living under BPL (Below Poverty Line). Poverty and Sustainable Development (SD) are two socio-economic phenomena drawing global attention of academicians, researchers, policy makers as well as human activists. Traditionally, the issues of poverty and SD have been treated separately and singularly but during last one decade there have been conceptual developments and paradigm shifts in these areas. They are now viewed as concepts that are multidimensional and more comprehensive. Also, there is some degree of convergence within and between the two in that the issue of poverty and food security is now considered an integral part of the bigger challenge known as SD. Further, most of the remedial aspects of poverty and SD required direct action and a pro-active involvement on the part of the government, the private sector, the civil society and the

NGOs at all levels – local, national and global. This paper seeks an attempt to examine an in-depth study about the degradation of common property resources, poverty and sustainable development in Arunachal Pradesh.

The paper is divided into three sections. The first section concentrates on Common Property Resources (CPRs) especially forest. The second section devotes to examine the meanings and some dimensions of Sustainable Development. The third section deals with the negative correlation between deforestation and sustainable development.

SECTION – I

Common Property Resources are those common resources in which a precise group of individuals have the rights as well as responsibility to use and conserve but not for individual possession. The resources are not under any management system and everybody has the equal right to use but no responsibility to conserve it, these are open access resources and termed as only commons. A variety of common resources such as forest lands, revenue lands, lands lying along side railway tracks, roads, water reservoirs, tanks, canals, irrigation ponds, rivers, lakes, streams, etc. are found to happen at varied degrees in rural areas. Majority of the rural poor depend on these commons for at least four purposes such as fishing, livestock rearing (grazing and fodder), fuel wood and irrigation of crops. Conventionally, the rural people of Arunachal Pradesh significantly depend on common resources (CRs) for their livelihoods and the duty of harvesting from the CRs lies on women and children of this impoverished class. It has been estimated that 84 to 100% of poor households are dependent on CRs for fuel, fodder and food items and they obtain 14 to 23% of their income from harvested CR products (Jodha, 1990). Most of these natural resources are 'open accesses and hence the destiny of these resources is supposed to be what has been described by Hardin (1968) as 'Tragedy of Commons'. However, in many parts of the world Hardin's hypothesis proved incorrect as communities, under certain conditions, are found to manage resources like water and forests successfully over a long period of time despite the fact that the resources and the management and use system are nearly everywhere facing increasing pressure from growing population and the effects of economic and political changes.

Forest has been playing an important role in socio-economic development of this region-specially hill tribal inhabited region, as a source of subsistence, employment, and raw-materials for industry. The indigenous people's role in ecological balance, environmental stability and sustainable development has been recognized in National Forest Policy, 1988. The forest resource of the region is under tremendous pressure due to increasing demand for human and livestock. Too much of extraction has led to forest degradation and disaster in ecological balance in recent time in this region.

The position of forest cover as per statement of Forest Report, (SFR) 1997 is in Table 1.

Table-1: Forest Cover in North Eastern Region in India

(in sq.km.)

State	*Total Geographical area*	*1991*	*1993*	*1995*	*1997*
Arunachal Pradesh	83743	68757	68661	68621	68602
Assam	78438	24751	24508	24061	23824
Manipur	22327	17685	17621	17558	17418
Meghalaya	22429	15875	15769	15714	15657
Mizoram	21081	18853	18697	18576	18775
Nagaland	16579	14321	14348	14291	14221
Tripura	10486	5535	5538	5538	5546
Total in NE Region	255083	165777	164842	164359	164043
All India	3287263	639364	639386	638879	633397

Source : The State Forest Report, 1997

The forest cover has decreased in all the states in this region in 1997 compared to 1991 except Arunachal Pradesh. The trend is observed in all India too. Forests may be regarded as capital stocks of such a nature that they yield two distinct flows of goods fundamentally different in nature-flow of private good such as timber, fuel wood, other minor forest produce and a flow of public goods like maintenance of environment, causation of rainfall, prevention of soil erosion, etc. There are some unique features of forest situated in Arunachal Pradesh. Around 61.5% of the total geographical area is covered under forest which is the highest among the seven states of North East India. The state contains nearly 16% of the total timber growing stock of the country (the highest among the individual states) and more than 20% fauna of India (Government of Arunachal Pradesh, 1995). In Arunachal Pradesh, the ownership of land as well as the forest land and the individual right to use it are governed by local traditions and custom of the tribes. Under the prevailing land tenure system, there are three types of land ownership namely [a] community land [b] clan land and [c] individual land. Regarding the forest land, almost all the tribes have the community forest land, almost all the tribes have the community forest which is controlled by the village council. In some areas, clan ownership is recognized in the forest areas falling within the village jurisdiction. That is why, if we look at the data on the basis of legal status of forest in the state, it is found that around 62.17% of total forest is under community ownership which is reported as Unclassified State Forest (USF). However, at present there is a growing tendency of individual ownership of forest which is a recent phenomenon in the state. For example, in the Apatani plateau of Lower Subansiri district, the forest has become increasingly privatized.

The reserve forest constitutes 19,236.55 sq. km, i.e., nearly 37.32% of the total forest area of the state. On the other hand, Anchal Reserve Forest covered only 256.08 square kilometers (only 0.5% of the total forest area). Such forests are managed by the forest department with the provision for sharing the net revenue in the ratio of 50:50 (share of village: share of government).

The classifications of Forests in Arunachal Pradesh are shown in Table 2:

Table-2. Classification of Forests in Arunachal Pradesh in 1990-91

Sl. No.	*Legal Status of Forest*	*Area (in sq. km)*	*% of total area*	*% of total geo. area*
1	*2*	*3*	*4*	*5*
1.	Reserved Forest	19,236.55	37.32	22.97
2.	Anchal Forests	256.08	0.50	0.30
3.	Protected Forests	7.79	0.01	0.0091
4.	Unclassified State Forest (U.S.F.)	32,039.00	62.17	38.27
	Grand Total	51,539.42	100.00	61.54

Source: Arunachal Pradesh Environment & Forest Department, Govt. of Arunachal Pradesh, 1993

SECTION – II

What is Sustainable Development?

It appears that the term Sustainable Development (SD) was first used in the context of environmental degradation across generations (Raskin, 1996). However, its scope has since widened to incorporate the new realities of changing times in almost all areas of human concern. Before elaborating on the various dimensions of SD we first explore its meanings.

The notion of SD is derived from two words – sustainable and development. SUSTAIN means 'to maintain' or 'to uphold' something (e.g., a life, a system, etc.) by providing a minimum necessary support and/or a conducive environment. SUSTAINABLE implies 'capable of maintaining' or 'capable of upholding' and has the objective and subjective dimensions of *viability* and *desirability* respectively. Finally, SUSTAINABILITY refers to the capacity or capability of systems for achieving the viable and desirable results from an activity under consideration.

Sustainable Development means 'development that meets the needs of the present without compromising the ability and future generations to meet their own needs. World Bank Report speaks about the sustainable development as "a process of managing portfolio of assets to preserve and enhance the opportunities people face". Sustainable Development includes economic, environmental, social sustainability which can be achieved by rationally managing physical, natural and human capital. This term being used by economists and politicians all over the world and the term is constantly being refined. 'Intergenerational' equity would be impossible to achieve unless the groups stop exploitation of other groups or community living in other parts of the world.

For example, Greenhouse gases generated by highly developed/ highly industrialized countries of the world leading to global warning and flooding of some islands resulting in displacement and impoverishment of entire islands. The situation of profiteering by the Pharmaceutical companies at the cost of millions of poor people being unable to offer medicines required to life threatening diseases. The live examples we can also quote in this regard are Bhopal gas tragedy of 1994, Chernobyl in Russia, Nuclear bomb attack on Nagasaki and Hiroshima during II World War in various forms.

The meaning of DEVELOPMENT is better understood when contrasted with the notion of GROWTH. Growth (or economic progress) means a vertical change in the economy requiring an efficient use of resources (based on the criterion or cost minimization). It is limited to an increase in the material production of goods and services produced in a year and can be measured quantitatively in terms of per capita income of a country. On the other hand, development is much more than just economic progress. It is a 'holistic' and 'multifaceted' phenomenon of horizontal change demanding a judicious use of resources (based on the notion of welfare maximization for the society as a whole). Of late, development levels achieved by different countries are approximated with human development index (HDI) that is currently based on three variables – literacy, life expectancy and gender disparity in addition to per capita income. Many other aspects of social concern such as poverty levels and gaps in income-distribution, etc. are also the desired variables of HDI but not included in its calculations so far. However, it is clear that the notion of development requires balance and harmony amongst various components of economy as well as society. Finally, it should be noted that growth is a necessary condition for development and not the sufficient one, i.e. growth is necessary for development but it need not always lead to development.

Historical example reveals that greater economic development was achieved at the cost of inequality, unemployment, weak democracy, loss of cultural identity, over exploitation of natural resources leading to ecological and economical imbalances resulting in a dire threat for both flora and fauna. To be sustainable, we must rely on certain amount of natural resources available in nature to absorb pollution and regeneration of resources.

Mainstream economists have been primarily concerned with growth and development and neglected the consequences of more production and output on the physical environment. While poverty has to be removed for accomplishment of development and economic development wants production of more goods and services which not only is the cause of environmental pollution but also leads to more extraction of renewable natural resources than their replenishment and directs to exhaustion of non-renewable natural resources that may deprive future generations from experiencing the benefits of those valuable resources. In economics little attention is paid on the problems of excessive natural resources exploitation in long run since to an economist sustainable economic development means extraction of maximum possible benefits over a fairly long period from the exploitation of the available resources in alternative uses. But given the fact that poverty, environment and development are closely connected; environmental problems which are largely caused by increased economic activities appeared as a serious threat to whole mankind across the globe in general and the poor in particular; hence, the costs of worsening environmental quality can no longer be ignored even in underdeveloped counties because unrestricted development may cause harm to environment which in turn may impair the scope of future development. In contrast to economic approach, ecologists are in favour of not using natural resources for economic purposes at least at the cost of loss of bio-diversity as biological sustainability implies conservation of environmental resources for maintaining wide bio-diversity which has vast option and existence values. The World Commission on Environment and Development (WCED, 1987) provided a balanced approach by defining sustainable development that "meets the needs of the present without compromising the ability of future generation to meet their own needs", which accepts obligation to pay attention on improving the economic condition of the poor for better environment recognizing the importance of people and their roles both in economic and ecological consideration. The definition of sustainable development given by Viederman (1996) which states "sustainability is a community's control and prudent use of all forms of capital to ensure, to the degree possible, the present and future generations can obtain a high degree of economic security and achieve democracy while maintaining the integrity of the ecological system upon which all lives and production depends" explicitly signifies management and use of capital by the communities in a democratic structure and may be regarded as an appropriate and comprehensive approach in the context of sustainable development. Though sustainable development needs reduction of industrial pollution, sustainable use of renewable resources and making certain the carry-over of non-renewable resources for all future generations, we will focus on the conservation of renewable natural resources in a participatory scaffold under the leadership of local level self-governing administration.

The equitable and balanced development must continue indefinitely by considering the interest of different groups within the same generations and among the generations taking into account the three interrelated areas i.e., economic, social and environmental. Blending or balancing, economic objectives – growth, stability, efficiency, productivity, per capita income, living standard and so on; social objectives – employment, equity, security, education, health, cultural identify, status and so on, and environmental objectives – healthy environment for both flora and fauna including human beings, rational use of renewable natural resources, conservation of non renewable natural resources, pollution control, treatment of effluents (solid, liquid and gaseous waste), etc., is becoming an enormous challenge for any country in the process of sustainable development; otherwise there will be irreparable damage on the environment. Many issues which are becoming more challenging and complicating, because the decisions which are taken at the local level have far-reaching consequences at global level – economic, social and environmental. When these consequences are negative, the situation is referred to as 'exporting un-sustainability'.

In Rio de Janeiro in June 1992, United Nations conference on Environment and Development, 1992, Para 2.1, it is declared, "Human beings are at the center of concern for sustainable development. They are entitled to a healthy and productive life in harmony with nature".

Sustainable development assumes high substitutability among different components of national wealth. Depletion of natural resources can be compensated with high investment on education i.e., human development and physical capital development which make ways for replacement of old technology to new technology to have effective usage of non-renewable resources at lesser level.

SECTION – III

Encroachment of valuable forest land, illicit felling, inter-state boundary disputes and their effect on deforestation, timber trade in the District Council areas, shifting cultivations and forest fires due to pressure of increase in human population and increase in urbanization are some of the reasons for the continuous loss of forest cover in Arunachal Pradesh. Due to population pressure, more and more forest lands are being brought under cultivation for increased food supply. The demand for fuel wood is increasing steadily. Virgin forests are being exploited for commercial purposes. The growth of population is shown in Table 3 and Table 4.

Table 3. Population Growth Since 1961

NEFA / State	*1961*	*1971*	*1981*	*1991*	*2001*
Arunachal Pradesh	336558	467511	628050	864558	1097968

Table 4. Decennial Population Growth Rate Since 1961

Sl.	*State*	*Percentage decadal*			
		1961-71	*1971-81*	*1981-91*	*1991-2001*
1	*2*	*3*	*4*	*5*	*6*
	Arunachal Pradesh	38.91	35.15	36.83	26.21
		(24.80)	(24.66)	(23.86)	(21.34)

Source: Census Report, Arunachal Pradesh, 2001.
Note: (i) Figures within bracket are at national level.

$$\frac{\text{(Population of previous census – Population of current census)} \times 100}{\text{Population of previous census}}$$

During every tenth year, population census is undertaken in India. The growth behaviour of population is shown above in Table 3 and Table 4 accounted for this period, which is known as decennial growth of population. From the standpoint of economic development, to know decennial growth rate of population is one of the most essential requirements. Because, the decennial growth rate and the economic benefit out of economic development at constant rate relate inversely considering that other things remain as constant. That is why, the technique of decennial growth rate is used as barometer to reflect the growth phenomena of population. In the absence of decennial population growth rate, the requirements can neither be identified nor quantified properly. Thus, population is the pivot around which all types of economic activities rotate.

Urbanization

Urbanization indicates technological, institutional, educational, communicational, industrial and organizational development from time to time and is being brought about by modernization and migration. It is so closely related with economic development and social transformation of the state or a region. Urbanization and economic development stimulate each other. Structural changes are linked with urbanization. Economic development is generally associated with the growth of urbanization.

Growth of Urban Centres

Till 1961 census of the State of Arunachal Pradesh was entirely rural. Census- wise trend in urbanization is shown in Table 5.

Table 5. Census-wise Urban Centres

Census	*No. of census Towns*	*Name of the census Towns*
1961	NIL	
1971	4	Bomdila, Along, Pasighat and Tezu

Census	*No. of census Towns*	*Name of the census Towns*
1981	6	Bomdila, Along, Pasighat, Tezu, Naharlagun and Itanagar.
1991	10	Bomdila, Along, Pasighat, Tezu, Naharlagun, Itanagar, Ziro, Roing, Namsai and Khonsa.
2001	17	Bomdila, Along, Pasighat, Tezu, Naharlagun, Itanagar, Ziro, Roing, Namsai, Khonsa, Tawang, Seppa, Daporijo, Basar, Changlang, Jairampur and Deomali.

Source : Census Report of Various Issues

All these towns are administrative centres in most cases and before the establishment of administrative centres, these places were full of jungles. According to 1991 census, 12.80% people live in ten urban areas while as per 2001 census 20.41 people live in seventeen urban areas. The decennial urban growth rate in the state has been recorded as 139.63 in 1971-81, 167.04 in 1981-91 and 101.24 in 1991-2001. The effect of urbanization brings deforestation for the establishment of urban centre.

Timber extraction in the state was taken up on a large scale till 1995-96. A large number of wood-based industries cropped up in Arunachal Pradesh. A timber trade in the state had also increased through the operation of tree permits. There was halt on this trade after a Supreme Court judgment on 12th December, 1996 on a writ petition (Civil) NO. 202 filed by Shri T.N.Godavarman Thirumulpad.

Forest is a renewable resource if properly husbanded, but it becomes a depleting non renewable resource once the process of deforestation brings the stock and its variety below a threshold. Deforestation does not take long, while a forest takes a very long time to develop into a self contained viable eco system. Preservation of the wealth of wild life depends on a scientific management of forest resources. Deforestation invites so many problems which are discussed below:

1. **Environmental and Socio-Cultural Problems:** Environmental concerns generally comprise of three factors:

(i) Depletion of natural resources.

(ii) Conservation of the natural state of the environment and

(iii) Pollution and its control.

These factors constitute the domain of environmental accounting.

The issue of natural resource accounting or environmental accounting becomes more pressing for a country like India where economic growth is significantly based on natural resources. In natural resource accounting, besides lack of awareness and proper database, one does not find set of rules which have universal application (which can be applied universally). Norway, France etc, have achieved remarkable success in this field but their geographical and political setup is so different that their framework cannot be adopted by most of the developing countries where the need of environmental accounting is much more pressing. This need becomes exigent considering the fact than in these poor countries the linkage between poverty and environmental degradation is very strong. In this context, World Resource Institute (WkI) has conducted some very useful studies, but it could not adopt a more sophisticated approach because the necessary data were not available. However absence of proper methodology to calculate the value of depreciation of environmental resources does not imply that we should wait for new techniques of natural resource accounting.

The concerns and doubts about environmental degradation were raised in Rome in 1972. These concerns have persisted since then and now it is widely recognized that the environmental degradation has essentially germinated from the failures/inconsistencies of the part of the decision makers. Some writers go to the extents of suggesting that the problems of environmental degradation is more serve than that of inflation, excessive foreign debt or stagnant economic growth. For less developed countries it has become much pressing where rapid deforestation, watershed degradation, loss of biological diversity, fuel wood and water shortages, water contamination, excessive soil erosion, land degradation, overgrazing, over fishing, air pollution and urban congestion are prevalent. Here a pertinent question arises that why this unwanted phenomenon occurs while no economic agent is willing to pay for this to happen.

It has been undisputedly accepted that shifting cultivation creates environmental and socio-cultural problems. The greater food requirements cannot be met out of dwindling yields from smaller plots of land devoted to jhuming with smaller and smaller fallowing periods. The over exploitation of forests for jhuming and commercial purposes also lead to a deterioration of the condition of the forests. The misuse and destruction of plants cover combined with great increase in human and livestock population has aggravated the problem of eco-system. Ecological damage in the hills, widespread poverty among hill-dwelling tribal, social discontent and the growth of extension has been the fall-out of the development of the hill economy.

There is an urgent need to study in-depth the present environmental crisis related with the misuse of natural resources. A thorough understanding, awareness and perception about environmental issues and natural resources management practices will help in designing suitable extension strategies to make the farmers aware and perceive better the issues concerned and adopt remedial practices. Further, studying the present utilization pattern of natural resources by farmers will also give an idea about the status of the existing resources and the exploitation level.

2. Soil Erosion: High rainfall and undulated topography is always associated with problem of severe soil erosion, which affects the environment adversely. The excessive deforestation caused by excessive cutting down of trees for commercial purpose as well as shifting cultivation are resulting in alarming and frightening signals for human survival. Estimates reveal that nearly 181 M.T. of soil is lost annually as a result of shifting cultivation from the north eastern hill region (Task Force Report, 1983). Developments in the hills and its fall-out on the ecology have caused soil erosion, landslides, floods and droughts in the plains. Without forest cover, there would be nothing to resist soil erosion during monsoon months. Forests are necessary to maintain the balance in the agricultural system in North East India and to increase agricultural productivity.

3. Soil Fertility: Burning of vegetation in the process of shifting cultivation chemically alters the plant nutrient supply from organic form to a mineral form in ash, major portion of which is often lost in course of run off. The effect of burning on some soil properties examined at laboratories shows the deficiency of soil fertility.

The shorter the jhum cycle preserves the lower level of soil fertility. Five year jhum *cycle* generates very low level of soil fertility. Thus, jhum cultivation becomes uneconomic progressively. This necessitates switching over to settled cultivation.

4. Loss of Flora and Fauna: Forest is a living resource. A large number of people of the hills and of plain area depend on forest resources. The forest eco-system is to be preserved and managed for wildlife improvement, soil and water resource conservation, maintenance and improvement of bio-diversity, medicinal plant and for what is now termed as eco-tourism to improve the economic potentiality of the people living in and around forest. The extent of deforestation of tropical forest has caused world wide alarm as tropical forests provide more than 50% of modern medicine. Tropical forests are living museums and laboratories that have yielded only a tiny fraction of their treasures to scientific study.

Arunachal Pradesh is a natural garden of more than 20,000 identified species of medicinal plants and many more still remain unidentified. In course of shifting cultivation remarkable varieties of flora and fauna are disappearing, which need immediate attention for extensive and intensive studies.

The type of vegetations destroyed depends upon the length of jhum cycle. A dense forest of long cycle has more tree species than grasses, whereas a forest of short cycle has more number of grasses. About 300 plant species out of native flora in North-Eastern India are used for edible purposes. Of these, over 25 provide tubers/rhizomes etc., which are eaten raw or boiled. Over 50 are consumed as green with their leaves/tender shoots cooked as vegetable; about 170 ripe fruits, which are pulpy and sweet/sub-sweet are eaten raw and many of these are used for pickles/ vegetables, when unripe; about 15 types of edible seeds are eaten raw or roasted.

Wildlife in the natural system constitutes the most important component of the ecosystem, which participates effectively in the energy flow and bio-geo-chemical cycling. Animal-plant, plant—plant and animal-animal interactions are the basic milestone of the success of an ecosystem and its productivity. As such, the richness of the ecosystem means the capacity of holding high species diversity but deforestation has threatened the very fabric of the survival of wildlife and the ecosystem in the region. This area is the habitat of as many as 55 major mammalian species of which 17 are rare or extremely rare. 21 rare species of extremely rare birds are found in this region and there are innumerable species of insects. As such, there are different species of wild lives found in this region. Almost all of them are dared as protected species under the protection Act of 1972. Like flora, other forest resources are also disappearing and becoming rare.

5. Water Resources: There are ample water resources in the North-Eastern Hill Region. Almost 10% of the total rainfall of the country is received in this region. Soil erosion and deforestation favour in less retention of under ground water and more run off water causing flood in the plains. This causes great loss to human and animal lives as well as crops. Now -a-days, supply of drinking water has become a serious problem in every town in the hill region. Due to its geographical location and its hilly terrain, Arunachal Pradesh has an immense hydel potential to use the power of water to produce electricity in comparison to the other states of the country. The state is having turbulent perennial rivers and major streams, which possess enormous hydro-electric generation potential. Therefore, Arunachal Pradesh, having untapped estimated hydro power potential of 49,000 MW, may emerge as Power House of India when this potential is fully harnessed. Deforestation which is seen in different remote areas of Arunachal Pradesh is abolishing the immense source of water not only for drinking but also for generating the hydro power.

Conclusion

Preservation of forest is a heavy task for the state. The interests of people depending on the forest products for their livelihood would have to be protected by providing training and employment opportunities in alternative occupations otherwise corruption would be rampant and the policy of protecting forests would be defeated by way of illegal felling of trees. Those who depend on forest products as a major source of fuel should also be provided with the alternatives. The Supreme Court Judgment has to be studied in the context of North East India's dwindling forest cover and needs of the people in villages. It is equally important to have a honest and strong forest administration prepared to stand up to the crime syndicates operating in the forest. No less important is the need of a sound statistical base on forest for a sound policy formulation to maintain a balanced eco-system and also for meeting the economic needs of the people.

Forest must be protected to conserve soil, environment, wildlife and biodiversity for sustainable development. At the same time, we should remember that the demand for resources yielded by forest is growing along with the growth of population and economic development in order to satisfy direct human wants and requirement of the forest based industries and construction activities. Only the sustainable use of forest products can ensure the sustainable development of forest taking into account of the problems created by shifting cultivation, indiscriminate destruction of forest. For sustainability of forest in Arunachal Pradesh, the state having enough potentiality can be developed through setting up of fruit processing industries and nature based tourism industries with least possible disturbance to the ecology in hill regions. As Arunachal Pradesh is one of the richest forest resources states in India, a vigorous study is required to make the people aware of how additional income and employment can be generated locally due to the existence of forest resources without disturbing its existence.

We must be satisfied with the intervention of the Supreme Court in preserving ecology and environment in North East India. The forest based industries can be properly planned now. But for achieving the objective of forest resource development, we feel that Forest Protection Force is very much required to check illegal felling of trees. The indigenous people may be trained for generation of entrepreneurial skill in forest based industry and maintaining the environment. The approach should be local need based, eco-friendly and accountability in environment management. There is now an urgent need to create awareness among the people that the forest resources including wildlife belong to the people and are essential for the survival and welfare of the societies of North East India located in a unique environment zone.

In view of such a fast depletion of natural resources, policy makers must recognize the impact of their macro policy on the environmental resources. For appropriate solutions, policy planners will have to see the whole problem in an entirely different framework. In a normative determination, policy planners will have to go for new set of economic framework starting from the concept of Environmental Accounting to the Benefit-Cost Analysis of each and every macro policy. In a nutshell all policy packages, yielding net economic benefit, should be preferred subject to the condition that depletion or deterioration in the quantity and quality of natural/environmental resources should be in non-positive.

Till now efforts for conservation of forest resources by strengthening the laws and law enforcement machineries have proved by and large futile. Our experience show that forest management, conservation and development could be successfully handled by concerned authority and decision making processes to the local communities. People oriented planning and management is necessary tools for the purpose. Sharing the responsibility with local forest communities and strengthening of local bodies can go a long way for sustainable management, preservation and development of forest resources in North East India in general and in Arunachal Pradesh in particular. Ownership pattern of natural resources, community participation in the management of natural resources etc, are such issues which should get its due importance.

REFERENCES

Ali, N. (2005), "An Institutional Approach for Sustainable Rural Development", Journal of Rural Development, Vol. 24, No.2, April-June, pp. 178-179.

Arunachalam. R & Radhakrishnan, T (2006), "Status and Concern for Natural Resource Management", Kurukshetra, April, Vol. 54, No. 6, pp. 42.

Azad, N.A. (2004), "Poverty and Sustainable Development", S.Bhatt (ed.), Poverty and Food Security in India, Aakar Books, Delhi, pp. 106 – 110.

Bhattacharjee, R.P. (2002), "Forest Resources in North Eastern Region of India – A case study of Arunachal Pradesh" in B. Datta Ray and K. Alam (eds.), "Forest Resources in North East India", Omson Publications, New Delhi, pp. 269.

Bhattacharya. R.N. (1999), "Economies of India's North-East Natural Resource Base and Globalization" in Banerjee, A. and Kar , B. (eds.) : Economic Planning and Development for North-Eastern States, Kanishka Publishers, New Delhi, pp. 113-14.

Govt. of Arunachal Pradesh (1990) : Arunachal Pradesh Forest Statistics, Department of Forest, Itanagar.

Government of Arunachal Pradesh (2003 & 2004), "Economy Review of Arunachal Pradesh", Directorate of Economics and Statistics, Itanagar

Government of Arunachal Pradesh (1990): Arunachal Pradesh Forest Statistics, Forest Department, Itanagar.

Government of India (1993): The State of Forest Report, Forest Survey of India, Dehra Dun.

Jodha, N.S. (1990), Rural Common Property Resources: Contribution and Crisis, Economic and Political Weekly, Quarterly Review of Agriculture.

Majumdar, D.N. (ed.) (1990), "Shifting cultivation in North East India, Omsons Publication, New Delhi.

Mandal, R.K. (2005), "Arunachal Economy: Socio-Economic Transformation", Champion Publications, Itanagar, p. 1.

Mitra, A. (2002), "An Evaluation of Forestry Planning in Arunachal Pradesh" in B. Datta Ray and K.Alam (eds.), "Forest Resources in North East India", Omson Publications, New Delhi, pp. 258 – 260.

Kumar, P. (2001), "Environmental Economics for Sustainable Development: Some Issues in Modeling, Accounting and Valuation", Manak Publications, New Delhi.

North Eastern Council (1992-1995), "Basic Statistics of North Eastern Region, Shillong.

Prakash, H, Venugopal, Ramesh Babu, R.K. and Paramashivaiah, P. (2005, "Integration of Environment for Sustainable Development", Southern Economist, Vol. 43, No. 21, March, 2005, pp. 17-18.

9

Sanitation Scenario in West Bengal

Abhijith Das

Introduction

Infrastructure can be treated as an engine of growth and provides a basic framework for socio-economic progress. Sustaining high rate of economic growth is clearly linked to infrastructure. Infrastructure may be physical or social. Physical Infrastructures (e.g. roads, railways, bridge etc.) are needed to attract more investments and helps in alleviation of poverty and unemployment through forward and backward linkage effects on three sectors (viz Primary, Secondary and Tertiary) of the economy. On the other hand social infrastructure (e.g. education, health, drinking water supply, sanitation facility) helps in improving the quality of the life of the people.

Access to sanitation facilities is an important factor which governs the quality of life. There are so many studies showing the existence of positive correlation between improved sanitation facilities and health quality. For example, a study on "Impact assessment of Rural Sanitation Programme in West Bengal" by ORG Centre for Social Research in the year 1998 (report published in the year 2000) pointed out that 45% latrine owners identified improved health and hygiene condition, a result of latrine use. Clean water and sanitation are among the most powerful preventative medicines for reducing child mortality.

In Uganda, access to an improved water source reduces the risk of infant mortality by 23%. In Egypt, access to a flush toilet reduces the risk of infant death by 57% compared with an infant in a household without access to sanitation. In Peru, access to a flush toilet reduces the risk of infant death by 59% compared with an infant in a household without access to sanitation (*Human Development Report*, 2006).

At the beginning of the 21st century, violation of the human right to clean water and sanitation is destroying the human potential in a large scale. In today's rapidly prospering and globalized world more people including children die for want of clean water and a toilet than from almost any other cause.

We make a clear distinction between rich world & poor world on the basis of access of clean water & sanitation facilities. In rich countries almost nobody dies for want of clean water or sanitation and women are not needed to walk long distance to find a suitable place for defecation in the absence of household or appropriate neighbourhood toilet facilities. In several cases, women are to wait till early morning or night before venturing out in open. More pathetic situation is the case of dropping out of girl students due to the lack of proper, safe & private sanitation in schools. Young girls particularly after puberty are also less likely to attend classes if the school does not have suitable hygiene facilities. Parents often withdraw girls from a school that does not offer adequate and separate toilets for girls because of concerns over security and privacy. On one estimate about half the girls in Sub-Saharan Africa who drop out of primary school do so because of poor water and sanitation facilities. That helps explain why improving school sanitation can increase the demand for education among girls; between1990 and 2000 a UNICEF school sanitation programme in Bangladesh was instrumental in increasing the number of girls enrolling by 11% (*HDR*, 2006).

Although there has been progress in water and sanitation picture throughout the world, yet at the start of the 21st Century 2.6 billion people almost half of the total population of developing countries do not have access to adequate sanitation facilities. Again, global aggregate for sanitation coverage varies across the region.

The Millennium Development Goals set by the World's leaders at the UN Millennium Summit in 2000, aim at halving the proportion of people without access to safe water and sanitation by 2015. To achieve this goal, Government of India have decided to reduce the number of people without access to sanitation by half by the end of the 10th plan itself (2007); and also decided to stop open defecation by the end of 2012. This paper based on secondary data highlights some facts that show as far as sanitation is concerned, full coverage may not be achieved by the stipulated time period.

National Status

The all India picture in this respect is not at all encouraging, since as per the estimates of the NSS 54th round survey on Drinking Water, Sanitation and Hygiene, more than 80% of the rural and more than 25% of the urban households do not have access to sanitation (latrine) facilities although such an access has improved from 11% to 17.5% in rural, and from 68.2% to 74.5% in urban areas between 1988 to 1998. According to the census report (2001), out of 191.96 million households in the country there are 22.07 million (11.50%) households are availing the facility of pit type of latrine within the house, whereas, 34.59 million (18.02%) and 13.21 million (6.88%) households have water closet and other type of latrine facility within the house respectively in the country.

Lack of sanitation facility is one of major causes of many diseases in developing countries like India. Comparatively high Infant Mortality Rate (national average:72 per thousand live births in rural India –NSSO 2001) and high levels especially among the most vulnerable (national average 47.7 percent of under -5 children –the India Child, MoHRD, 2002) are also attributed to poor sanitation, and water borne diseases. According to World Health Organisation (WHO), more than 80% of all sickness and diseases lead to high socio-economic losses in the country. WHO estimates the annual loss of 180 million man-days and Rs 12 billion to the economy owing to sanitation related diseases.

Sanitation Status in West Bengal

Drinking water and sanitation are state subjects, included in the Eleventh schedule among the subjects that may be entrusted to panchayats by the states. Emphasis on sanitation facilities was given from Eighties. Central Rural Sanitation Programme (CRSP) was launched by the Government of India on 1st October, 1986. This programme was highly subsidized and supply driven. During 1987-88, rural sanitation programme was included in the minimum needs programme. But no significant success was achieved. From1991 censes report, we came to know that only 12.3% of the rural West Bengal (9.45% for rural India) having sanitation facility. After 14 years (1999), a new programme known as Total Sanitation Campaign (with effect from 1.4.1999) was launched due to not satisfactory output from CRSP. Total Sanitation Campaign (TSC) moves away from the principle of supply driven approach to a demand-driven approach. TSC also gives more emphasis on information, education and communication (IEC) for demand creation of sanitation facilities. It has been decided through the TSC that every primary school, every upgraded Shishu Sikhsha Kendras (SSK), every Madrassah with two sanitary toilets, one for boys and male teachers, and the other for the girls and lady teachers. To give a tremendous boost to TSC implementation, some initiatives are taken. "Nirmal Gram Puraskar" is one of them. 100 percent (i.e. fully) sanitized and open defecation free Gram panchayats, Blocks and Districts are eligible for "Nirmal Gram Purusakar". As long as people have not been prevented completely from urinating or defecating in the open, no declaration of Nirmal Gram or district can be made. The first Nirmal Gram Purusakars (NGPs) were given on 24th February, 2005, by the president of India, Dr. A P J Abdul Kalam to 12 Panchayati Raj Institutions (PRIs) of West Bengal for their outstanding performance to eliminate the practice of open defecation in their respective panchayats. In 2006, the number of such Nirmal Grams has increased to 134 in West Bengal. Thus, due to TSC, some improvement has been taken place in rural India. Rural sanitation coverage increases from 22% in 2001 to 38% in 2006 (*Yojana,* June-2006).

Let us now see the district level rural-urban scenario of sanitation facility in West Bengal (Table1). From table 1, we see that about 73.07% of the rural households are without sanitation coverage. Except two districts (viz Nadia & N-24 Parganas), other remaining districts, having more than 50% of the rural households remain without sanitation facility. Sanitation Situation is more alarming for Purulia and Bankura districts (where 90.16% & 88.12% rural households are without sanitation facilities). Table 2 shows the percentage of households having sanitation coverage during 1991 and 2001. Except Midnapur, the percentage changes in sanitation coverage (1991-2001) in other districts of West Bengal are lower than the percentage change in population size. In fact, Midnapur (only one district in West Bengal) received Nirmal Gram Puraskar in November, 2006. Although some rapid changes have taken place in Howrah, Hooghly, Darjeeling, Nadia and South 24-parganas but the percentage changes in sanitary position in Purulia, Malda, Dinajpur, Murshidabad, Birbhum, and Bankura are very low. Up to August 2006, Murshidabad has reached only 37.03% of its target for sanitary toilets, and Purulia an even more dismal 5.56% (*FOOTSTEPS*, August, 2006)

Table 1. Distribution of Households without Sanitation Facilities in West Bengal

District	No. of Households			No. of Households without Sanitation Facility		
	Total	Rural	Urban	Total	Rural	Urban
1	2	3	4	5	6	7
Darjiling	310149	212082	98067	127965 (41.26)	112707 (53.14)	15258 (15.56)
Jalpaiguri	681435	554114	127321	422256 (62.00)	401729 (72.50)	20527 (16.22)
Cooch Behar	521425	475138	46287	370098 (71.00)	364112 (76.63)	5986 (13.00)
North Dinajpur	461744	411308	50436	367526 (79.60)	359425 (87.39)	8101 (16.06)
South Dinajpur	316939	278991	37948	241447 (76.18)	236870 (84.90)	4577 (12.06)
Malda	629916	580336	49580	495858 (78.72)	487296 (83.96)	8562 (17.27)
Birbhum	593886	540822	53064	498334 (83.91)	477861 (88.36)	20473 (38.58)
Burdwan	1380873	862458	518415	806136 (58.38)	629818 (73.03)	176318 (34.01)
Purulia	452897	406674	46223	408340 (90.16)	388889 (95.63)	19451 (42.08)
Bankura	604605	557646	46959	532770 (88.12)	511923 (91.80)	20847 (44.40)
Midnapur	1798361	1606438	191923	1239175 (68.91)	118576 (73.81)	53414 (27.83)
Murshidabad	1129593	991967	137626	868610 (76.90)	813678 (82.03)	54932 (39.91)
Nadia	943651	736063	207588	436464 (46.25)	413319 (56.15)	23145 (11.15)
Hooghly	1020618	665263	355355	455792 (44.66)	411470 (61.85)	44322 (12.47)

1	*2*	*3*	*4*	*5*	*6*	*7*
Howrah	838235	399845	438390	327599 (39.08)	256521 (64.16)	71078 (16.21)
N-24 Parganas	1797814	802407	995407	443540 (24.64)	373590 (46.56)	69959 (7.03)
S-24 Parganas	1312279	1080318	231961	764393 (58.25)	731097 (67.67)	33346 (14.38)
Kalkata	921495	....	921495	39826 (4.32)	....	39826 (4.32)
West Bengal	15715915	11161870	4554045	8846138 (56.29)	8156016 (73.07)	690122 (15.15)

Figure in the parentheses indicates percentage distribution.
Source: Census of India (2001)

Table 2. Percentage of households having sanitation facility during 1991 and 2001 in West Bengal.

District	*Percentage of households having sanitation Facility(1991 census report)*			*Percentage of households having sanitation Facility (2001 census report)*			*Percentage change in sanitation coverage between 1991 to 2001*	*Percentage change in Population size between 1991 to 2001*
	Rural	*Urban*	*Total*	*Rural*	*Urban*	*Total*		
1	*2*	*3*	*4*	*5*	*6*	*7*	*8*	*9*
Burdwan	15.32	60.38	32.12	26.97	65.99	41.62	9.5	14.4
Birbhum	6.79	49.8	10.69	11.64	61.42	16.09	9.4	17.9
Bankura	3.94	47.69	7.62	8.20	55.60	11.88	4.26	13.8
Midnapur	4.74	56.61	10.22	26.19	72.17	31.09	20.87	15.7
Howrah	13.6	77.9	47.93	35.84	83.79	60.92	12.99	14.6
Hooghly	21.34	82.87	41.89	38.15	87.53	55.34	13.45	15.7
24-parganas(N)	28.33	86.84	58.72	53.44	92.97	75.36	16.64	26.6
24-Parganas(S)	13.7	70.87	22.38	32.33	85.62	41.75	19.37	20.9
Kolkata	—	94.98	94.98	—	95.68	95.68	0.07	04.1
Nadia	22.71	75.51	35.17	43.85	88.85	53.75	18.58	19.5
Murshidabad	8.36	51.11	12.94	17.97	60.09	23.10	10.16	23.7

1	2	3	4	5	6	7	8	9
Uttar Dinajpur	6.15	75.45	14.05	12.61	83.94	20.4	6.35	28.7
Dakshin Dinajpur	6.15	75.45	14.05	15.10	87.94	23.82	9.77	22.1
Malda	7.84	71.55	12.6	16.04	82.73	21.28	8.68	24.8
Jalpaiguri	15.43	72.25	24.96	27.5	83.78	38	13.04	21.5
Darjeeling	27.23	69.03	39.21	46.86	84.44	58.74	19.53	23.5
Cooch Behar	9.69	83.36	15.3	23.37	87	29	13.7	14.2
Purulia	3.27	53.91	8.22	4037	57.92	9.84	1.62	14.0
West Bengal	12.3	78.8	31.5	26.93	84.85	43.71	12.21	17.84

Source: Census of India (1991, 2001)

In each block of West Bengal a sanitary mart is organised to provide a low cost sanitary latrine and components on one hand and to generate awareness within the rural poor common people regarding the need to have a sanitary latrine. Sanitary marts are visualized as social marketing outlet where on demand people can get a latrine according to their choice and capacity. Sanitary mart is actually a part of CRSP and TSC. Table 3 shows the formation of sanitary marts and household coverage under total sanitation programme. It is seen that the number of sanitary marts gradually decreases but the household coverage increases (except in the year 2004-2005).

Table 3. No. of sanitary marts and household coverage in West Bengal.

Year	*No. of sanitary marts*	*Household coverage*	*Percentage change over the previous year*
1993-94	68	19565	–
1994-95	42	36940	88.80
1995-96	28	74761	102.38
1996-97	23	1,17,053	56.57
1997-98	17	1,47,072	25.64

1998-1999	17	1,96,737	33.37
1999-2000	41	2,31,678	17.76
2000-2001	21	2,72,567	17.65
2001-2002	27	3,53,605	29.73
2002-2003	28	8,47,094	139.55
2003-2004	8	10,99,732	29.82
2004-2005	8	10,45,319	- 4.95
Total	328	44,42,123	

Source: 1.Towards a District Development Report for W.B
2. Department of Panchayats and Rural Development, GoWB.

Let us now see the West Bengal sanitation scenario during three consecutive census periods-1981, 1991 and 2001. Although the state government has considered several programmes for improving sanitation coverage in West Bengal, Table 4 reveals that no remarkable change is occurred during these three decades.

Table 4. Sanitation status in India & West Bengal in 1981, 1991, 2001.

Country / State	*Total / Rural*	*1981**		*1991*		*2001*	
		with	*without*	*with*	*without*	*with*	*without*
India	Total	...	...	23.7	76.5	36.4	63.6
	Rural	...	...	9.50	90.5	21.9	78.1
	Urban	58.1	41.9	63.9	36.1	73.7	26.3
West	Total	...	...	31.5	68.5	43.7	56.3
Bengal	Rural	...	...	12.3	87.7	26.9	73.1
	Urban	77.7	22.3	78.8	21.2	84.8	15.2

Source: Census of India, 2001
*In 1981 sanitation facility was estimated only in urban areas.

From the above data, it is clear that more then 60% of the rural population is beyond the sanitation facility. After sixty years of our independence, such sanitation scenario is very much disgraceful especially when we are trying to increase our National Income to 10%. Not only that, this picture is not healthy for our Environment also.

Millennium Development Goal

The Millennium Development Goals, set by the world's leaders at the UN Millennium Summit in 2000, aim at halving the proportion of people with out access to safe water and sanitation by 2015. Following the MDG, the government of India has decided to reduce by half the number of the people without access to the sanitation by the end of the 10th plan itself (2002-2007); and as decided by ministry for rural Development, GOI, to complete implementation of TSC stop open defecation in the entire areas of the country by 2010.

Can we stop open defecation in West Bengal by 2010?

On the basis of the given data we can say it is very difficult task to achieve the target within the stipulated time period. According to 2001 census report, total number of households in West Bengal is 15715915. Only 6869777 households have latrines. This indicates that 8846138(59.29%) have no latrines. In rural West Bengal it is 8156016 (73.07%). The task is huge in relation to the target. This can be explained as follows: On an average if 6 lakhs construction is possible in a year then it will take approximately 15 years (assuming that population remains constant) to make 100 percent sanitation coverage. If we can do, then that will be good news for country as well as for our environment. Lastly, I quote a statement of Pandit Jawaharlal Nehru "*The day everyone gets a toilet to use, I shall know that our country has reached the pinnacle of progress*".

10

The 'Kudumbashree' Weapon of Poor : Grassroot States and Self-Developmentalism in Kerala

Sajan Thomas and
Jayaseelan Raj

In this paper, we attempt to show the link between the 'reconstituted self' within Human Development framework and the reconfiguration of developmental state at the grassroot level. At the outset, our focus is on this reconfiguration process in Kerala[1] in wake of the restructuring of its *welfare state's* much acclaimed developmental role. The grassroot level changes in Kerala associated with the subsequent bottom-up, community based, participatory and decentralized approaches to development has been in scholarly focus[2] for quite a long time, particularly within economics, political science, sociology and in broader developmental studies. One prominent interpretation in this direction (Veron 2001) has explained the transition in the practice and conceptualization of Kerala's development as a transition from *old Kerala model*, which was characterized by socially sustained redistributive policies of the native and democratic state, to a *new Kerala Model* that 'seeks reconciliation of social, productive and environmental objectives at the local level, and tries to develop synergies between civil society, local governmental bodies and the state government'. The ideological moorings of new Kerala development model and the potential role of international development agencies in sustenance of the same has triggered political controversies and academic discussions at various levels[3]. Although Veron's (2001) depiction of a dichotomous transition (i.e. from the state-led development process to a community driven one) offers only a limited explanation, it could be of use as an entry point into Kerala's trajectorial shift in development. It is relatable to note that most of these second generation academic debates on Kerala development experience focus on people's participation at the grassroot level and the facilitational role of institutional transformations such as decentralization and people's planning.

This paper is organized into three sections. Section I deals with the state developmentalism in Kerala, especially its historical trajectory and its reconfiguration in the wake of the emerging human development paradigm. As an institutional case, the Kudumbashree in Kerala has been presented for further examination in the subsequent sections. Section II defines and discusses the relationship between two new concepts, *grassroot states* and *self-developmentalism*. This section also analyses Amartya Sen's Capability Approach (CA) —which is considered to be the philosophical basis of human development paradigm — to explain the trajectorial shift of Kerala from state developmentalism to self developmentalism. The third section on concluding observations are largely based on the susceptibility of Kudumbashree to religious interests. This section also presents our strong case for ethnographic inquiries into these reconfiguration processes in Kerala.

SECTION I : STATE DEVELOPMENTALISM IN KERALA

State has always been a contested concept. Although the timeline of such divergences can be traced to the Platonic phase or even before, the emergence and consolidation of the modern state system has been the basis of our discussion[4]. Among these contestations, the transformation of *State* and its interventions in specific spatial and temporal contexts has been a dominant one. In order to explain the transformation and transmutation of modern state, especially the reconfigured state-society relations in the context of human development framework, we are focusing on the case of Kerala[5]. The developmental attributes of the state in Kerala had been in the forefront of the post 1950 discussions on social and human development[6]. To quote Ramkumar (2006) "the most important lesson that development economists have drawn from Kerala's development experience is that the attainment of high levels of social indicators need not wait till an economy generates adequate resources through economic growth to finance programmes for social development". And so, despite the shift in the conceptualization of 'non-economic' dimensions of development, for instance the overriding of social development with human development since 1990s, Kerala has been widely projected as a case for state interventionism in development. As Desai (2005) puts it "Kerala's welfare state thus became widely renowned as a model to those who argued that redistribution rather than growth was the fastest avenue to reducing mass poverty". No wonder, the role of state in regard to the evolution and sustenance of Kerala development experience has always been in the scholarly focus; the best illustration is Heller's (1999) conceptualization of a *democratic developmental state*.

As grassroot transformations were central to the evolution of State developmentalism in Kerala, the historical trajectory of the developmental state is fundamental to analyze its present-day reconfiguration at the grassroot level. Kerala *model* can be viewed as "a post facto generalization of an experience historically evolved but promoted by public action (which inter-alia includes socio-religious reform movements, wide and active press, adversarial politics) and sustained by social demands" (Ommen 1999 xvi). The popular base and inclusive character of this model owes much to active societal interventions, particularly through sustained socio-political mobilizations from the grassroots (Varkey and Thomas 2006). According to Tharakan (2004), political activity in the State is largely evolved as sort of local group demands that habitually expressed through *conscious* collective struggles. These bottom-up mobilizations, particularly from underprivileged groups have limited the options of democratized state to supply basic services. Kerala's prior legacy of welfare has been analyzed in detail in Desai (2005), where he examines "the relationship between a strong nineteenth-century welfarist expansion between the 1860s and early 1940s, in Kerala, India, under indirect British rule, and the "exceptional" antipoverty regime that democratically elected Communists implemented during the postcolonial (post 1947) era in the state." Despite the prevailing discord in regard to the causation of Kerala exceptionalism[7], scholars and observers of this development experience has directly or indirectly emphasized the role of the historical grassroot action in the state. The influential explanation by Amartya Sen[8], based on his concept of Public Action, can be considered as an ideal case for this. In his Tanco memorial lecture (1990), Sen clarifies that "public action includes not only what is done for the public by the state, but also what is done by the public for itself. It includes, for example, what people can do by demanding remedial action and through making governments accountable". Moreover, extending the contours of public action, Dreze and Sen also argued that in a strategy of public action for development outcomes, multiple layers have to be considered - (a) the state (b) the market (c) non-Governmental organizations; and (d) public activism for swaying Government policy as well as influencing social and personal behaviour. Grassroot action and networks, particularly mobilizations, campaigns, deliberations etc., are fundamental to any sort of public action and the Kerala case is not an exception.

State developmentalism in Kerala, in particular since 1990s, has entered into to a new phase with the governmental drives to institutionalize grassroot democracy through the devolution of political and economic power. Kerala's relatively successful experience with decentralization has resulted in a notable shift in the development literature. There is a whole gamut of literature on various aspects of grassroot democracy in the wake of decentralization and the practice of participatory planning and implementation in the context of a mass campaign throughout the state. Since lion's share of these works was done within the disciplinary boundaries of economics, political science and sociology, the conclusions are often based on either discourse analysis or questionnaire based field works. Very few attempts have made to conduct ethnographic investigations; a crucial exercise for understanding the multifaceted transformation of state interventionism at the grassroot level. Moreover, very few analyses have perceived the grassroot level changes in Kerala, given the context of a re-conceptualization of the state-led development framework — including the role of state, society and individual within the development processes— within the multilaterally set Human Development paradigm. The dominant tendency is to perceive all grassroot formations/reconfigurations within the decentralization framework, which is supposed to be an all-encompassing one with regard to grassroot level transformations. Analyses on Kudumbashree in Kerala — the women based state poverty eradication mission of Government of Kerala since 1993 – is an illustration of this *decentralization wave* in grassroot studies[9]. Our argument is that the governmental drives to operationalize the Human Development paradigm is accompanied with a reconfiguration of developmental state at the grassroots. In order to explain these scantly researched processes, we are introducing two concepts – 'grassroot states', 'self-developmentalism'.

SECTION II: CONCEPTUAL ISSUES

Grassroot States

There is a near unanimity among scholars with regard to the transformation and transmutation of modern state system in the wake of an unfolding globalization process. Despite the divergences over its extent and nature, a good number of academics perceive globalization as a disjuncture that alters the interventions of developmental states, both its capacity and institutional structure However, majority of the arguments is rooted in the reconfiguration of state interventionism at a macro level; economic, political, social and even ideological. The aforesaid analyses oftentimes give less emphasis to the micro level processes accompanied with reconfiguration of existing state structures in the local level, which we would like to term as 'grassroot states.'

A grassroot state can be defined as the reconfigured development unit of developmental state at the local level, which is characterized by globally homogenized institutional structure and priorities; but with locally specific interventionist strategies. By and large these development units function through neighborhood based self-help groups, whose nature of interventions are spatial and temporal specific. The territoriality of grassroot states is largely based on the political/administrative boundaries of the nation state, especially those of the decentralized state bodies. But it has an 'exclusionary citizenship' as the membership is often based on gender, class position and in some cases their positioning in the social hierarchy. Eventhough the global-local interface of the times has been explained through a lot of related concepts (for instance, grassroot globalization, grassroot democracy and grassroot movements), Kudumbashree in Kerala provides a strong case for arguing the reconfiguration of nation-states at the local level as grassroot states.

Contextualizing the state driven self-help groups is problematic in the Kerala case. Different variants of state backed self-help groups among the *poor*, which is the precursor of the contemporary *empowering mechanisms*, had been active in the Kerala since 1960s. However, the recent spurt of state driven self-help groups, which function in close association with decentralized bodies, have to be seen in the context of the ongoing discussions on *globalization from below*, *think globally act locally* and *glocalisation*. These discourses often perceive the grassroot transformations associated with globalization as a new social phenomenon that can be an alternative to corporate globalization. Appadurai's (2000) concept of *grassroot globalization* to explain the emerging social forms, which proceeds independently of the actions of corporate capital and the nation-state system, is a prominent one in this regard. Although this can partially explain the emergence of self help groups institutionalized by non-state actors (predominantly development agencies and religious institutions), it can't explicate the grassroot level reconfiguration of the contemporary developmental states. As state driven self help groups has emerged as the main development unit at grassroot level, at many times replacing the erstwhile counterparts, the concept of grassroot states is of more use to understand the reconfiguration process.

The reasons for viewing the state driven self help groups as a disjuncture from the grassroot level structures of the developmental state are manifold. First of all, these self help institutions has a different 'grassroot level development schema' than that of the developmental state for the well-being of its populace. Although this development schema has locally specific interventionist strategies, its institutional structure and priorities are largely in lieu with the multilaterally set Human Development framework. The human development paradigm, which conceives development as widening of choices, largely relies on the reconfigured state structures for accomplishment of its global and local targets. Grassroot states are the main choice in this regard because of its firm enmeshment in the local cultures compared to the superimposed structures of the developmental state[10]. Secondly, there is the centrality of certain dimensions of human well being over others, for instance poverty eradication has been the main concern for a substantial number of self help groups. Depending on the core focus, grassroot states has their own approach to the production and redistribution question, the role of individuals and groups in social processes, mobilization of resources and local level planning. However, the main difference lies in the emphasis on *self* in development processes, which would be taken for further analysis in the subsequent portion.

Self Developmentalism

Different dimensions of 'self' had been so central within the liberal thought. Ranging from the socio-cultural self-constitution of Locke's liberal individual to the self-centered pursuit of economic activity in Smith's self-regulating market[11] , assumptions of a particular kind of 'self' and the practical and institutional means by which that 'self' is constituted and realized has been central to modern political theories. However, the settling in of territorial nation-states and the emergence of a population to be *welfarely governed* has made *art of government* an important subject matter in regard to the state-society interface.[12] Focouldian notion of *governmentality* is largely based on the transition from a (repressive) sovereign power to a welfare regime (Sharma and Gupta 2006) where Kapferer's (2007) reading of Foucault seems fit – "the state is integral to the self of its subjects", although one is opposing state power. This trend has reinforced in the twentieth century, particularly owing to two reasons. The instantaneity of Soviet experiment to embark on a classless society and the grooming crisis with in the global capitalist system has led up to revisionism within macro-economic theory in favor of state intervention in the economy. Keynesian economics stresses state intervention to discipline the market and ensure full employment level through fiscal and monetary policies[13]. Secondly, the emergent post colonial states across the Afro-Asian and Latin American world have resorted to a state-led development schema, despite its diverse nature of state interventionism. However, all sorts of state developmentalism have undergone challenges within the period of *advanced liberalism or neo-liberalism*. 'Discourses during this period were marked by market mentality and its related thinking of small government, efficiency and competition. This has refocused the attention on newly constituted individuals who exercise free choice in pursuing their own well-being and advancement. Subsequently, the mechanisms of governments has shifted to these individuals and the communities to which they belong; mechanisms of power and systems of rule that produce self-governing, self empowering, self-fulfilling individuals and communities' (Rose 2006; Gupta and Sharma 2006). The recent spurt of self help institutions, especially state driven self-help groups, is an ideal case to explain the concept of *self-developmentalism* within the broader context of the reconfiguration of states at the grassroot level. Although there are multiple dimensions, our conceptualization of self-developmentalism is in relation to Human Development framework.

Contemporary development thinking, especially those triggered by the multilateral institutions, had undergone a human development turn since 1990s. Human development, which has its theoretical basis in the capability approach, has been projected as an alternate development paradigm with extensive applicability in the policy sphere, both at national and global levels. According to a 'radical re-conceptualization', development is seen as a process of expanding the real freedoms that people have reason to value in a milieu of *free agency*. The approach is evolved out of Amartya Sen's critique of traditional welfare economics, which typically conflate well-being with either opulence (income, commodity command) or utility (happiness, desire fulfillment). Detaching himself from the utilitarian ethics, Sen has invoked a choice based approach to human flourishing with an emphasis on pluralism. Given the increasing efforts to operationalize Sen's capability approach, especially to confront global poverty, it is of need to look into the impact of human development paradigm on the existing forms of state intervention. This is especially significant in a context when the operationalization of human development framework is predominantly through the reconfigured state institutions at the grassroot level.

Human Development Framework have been characterised with a reconceptualisation of the existing notions of *self* within a new spatial and temporal context. Placing individual's self-realisation at the corner stone of development, these discourses often focus on the reduction of internal,institutional and social constraints that prevents an inividual from exerting his/her agency. Moreover, delinking the individual from broader societal structures, the operationalisation of human development approach oftentimes uphold the partial realisation of *self* within regulated spatio-temporal context, for instance in development projects. Through a reconceptualisation of the role of *self* within the development process, Sen recognized people as active agents of change, rather than as passive recipients of dispensed benefits. Subsequently, the capacity of the existing social arrangements, including the state, in regard to 'the removal of various types of unfreedoms that leave people with little choice and little opportunity of exercising their reasoned agency' has been revisited under the human development framework. This re-examination pushed for the reconfiguration of the existing state structures and the case of new institutions based on self-help at the grassroots[14] . Self-help groups (SHGs) organized on the neighborhood basis has been projected as the institutional base to reduce internal, institutional and social constraints that prevents an individual from exerting his/her agency. Consequently, there has been a surge of grassroot institutions, both sponsored by state and non-state institutions, across the developing world. Majority of the self help groups are also directly or indirectly related to global poverty reduction efforts, which has emerged as a global movement ever since the inception of Millennium Development Goals (MDGS) to halve global poverty by 2015.

SECTION III : CONCLUDING OBSERVATIONS

Our discussion in regard to the reconfiguration of developmental state at the grassroot level can be represented in a simple diagram:

State Developmentalism $\xrightarrow{\text{Grassroot States}}$ Self Developmentalism

Grassroot states with Self developmentalism as its *invisible hand* is a crucial disjuncture from the nation-states characterized with state developmentalism. This disjuncture has ramifications concerning the state power in relation to the demarcation the boundaries between state and religion in the development process. State has mostly been understood as an umbrella entity which is spatialised in terms of verticality and encompassment (Ferguson and Gupta 2002).The macro level imagination of state has also reflected in the understanding state-religion interface, even in studies based on field work. However, the functioning of Kudumbashree is an illustration of the religious inclinations of a grassroot developmental order based on self-developmentalism in Kerala.[15] Whether the susceptibility of Kudumbashree to the appropriation and maneuvering of religious and political institutions has any connection to the epistemological basis of Human Development paradigm?

Human development framework has revisited the relationship between religion and development in such a manner that religious freedoms should also be part of the development process[16] . When development is perceived as the expansion of freedoms that people has reason to value and choose, there is no point in disassociating religious groups from development if they value the same[17] . It is argued that religion can play a crucial role in poverty reduction as faith communities have often developed effective grassroots institutions that serve and care for those in extreme poverty. To them faith, traditions have often inspired followers to alleviate human suffering, to nurture solidarity and transnational bonds of affiliation. Many empirical inquires in this regard have been asserted faith based development programmes as being more compassionate, effective and efficient than secular programmes. It is pertinent to note that one emerging area of study within Human Development is those linking Amartya Sen and Catholic social thought in general and liberation theology in particular[18].

References

1. By reconfiguration processes in Kerala we mean the transformation of both structure and mechanisms of developmental state at the grassroot level, with a focus on the changing patterns of state interventionism.
2. Regarding the Indian case in general, arguments in this direction are largely based on *new social movements* active at the grassroot of politics that resist global capital using the new political spaces opened up by the retreat of the state from socio- economic areas. Despite the quagmire over the nature of Indian state, *state-led developmentalism* has been an important part of the state formation in India's predominantly religious society. A state-led capitalist development schema with public sector in the commanding heights of economy was concomitant with the Nehruvian attempt to superimpose 'a secular, scientific and amoral ideology of nation-building'. The dependence on the developmental interventions of a modernizing state for the secularization project is best reflected in Nehru's controversial statement-"dams are temples of modern India". Nevertheless, the emergence of grassroot mobilizations and groupings since late 1960s, of which many of them were based on parochial identities, has challenged an intervening state in many respects. The argued out reasons for the grassroot transformation are: structural

context of brutal dislocation associated with the capitalist development; decline of the Congress system, the culmination of honeymoon phase and so on. Many of these grassroot mobilizations with redistributive social, political and economic agenda have become incorporated into the political processes and later into electoral fray. This has resulted in a shift in the Indian political system, i.e. a shift in the social basis of political power. Although there had been interstate disparities, these processes were largely facilitated by the different spells of the decentralization of political power at the grassroot level; the notable change was followed by the 73rd and 74th constitutional amendments of 1993 and 1994.

3. Majority of these discussions are politically charged ones and various academics were alleged to receive funding from Centre Intelligence Agency (CIA) and some other multilateral agencies.

4. Defining state in complex societies has always been a problematic exercise. As Kapferer (2007) notes in regard to Foucault's monolithic totalizing vision of the modern state, "state itself may contain processes that are subversive of it". For him this includes democratic forces and Deleuze and Guattari's rhizomic and ahierarchical forces that found in most social formations. We argue that inter-state developmentalism, particularly in regard to human development framework and multilaterally set targets like Millennium Development Goals (MDGs), can also subvert the erstwhile intra-state developmentalism due to its reconfiguration through a different developmental process (grassroot state and self- developmentalism in this case).

5. We think Kerala is an ideal case to analyze how "the processes connected with globalization have reconfigured identities and territories at multiple scales, connecting and disconnecting places in complex ways and re-enforcing old while producing news forms of segregation and polarization. The spaces, territories and identities (re)produced in the complex contexts in which the global, national, regional and local meet"

6. Ever since the publication of UN study *Poverty, Unemployment and Development Policy* (1975) by K.N Raj and his colleagues at Centre for Development Studies, Thiruvananthapuram, Kerala's high achievements on the statistical indicators of development despite continuing low incomes (Franke 1995) received much international attention. The paradoxical relationship between social and economic development in this South Indian state, often characterized as a model for developing societies, has been in the forefront of post-1970 development discourses. Discussions on Kerala's pathway of development are broadly clustered around four questions: Does a Kerala development model really exist? What are the factors that contributed to the evolution of this development experience? How much inclusionary is this development framework? Whether it can be sustained over generations or be replicated elsewhere? The questions on evolution is centered around endogenous explanations such as public action (Sen 1989), class mobilization (Heller 1999, Reynolds and Harilal 2006) and radical reforms (Franke and Chasin 1989) and the exogenous interpretations emphasize on the foreign links over centuries (Kawashima 1998, Raman Kutty 2000, Kannan 2005, Harilal and Joseph 2000). Meanwhile, the queries on sustainability and replicability focuses on concerns such as fiscal crisis (George 1993), environmental sustainability (Chattopadhyay and Franke 2006), and demographic transition (Zachariah and Rajan 1997). However, there were also discussions with regard to the rationale of conceptualizing development on the basis of certain quantifiable variables and the exclusionary tendencies inherent in Kerala's development experience. The latter debates are going on in relation to the multifaceted marginalization of *outliers* i.e. Dalits, tribals, fisher folks, and certain other socio-economic groups (Kurien 1995, Kunjaman 2002)

7. The best illustration of this disagreement is Franke and Chasin's critique of Amartya Sen's analysis of Kerala exceptionalism, particularly his minimization of Kerala's radical political traditions and the long history of mass mobilization. For Sen, "the causal chain of Kerala's exceptional record goes back in history and includes among

other things such steps as the public policy of "enlightenment" and "diffusion of education," clearly articulated by the reigning queen (Rani Gouri Parvathi Bai) of Travancore as early as 1817 ". A number of explanations clustered around the agreement that Communists were responsible for institutionalizing a policy regime that greatly reduced poverty and led to more egalitarianism.

8. "Sen invariably uses Kerala to illustrate (1) the existence of Development in terms of non-income freedoms like education and health, though incomes of people are low - highlighting the government's role (2) the importance of education - for example, how literacy helps women gain more control over family planning (3) the importance of political freedom - for example, how the freedom to protest can be used to monitor and ensure good medical services".

9. Kudumbashree in Malayalam means *prosperity of the family*. Envisioned to eradicate poverty by means of the empowerment of women through community based organizations, the Kudumbashree aims to 'reach out to the family through women, reach out to the community through family'. It has a class character as its membership is restricted to the women in families that are 'below the poverty line' (BPL) and those hailing from other low income groups. Kudumbashree is institutionalized "to eradicate absolute poverty in ten years through concerted community action under the leadership of local governments, by facilitating organization of the poor for combining self-help with demand-led convergence of available services and resources to tackle the multiple dimensions and manifestations of poverty, holistically." It is envisioned as a secular institution that has to function in close cooperation with the decentralized state bodies. Within a short span of time Kudumbashree became projected as the largest 'women movement in Asia' with a membership of 3202385, representing equal number of families, and has selected for numerous awards including *We the People* award of United Nations in 1995.

The encompassing nature of Kudumbashree is evident from the data on a Village Panchayat in Kerala – Amboori. Amboori is a village panchayat in Thiruvananthapuram district with a population of 21914. This panchayat has around 200 active Kudumbashree units that spread across 4000 families and twelve wards. It is interesting to note that almost 700 religion based women and men based self-help groups are also in the region.

10. The growing literature in *culture and public action* explores different dimensions of the importance of local culture while comes to the implementation of development projects.
11. To Adam Smith "It is not from the benevolence of the butcher, the brewer or the baker that we expect our dinner, but from their regard to their own interest. We address ourselves not to their humanity but to their self-love, and never talk to them of our necessities but of their advantages."
12. The care and security of the aggregate population, in other words becomes the object of government intervention.
13. It is widely heralded that John Maynard Keynes has saved capitalism by using the Marxist pillars.
14. According to Amartya Sen, the resources available to the poor people are not only income, land, credit, etc. but they would also include various other aspects of human capital such as nutrition, health, training, education and social networks, etc. which are available to poor to draw on in their search for survival, security and dignity (quoted in Kabeer, N., 2003). By using the cases of Self-employed Women's Association (SEWA) and participatory credit and cooperative organizations associated with the Grameen Bank in Bangladesh, Sen has illustrated the importance of self help based group activities in bringing about substantial social change.
15. The Kudumashree experience demonstates the susceptibility of state backed 'empowering mechanisms' to religious institutions and organizations. This is exemplified in the increasing involvement of Christian church, Vishwa Hindu Parishad (VHP) and several Muslim organizations in the functioning of neighborhood networks of Kudumbashree. This association ranges from the direct engagement in mobilizing Kudumbashree units to encouraging its members to associate with its neighborhood groups. Moreover,

different religious establishments have their own versions of neighborhood initiatives that set to accomplish economic, social and spiritual objectives. The neighborhood prayer groups and the Mathrujyothi networks of Catholic Church is an example for this 'overlap'.

16. Human Development and religion is a thematic group of Human Development and Capability Association (HDCA) and Faith & Development groups have been active in development studies for quite a long time.
17. Amartya Sen once opined that he does not believe in religion, but he respects those who work for the welfare of human being even in the name of religion.
18. Discussions on Putnam's version of social capital with emphasis on values and virtues are also important in this regard. Although Putnam viewed that Catholicism is a poor foundation for social capital, later adherents of his version conceptualized faith and religion as a social capital.

11

Decentralization and Local Governance: Initiatives in Kerala

G. Lakshmi

Introduction

Welcome to Kerala, God's Own Country. With the Arabian Sea on the west, the Western Ghats towering 500 - 2700m on the east and Kerala is networked by forty-four rivers. It is a very easy place to simply sit back and enjoy. The name means "land of coconuts" and the palms shade nearly the entire state from the tropical sun; many call the beach at Kovalam the best in India, tranquil stretches of emerald backwaters, lush green hill stations and exotic wildlife, ayurvedic health resorts, enchanting art forms, magical festivals, historic and cultural monuments, an exotic cuisine all of which offers a unique experience.

Kerala is one of the ten 'Paradises found' declared by the National Geographic Traveler, for its diverse geography and overwhelming greenery. It is a land much acclaimed for the contemporary nature of its cultural ethos, and much appreciated for the soothing, rejuvenating paradise that it is. Health and medical tourism is perceived as one of the fastest growing segments in marketing 'Destination India' today. While this area has so far been relatively unexplored, we now find that not only the ministry of tourism, government of India, but also the various state tourism boards and even the private sector consisting of travel agents, tour operators, hotel companies and other accommodation providers are all eying health and medical tourism as a segment with tremendous potential for future growth.

Kerala is not only a beautiful destination in Southern India known for its scenic beaches and serene backwaters. Of late it has gained international attention for Medical Tourism and is becoming a popular international medical tourism destination. Kerala - the Pioneer State: Kerala, or God's Own Country as its corporate slogan goes, has pioneered health and medical tourism in India. They have made a concerted effort to promote health tourism in a big way, which has resulted in a substantial increase of visitor arrivals into the state. Kerala and Ayurveda have virtually become synonymous with each other. However, though it has strongly focused on Ayurveda and its wide array of treatments and medications, good facilities are also available in the other traditional forms of medicine as well as in modern medical treatment.

Throughout most of the 20th century, health conditions in Kerala were better than other Indian states, but not markedly so. It was after the amalgamation of socially-advanced Travancore-Cochin with more-backward Malabar in 1957 that Kerala experienced a health take-off, diverging from the rest of India. Good health with equity was attained through political will, strong public policies, and wise social investments. For the world community, the intellectual impact of Kerala has been enormous — an inspiration to an entire generation. The Kerala story countered the prevailing thinking that economic growth was the major route to development success. Kerala demonstrated that high income and economic growth were no guarantees of social development. Good health depended on a combination of political, social, educational, and health advancement.

By nineties the much-acclaimed Kerala model of development aimed at bringing about human development, started facing the sustainability crisis. It became difficult to maintain the level and quality of governmental services in the absence of rapid economic growth. These problems were further compounded by the sharply adversarial political relations in the State. It was felt that decentralization could shake up the system and help in a thorough overhaul. In this context the objectives of the decentralization experiment in Kerala could be listed as follows:

1. To improve the quality of investment by allocating resources for priorities fixed by the local people.
2. To facilitate emergence of local solutions, developmental problems through improved planning, better implementation, use of traditional knowledge and appropriate technology etc. and to exploit local production possibilities and enable people's participation leading to better vigil in execution of schemes, followed by better upkeep of assets.
3. To provide the enabling environment for people to make contributions in kind and cash for development programs identified by them for priority action and to bring about a convergence of resources and services to tackle development problems with greater vigor.
4. To unleash public action resulting in a demand led improvement in the delivery of developmental and welfare services. In the process of realizing these objectives it was felt that it would lead to a new politics of development emerging out of dialogue and consensus rather than conflict and collision and help forge a realistic approach to development, based on a clearer understanding of problems and issues at the grassroots level.

Kerala is also innovating in local governance. Over the past decade, the State has decentralized power to local Panchayats. Facilitated by constitutional amendments, 40% of Kerala's state budget is now transferred directly to local

Panchayats in support of more than 20 key functions following the principles of subsidiary, devolution of decision-making and local capacity building. Health and education are central components of decentralization. Devolution has been not just technical and financial, but it is also backed by mass social mobilization. Community participation has followed the approach of Kerala's pioneering people's science movement and mass literacy campaigns.

Kerala's decentralization underscores a critical gap linking local and global governance. Ironically, while Kerala's Panchayats are empowered by decentralization, national governments and global institutions are being overwhelmed by transnational flows. The crisis of global institutions is reflected by social protests last fall at the World Trade Organization meeting in Seattle and at the recent World Economic Forum in Davos. These protests mix multiple concerns — global equity, "Americanization," and environmental and labor standards. The concerns appear to focus less on global flows per se and more on the fairness of the ground rules for global engagement, which are perceived to be detrimental to the poor in developing countries.

Will decentralization accelerate Kerala's progress in an era of globalization? Or will global forces overwhelm local initiatives? One problem of globalization, in my opinion, is not global connectivity but rather the lack of democratic governance to ensure fairness in global engagement. Global decision-making is excessively concentrated among only a few power centers. These biases fuel a sense of powerlessness among world citizens who feel unable to control global decisions that shape their destiny.

Development of Tourism in Kerala

Almost simultaneously Kerala discovered its tourism potential and through proper positioning (Back Water Tourism, Beach Tourism etc.,) and strategic marketing it was able to achieve remarkable growth since mid 80's showing an average rate of 30% for foreign tourists and 70% for domestic tourists. Kerala has been declared as one of the 50 must-see destinations by the National Geographic Travel. The Government has been rightly playing a facilitators role encouraging private entrepreneurs and providing the required infrastructure and guiding preparation of proper spatial planning of tourism sites. Tourism with an employment generation of 0.7 million and with a revenue contribution of nearly $ 100 million which is equivalent to 6.29% of the Gross State Domestic Product now bids fair to become the new engine of growth. Sunrise areas like health, tourism and eco tourism are being tapped. However this sector has not been decentralized.

Strategy of Decentralization in Kerala

Traditional wisdom calls for capacity building of local governments and then giving power to them in degrees to match the improvements in capacity. But real and effective decentralization probably calls for a big bang approach – functions, powers and resources are transferred at one go. If decentralization is effected in one fell blow the suddenness would stun potential dissenters into silent acceptance; before people realize what they have lost, decentralization would have become a fait accompli. The 'reversals' - of giving responsibility and then building capacity, of giving powers and then creating procedures and systems, of giving funds and then setting up umpiring systems – help in another way. If government transfers a lot of responsibilities and funds considerable pressure would build on government from various sides to ensure that the responsibilities are carried out effectively and the funds are utilized properly. It would then become Government's responsibility to ensure that decentralization works. Kerala followed this approach and hindsight shows that strategically it was a sound decision as it would have been impossible to transfer power in small dozes.

To operational decentralization, Kerala chose the path of participatory local level planning as the entry point. This succeeded to a considerable extent in harnessing public action in favor of decentralization. In order to push the system and force the process a campaign approach was followed for decentralized planning - known as the 'People's Planning Campaign'. This campaign created a powerful demand factor for decentralization to be guided along the right path. To a large degree the campaign succeeded in setting the agenda for decentralization.

THE PROCESS OF DECENTRALIZATION

1. Steps in Decentralization

(i) Defining the functional domain

This is a very difficult activity and it is totally dependent on the political vision of decentralization. Also, the size of the local government particularly that of the Village is a critical factor in assigning its functions. Most of the State legislations give more or less the same functions to all the three tiers of local governments. It would be a healthy practice if a legislative definition of the functional domain is done with as much precision as possible. But this is a rather difficult task. In Kerala, functions in practically every development sector like agriculture and allied sectors, village industries, rural development, health, education, social welfare and poverty reduction have been devolved almost fully to the local governments. Kerala found that it is easier to define the functions in the management of institutions, creation of infrastructure and provision of services but when it came to the question of defining the functional areas in sectors like agriculture and industries there is bound to be certain overlaps, and only based on several years of experience can the comparative advantage of each tier in performing various functions would be known clearly. Thus a process approach is called for in demarcating the functions of different tiers of local government as also the role of the State Government in such development areas.

Freedom and its limits for each function and each kind of activity the freedoms of local governments as well as the limits to the freedom need to be indicated. This is best done through a process of experimentation followed by consultation with local governments to reach a consensus. Such an exercise was undertaken by Kerala when it was found that local governments were giving abnormally high subsidies to individual beneficiaries of various schemes.

Need for appropriate administrative operating systems.

Development programs and development administration run essentially on the basis of executive instructions which constitute the flesh and blood of administration with the Acts providing only the skeletal framework and form. Therefore any number of legal provisions and rules would remain on paper if they are not followed up with clear-cut administrative instructions in the form of Government Orders, Circulars, Manuals etc. It would not be appropriate if the existing administrative systems and executive orders are just transplanted on to local governments. The deep structure of such instructions is oriented towards centralized governance and is tailored for hierarchy; eg., procurement instructions, accountability systems, reporting systems etc. These need to be harmonized to local government conditions without sacrificing accountability or efficiency.

Transfer of Resources

Human Resources

Often one comes across vague conceptualization of local governments particularly village level ones as "doers", but actually they should be the 'deciders' and the 'doers' should be personnel under their control. Expecting local governments to do functions without assigning at least the staff who was hitherto performing those functions would be futile. This was done in Kerala on the principle of work and worker going together. As a compromise the cadres and service conditions are not disturbed and government continues to pay salary.

Financial resources

Kerala's experience in fiscal decentralization is worth noting. Its salient features are enumerated below:

(i) The cutting edge local governments at the Village level and Municipal level have been given the right to collect certain "own" taxes viz., property tax, profession tax, entertainment tax and advertisement tax. In addition the State Government fully or partly shares its land tax, motor vehicle tax and tax on registration of property. The local governments are given the freedom to fix tariffs and levy user charges without reference to the State Government.

(ii) The remarkable feature of fiscal decentralization in the State is the transfer to local governments of what is called Plan grants. In India Plan signifies new investment both capital and revenue and Non-Plan means maintenance and running costs. 1/3rd of the Plan resources which are mostly borrowings is earmarked for local governments with the urban and rural areas getting shares equivalent to their population and among the rural local governments, the Village local government getting 70%. The grant is practically untied and gives freedom to the local governments to plan and prepare their own development programs. The entire money is invisible and local government-wise allocation is passed along with the State budget and every single rupee is devolved according to a formula without any political or executive discretion whatsoever.

Setting up Accountability Systems since substantial funds have been given to the local government's accountability system acquires special importance. In addition to the traditional systems new checks and balances need to be evolved. To a large extent, accountability can be ensured through open government. In a sense transparency is the best form of audit. Corruption in local governments is to be addressed right at the beginning. It is felt that decentralized corruption is more harmful than centralized corruption for it permeates every part of the society and causes widespread moral degradation. In addition to traditional accountability mechanisms like audit and inspection, Kerala has attempted two innovations – first, setting up Performance Audit to conduct regular auxiliary audit with a view to correcting mistakes as and when they occur and guiding local governments in maintaining the proper systems; second, setting up of a technical audit team consisting of senior engineers selected for their integrity to investigate complaints of malfeasance in public works. An Ombudsman for Local Governments has been created. More significantly new accountability mechanisms have also come up. Regular IEC campaigns, participatory structures right from planning up to monitoring, transparency provisions and scheme formulation framework and spelling out the due process in various kinds of decision-making, which fix the rational boundaries to autonomy, are the important examples. Reforms on the anvil relate to semi structured social audit, insistence of compulsory information giving, publishing of Citizen entitlements and Charters and use of information technology.

Operational Decentralized Participatory Planning

The People's Planning Campaign has succeeded in providing a concrete methodology for participatory planning for local level development. The salient features of this methodology include participatory priority determination through assemblies of electorates at the Village/Municipal Ward level, preparation of a development status report using primary and secondary data, determination of broad strategies through interaction with selected members of the public, experts both official and non-official and political leaders, preparation of project profiles by joint teams of elected leaders, government officials and non-government experts, vetting of the projects by similar teams and finally implementation in a transparent manner.

Role of Government

Paradoxical though it may seem the role of Government increases considerably in the early years of decentralization; it has to play the role of an activist facilitator. Decentralization is a process and throws up several unexpected challenges during its course. The Government should have the readiness and flexibility to respond quickly. Capacity building for managing the change is a tremendous administrative responsibility of the Government. There are so many persons to be trained both officials and non-officials. Capacity building has two components – training as well as providing professional support. In Kerala for training the institutional framework of the State Planning Board and the Kerala Institute of Local Administration is being used. Sufficient funds are earmarked for this activity. There is a pool of master trainers identified from government officials, retired officials and NGOs who provide a kind of cascading training to the staff and elected representatives of local governments. How-to-do handbooks and case studies of best practice enrich the training process. Professional support is being provided by tapping barefoot expertise, non-government sources as well as academic institutions especially for fresh graduates who could serve the local governments as apprentices.

Genuine decentralization demands that there should be a gradual withdrawal of direct executive control over local governments. This has to be balanced with the need for accountability. The best option is to create independent regulatory institutions or strengthen existing ones. Kerala has gone considerable ahead in this process.

As decentralization progresses, the attitude of the government towards the local government has to go through appropriate phases which has administrative implications. In the initial days patience and tolerance are highly essential as several mistakes could be made – some of them bonafide and a good number of them malafide. Government should have all eyes and ears to grasp the complexities of the process. Quickly this should be followed by a corrective phase where the focus is on helping local governments to set their house in order. This would mark the period of stabilization and institutionalization. Thereafter the regulatory institutions should take over and have both preventive as well as punitive systems in place to avoid maladministration and malfeasance.

Good Governance Features

Government has to play a conscious role to improve governance in local governments. Experience shows that it is relatively easier to introduce good governance features at the level of the local government. To recapitulate, some of the good governance features in the Kerala experiment are—

- Transparency and right to information
- Insistence on due process
- Participation in all stages
- Giving opportunities to young professionals to serve as apprentices in local governments eg: Civil and agricultural engineers, IT professionals etc. _ Recognition of best practices by selecting Beacon Panchayats
- Strengthening independent umpiring institutions
- Introducing code of conduct for elected representatives and officials
- Making Citizen's Charter compulsory
- Revising office management systems to make them people friendly
- Simplification and modernization using information technology.

Implications—Initial Evidence from the Field

The Achievements and the experience of the first few years of decentralization has proved that in providing basic minimum needs infrastructure like housing, water supply, sanitation and connectivity, the Local Governments have performed creditably. The speed and extent of coverage as well as efficiency in implementation in respect of provision of minimum needs has been superior to that of Government. Next to minimum needs, the local governments have done reasonably well in natural resource management particularly in utilization of water resources for productive purposes. As regards the productive sector there have only been isolated successes where agricultural production and productivity has been increased manifold. However in providing services like health and education, success stories have been relatively less in number. Of course outreach of health services as well as remedial coaching for laggard students has definitely improved and the infrastructure for health and education has rapidly been upgraded. But management of professionals and other staff to provide better quality services requires further effort. On the whole an encouraging feature is the fact that in most of the sectors there have been viable models evolved by individual local governments. A major challenge would be to upscale and replicate them. It is pertinent to note that funds spent on poverty reduction program by local governments significantly exceed earlier investments. This is suggestive of the higher priority given to anti poverty programs by local governments. The spread of this investment is also much wider and generally more equitable.

Another significant area relating to poverty reduction where the local governments have performed well is the implementation of social security schemes like pensions. The coverage has improved and the targeting has been fairly satisfactory. The good governance aspects of decentralization particularly transparency as well as the opportunities for participation have improved the quality of the programs formulated and implemented by local governments. There is considerably less leakage and definitely the identification of beneficiaries is better.

The Potential in terms of local level development, decentralization has certain definite advantages which are evident from practice. They are:-

(1) Resources have flowed into every nook and corner and if the formula of devolution and distribution is a progressive one with earmarking of funds for the disadvantaged groups, greater equity can be achieved.

(2) The outreach of a developmental service has improved a lot.

(3) There is less of sectoralism in decentralized programs. Greater convergence has contributed to reducing the ratchet effect of poverty. Local Governments particularly Village Panchayats, tend to view problems holistically and come out with a solution first and then only decide on the agency of implementation.

(4) In view of the financial constraints and skill limitations there is greater emphasis on locally appropriate, affordable solutions.

(5) There is great realism in tackling problems of poverty. There are no tall promises. The problem of poverty is perceived in its stark reality. It cannot be submerged in academic debates or hidden in statistical sophistry.

(6) The innumerable opportunities for participation which has been structured into Kerala's decentralization process has helped the poor in gaining confidence and in moving from lower levels of participation into higher forms of direct social action like management of facilities, creation of demand for services and so on.

(7) The participation of people has definitely improved accountability.

The Limitations

There have also been certain problems, which are enumerated below:

(1) The outliers like Scheduled Tribes are still to gain from decentralization. In scenarios where one section of the poor lives off another section, then decentralization has certain inbuilt limitations.

(2) The poorest among the poor need social safety nets particularly for food and health emergencies. This cannot be provided by local governments.

(3) The management of services particularly health and education have not been more efficient than before and these services have direct implications for local development especially poverty reduction.

(4) The flow of bank credit into local schemes has been rather limited resulting more from bankers' reluctance to deal with local governments than from inadequacies of project formulation. This has resulted in higher subsidies.

(5) In a State like Kerala where the number of educated poor is very high there is an inherent limitation in local government action for creating jobs. The role of local governments in bringing about economic development and creating employment opportunities on a large scale needs further study.

(6) There is a tendency to spread resources thinly with preference being given to every electoral constituency whenever a development scheme is taken up.

(7) Participatory aspect of planning is often limited to airing of needs and sharing of benefits. There is need for enhancing the quality of participatory planning so that there is a healthy discussion by all sections of the population based on data and norms, generating a prioritized list of developmental needs.

The Role of Local Governments in Development of Tourism – the Potential and Possibilities

Before the local governments were created decentralized tourism development activities were taken up at the District level through District Tourism Promotion Councils. These Councils took up activities like promoting back-water tourism, eco tourism, maintained scenic spots and parks, provided tourism information and developed tourism infrastructure related to sanitation and hygiene. Though tourism has not been transferred as a subject to the local governments they have started showing keen interest. Some of the areas where some initiatives have been taken are:

(a) Local Governments especially near the sea coast or back-waters or in the hills have taken several steps to develop infrastructure needed for tourists like electricity, water supply, roads etc., and to maintain environmental sanitation.

(b) Local governments have started identifying heritage spots and nature tourism spots for protection, promotion and proper upkeep.

(c) In some cases group entrepreneurship by the relatively poor sections have been directly supported by local governments through skill development training and financial assistance to start tourism related enterprises. This is turning out to be an area of tremendous potential. Families below poverty line covering about a third of the population are networked into Neighborhood Groups at the local levels, Area Development Societies at the intermediate level and Community Development Societies at the Local Government level with each family being represented only by women folk. These self-help organizations of women have taken up several activities like revival of traditional cuisine, development of local handicrafts, taking up environmental sanitation activities as group effort providing IT services and so on. Since the women below poverty line are properly organized they can be trained to reap the direct down stream benefits of tourism. It is a good example of making tourism development pro-poor. More linkages are expected in the coming years.

(d) Development of local cultural activities, preservation of traditional art forms is two activities in which local governments have done quite well. Without much investment they are able to ensure local level action in these areas.

(e) Eco tourism is an area where partnership with local governments shows much potential. Local governments can train tourism guides as a means of self employment. They can provide minimum required infrastructure like drinking water and toilets in these tourism spots.

(f) The State Government is now in the process of building long-term perspective on tourism development in partnership with local governments. Learning from experience the State is now bringing about proper spatial planning in tourism sites to prevent overcrowding and inappropriate architecture. This joint planning exercise with local governments is expected to improve destination tourism in the selected local governments. As local governments are moving into finding avenues to push local economic development tourism development would be getting natural preference.

CONCLUSION

INITIATIVE TOWARDS DECENTRALISATION

Kerala captured the world's imagination for its success in health and development. What lessons will Kerala offer for the future? How will Kerala's people, both residential and non-resident, exploit the opportunities of globalization? How will Kerala's decentralization perform in the face of changing global governance? How will Kerala and India balance entering the competitive global economy while improving global systems of governance? Kerala's people may show that its human talent, skills, and enterprise can compete in the global economy. Kerala's experiment in local governance may demonstrate that decentralization can help democratize decision-making at both the local and global levels. Yet, Kerala's future must be navigated in a world lacking in genuinely democratic institutions. Without the democratization of health, global health equity built on consensus and shared values will be difficult and people will continue to feel unable to shape their health future. Krishnan was visionary about these challenges. When India began economic liberalization in 1991, he did not oppose the expansion of private markets in India per se.

Rather, he became a passionate defender of public provisioning to protect the poor. He advocated for maintaining India's public food distribution system; indeed, he was a founder of the Food Corporation of India. In our UN-Harvard-Government project on health and development, Krishnan created partnerships among the actors and linked them to young social scientists throughout India. True to his values, his last paper on the crippling cost of family health crises moved him to propose the introduction of catastrophic hospital insurance for the poor. These intellectual contributions were based on Krishnan's understanding of Kerala's history of participatory democracy, tolerance among groups, and pluralism of ideas. Everybody is confident about the resilience of Kerala society increasingly connected to a rapidly changing world.

The decentralization process in Kerala has moved from the experimentative phase through a corrective phase and has now entered the critical institutionalization phase. In the first stage which was based on trial and error, several mistakes were made and several new areas discovered. At this stage adhoc systems were designed to facilitate operational flexibility at the local level. Now from the campaign mode decentralization is entering the systems mode. This is the time for weeding out worn out procedures and systems and planning modern systems, which are simple, transparent, fair, providing easy upkeep while at the same time ensuring accountability of the highest degree. The Peoples' Planning Campaign has been sustained through a host of activist volunteers. Soon these volunteers would move out of direct leadership and play the role of facilitators. Regular support systems appropriate to local government functioning would be in place.

The local governments which are by now reasonably adept in preparing plans are expected to further improve their capacity to implement them efficiently and economically. A major challenge ahead would be to build capacity in the local governments to manage provision of various services to the people. Participation of the people needs to be further institutionalized and the question of integration of plans among the tiers needs to be dealt with. From incremental annual planning, the local governments are expected to switch over to five year planning from the year 2002. For this purpose they have to be conditioned to develop a strategic vision. In this phase they have to graduate from creation of infrastructure to promoting local economic development including tourism. While doing so they have to increasingly rely on local resource mobilization as well as innovative methods of financing projects.

References

Aravindan, KP and TP Kunhikannan (eds) (2000): Health Transition in Rural Kerala: 1987-1996, Kerala Sastra Sahithya Parishad, Trivandrum.

Caldwell, JC (1986): The conditions of unusually low mortality: Optimum paths to health for all. Population and Development Review 12(2).

Centre for Development Studies (1975): Poverty, Unemployment and Development Policy: A case study of selected issues with special reference to Kerala, United Nations, New York.

Chandrasekhar, CP (2000): "ICT in a developing country context: An Indian case study," Background paper for the Human Development Report 2000, Human Development Office, UNDP, New York. Chatterjee, Mirai: "Taking care .

Isaac, TM Thomas. "Campaign for demographic decentralization in Kerala: An assessment from the perspective of empowered deliberative democracy," Centre for Development Studies, Trivandrum, January 12, 2000.

Menon-Sen, K and AK Shiva Kumar (2001): Women in India: How Free? How Equal? Report commissioned by the Office of the United Nations Resident Coordinator in India, New Delhi.

Panikar, PGK and CR Soman (1984): Health Status of Kerala: The Paradox of Economic Backwardness and Health Development. Centre for Development Studies, Trivandrum.

Radhakrishnan, T, KR Thankappan, RS Vasan, and PS Sarma (2000): "Socioeconomic and demographic factors associated with birth weight: A community based study in Kerala,." Indian Pediatrics 37:872-875.

Raman Kutty, V (1989): "Women's education and its influence on attitudes to aspects of child care in a village community in Kerala," Social Science and Medicine 23:11.

Raman Kutty, V (2000). "Historical analysis of the development of health care facilities in Kerala State, India," Health Policy and Planning 15 (1):103-109.

Thankappan, KR and MS Valiathan (1998): "Health at low cost: the Kerala model." Lancet 351:1274-1275.

12

Democratic Decentralisation and Participatory Planning in Kerala: The Locomotive of a New Development Culture

B. Mohanan

Introduction

Ever since the launching of the campaign for democratic decentralization and participatory planning by the CPI(M) controlled Left Democratic Front (LDF) Government in 1996, Kerala has, once again, become the locus of international attention thanks to the sudden transformation of the state as the location of innovations in local democracy and participatory development, in the age of globalization. Development thinkers, social scientists, policy makers and activists from other states in India and abroad have detoured the charming villages of Kerala to get a feel of the nature and dynamics of decentralized democracy at the grassroots level. All of a sudden Kerala has become the most favoured destination of academic tourism as everyone wanted to know what is happening in the red-bastion in the South –west strip of India.

Many western writers who have been studying Kerala for several years have show- cased the decentralized planning campaign as an alternative to the economics and politics of corporate dominated globalization. For writers and activists from other states in India, Kerala has emerged as a replicable model of democratic decentralisation within the framework of 73rd and 74th amendments to the constitution of India that came into effect in 1992.

Back home the people's plan campaign for decentralized planning (PCDP) generated heated arguments, debates, discussion as also controversies of unprecedented nature. The Left intellectuals in Kerala who took positions in the 'right' of the 'left -centre' and 'left' of the 'left- centre' and 'far- left' of the 'left -centre' enriched the intellectual horizon of Kerala with illuminating ideas and arguments. Interestingly, there was virtually no participation in the debates from the side of the leaders and supporters of the non-left formations in Kerala represented by the Congress (I) party led United Democratic Front (UDF).

The media in Kerala, both print and electronic, sensationalized the whole debate by crossing even the fault-lines of decency and civility. Two of Kerala's most circulated newspapers have substituted meaningful discussions with personal attacks and mudslinging. They found in the debate a handy stick to beat the CPI (M).

It is evident that some comrades, friends and fellow travelers of the CPI (M) seemingly failed to comprehend the development implications of the politics of democratic decentralisation in its proper spirit. For instance, the far-left deviation of M.N. Vijayan, a Professor of Malayalam language and literature, who served as Editor of CPI (M)'s weekly Magazine, is noteworthy. In fact, Vijayan was resigning as Editor of *Desabhimani weekly* in protest against what he perceived as the party's deviation from conventional party programme and strategy. At the same time, CPI (M) had expelled one of its committed comrades, the people's science movement activist and scientist M.P. Parameswaran for his over enthusiasm for decentralized planning programme which the party thought a kind of right deviation. The CPI (M) leadership in unequivocal terms made it clear that right deviation is not the answer to far - left adventurism. What was perceived as 'far - left' adventurism and right deviation of two of CPI (M)'s prominent intellectuals in Kerala combined with the unethical journalism of certain newspapers and news channels have given enormous amount of embarrassment for the state unit of CPI (M) at a time when the party was engaged in a process of repositioning itself in the society and polity of Kerala with a new political strategy. Why CPI (M) thought of initiating a new political strategy in 1996? What exactly is the 'new' in the strategy initiated? What is the meaning and content of the new development culture that the CPM was talking about during the late eighties?

Overview of Literature

The debate on decentralization in Kerala is very active and vibrant from the 1990s. E.M. Sankaran Namboodiripad (1992) has suggested that Panchayati Raj Institutions (PRIs) should be made important instruments for the extension of democracy at all levels of administration and for the solution of serious problems in socio-economic development. He pointed out that PRIs could be micro- level institutions for development of agriculture and petty production sector. V.K. Sukumaran Nayar (1992) argued that decentralisation should start with political parties. V. Ramachandran (1992) drew the attention to the need for enough preparation before implementation of any programme on decentralisation.

Jos Chathukulam and P.G. Padmanabhan (1998) brought out a critical analysis of Kerala Panchayati Raj Act 1994. Jose Chathukulam and M.S. John (1998) examined the Sen Committee Recommendations on devolution of powers and identified certain problems with it. They have expressed the view that we cannot set up local self government by extending sectors of activities or by providing more funds to local bodies. Self governance could be realized only through creating institutions in which there should be complete freedom for decision making and for utilizing financial resources without external control and interference.

People's campaign for development planning added a new chapter in the annals of democratic decentralisation efforts in Kerala. This has also been extensively reviewed by academics and activists in the fields of Development Studies. These include Thomas Issac (2000) Isaac & Franke (2000), S. Mohanakumar (2000), V Rajendran Nair (2000), Sajith Sukumaran (2001), Rashmi Sharma(2003), B. Mohanan (1998,2003,2005), Richard Franke and Barbara Chasin (1995). All these writers have praised PCDP, identified certain weaknesses of the programme and suggested measures for further improvement. However, John and Chathukulam observed that institutions created with state patronage would not serve the interest of democracy at the grassroots level. B. Mohanan (2002) studied the reasons for low participation in the *gramasabha* meetings in Kerala and arrived at the conclusion that people's participation in *gramasabha* in Kerala was drastically low because of the effect of civil society.

The extensive literature on Kerala's decentralisation movement can be grouped into two distinct categories. The academic writings on Panchayati Raj Institutions and democratic decentralisation up to 1996 constitute the first category. The second category of literature started burgeoning ever since the launching of people's campaign for decentralized planning and development. The post -1996 literature could be classified into four groups. Firstly, the insider's view as presented by Thomas Isaac and his associate – activists in the campaign for decentralisation. The extensive writings which have assessed and reassessed the merits and demerits of PCDP from a purely academic point of view form the second category of literature. The debates on the ideology of people's plan campaign represent the third category. Analysis by the intellectuals of the far-left school viewed it as the implementation of the neo-liberal agenda of governance. Finally, the writings of the foreign scholars who projected Kerala's decentralized democracy as a viable alternative to corporate dominated globalization. However, the contextual and domestic compulsions that necessitated the launching of the programme have not received adequate attention.

Efforts at Democratic Decentralization in Kerala

The history of efforts at democratic decentralisation in Kerala goes back to the early days of formation of the State. The Administrative Reforms Committee (1958) under the Chairmanship of the then Chief Minister, EMS Namboodiripad , suggested a two-tier local government set up with Panchayats and Municipalities at the grassroots level and District Councils at the district level. The District Council Bill was introduced in the Kerala State Assembly in 1958. But the bill could not get passed because the EMS Government was dismissed by the Central Government and the Assembly was dissolved in 1959. In 1967 the second EMS Government wanted to enact the two-tier local government set up. The Kerala Panchayati Raj Bill was introduced in 1967. The Government resigned in 1969 and the bill lapsed. A Kerala District Administration Bill was passed by the Congress Government headed by A. K. Antony in 1979 which was originally introduced in 1971 and re-introduced in 1978 but no attempt was made to implement it till 1987. The LDF Government of E. K. Nayanar (1987-91) took measures to implement the Act. Elections to District Councils were held in February 1990. In the next Assembly Elections the LDF lost power and UDF Government under the leadership of Congress leader Karunakaran came to power. The UDF Government of Karunakaran took back all functions and powers transferred to the District Council in the very first decision of the new government.

It is at this juncture that the Government of India came out with the 73rd and 74th Amendments to the Constitution of India to have uniform pattern of local bodies all over India and to provide constitutional status to them.

Kerala's experiment with decentralisation has always been affected by the sharp political division in the state on rightist and leftist lines ever since the dislodging of the first

Communist Government through the so called liberation struggle. The two major coalitions of Political Parties the Left Democratic Front (LDF) and the United Democratic Front (UDF) have approached the question of democratic decentralisation with contrasting interests and ideas. It has been well documented that the LDF tried to push forward the decentralization programme earnestly whenever they controlled the state government. However, Kerala could not succeed to present a viable model of decentralized governance till the PCDP was launched in 1996 because of the alternating of governments between LDF and UDF on every five year intervals. The PCDP has provided an opportunity for both protagonists and opponents of decentralization for learning and experiencing grassroots democracy.

The campaign for decentralized planning and local democracy was in fact, a clear departure from the existing strategies and programmes of the left in Kerala. In the context of the serious setback suffered by the Communist movement at the global level in the aftermath of the demise of Soviet Union, the CPI(M) leadership in the state might have felt that if the CPI (M) was not addressing the development crisis of the state the party might be facing the threat of redundancy. In fact, this is not the first time that the CPI (M) is coming out with a new agenda for action for the attainment of its brand of socialism. Krishnaji has identified three such phasesin the history of communist movement in Kerala. The first one was before the formation of the State in 1956 when the communists were engaging exclusively in class struggle along "orthodox" lines on behalf of workers and peasants, marked by much violence. In the second period from 1957 to the early 1970s the communists experimented with ways of both ruling the state under the Indian democracy and transforming property relations to the extent possible with out giving up militancy. The third phase is from 1970s which is characterized by the total absorption of the communists in the electoral politics (Krishnaji

2007).The kind of total absorption of the communists in the electoral politics as encapsulated by Krishnaji is the creative response to contextual compulsions and challenges.

The Crisis Narrative and the Left Response

In the late eighties and early nineties several studies questioned sustainability of the celebrated Kerala model of development because of the absence of the support system of required level of economic growth.

This phenomenon of social development sans economic growth has been explained in terms of the redistribution strategy adopted by successive progressive governments of the State in response to public action through mass mobilization. In the eighties and early nineties, the left intellectuals in the state had also started subscribing the view that Kerala model of development was facing a severe crisis of sustainability. Social sector achievements could not be maintained further without addressing the issue of sluggish economic growth. They had arrived at the conclusion that without increasing production and productivity in agriculture and petty production sectors, the state would fall into the morass of deep crisis.

At this juncture it is pertinent to have a look at the left response as explained by Thomas Isaac, the chief activist of the people's plan campaign. He refers to various studies undertaken by scholars of the Centre for Development Studies (CDS, Trivandrum) and the speeches and writings of EMS Namboodirpad.

In 1991, CDS Economist, Dr.Krishnan came out with empirical evidence that the rate of growth of wages was higher than the rate of growth of productivity in the state.

Even before that in 1989 EMS Namboodiripad published a pamphlet entitled *Politics of Development* in which he proposed the need for a new political culture in the state for development. Since then he had been articulating his views for a new strategy. For instance in 1991 as a response to Dr.Krishnan's findings he said self critically:

> "I don't claim that the approach of the workers and peasant organizations and political parties leading them are above fault. While they struggle for their rights and demands they have to realize the importance of improving production and productivity in agriculture and industry. Mass organizations of workers and peasants and other sections of people and political parties giving leadership to them have to come forward to increase production in the public and private sectors and help to mobilize capital for social investment. I want to publicly state our commitment to rectify mistakes, if any, in this respect from our side" (EMS in 1991 as quoted by Thomas Isaac, 2000:45). EMS was bold enough to admit the fact that the problem of sluggish economic growth, was partly due to the mobilization strategies of the communist party. He candidly admitted that while organizing struggles for rights and demands, the mass organizations did not pay due attention to issues related to production and productivity. He further publicly expressed his commitment to rectify mistakes, if any.

Further, he said that leaders and workers of mass organizations had to come forward to increase production and productivity in both public and private sector. Another most significant point in the statement quoted above is his views on the role of mass organizations in helping to mobilize capital for social investment. In another occasion he said: "Kerala faces today an intense economic crisis in production – agricultural and industrial. I am inclined to believe that while we have spent much time and attention on "social sector' issues of welfare and improvement of the living standards of the people we have not paid enough attention to or adequate concern for pressing problems of economic growth and material production. I make a request: let not the praise that scholars shower on Kerala for its achievements divert attention from the intense economic crisis that we face. We are behind other states of India in respect of economic growth and a solution to this crisis brooks no delay. We can ignore our backwardness in respect of employment and production only at our own peril" (EMS 1994 as cited in Isaac 2000:44).

He admitted that Kerala is behind other states in India in respect of economic growth and generation of employments. He had reasserted his views that the organized strength of the mass organization could be mobilized for increasing production and productivity:

> "Our greatest assets are our mass organization and the democratic consciousness of our people. The combined strength of all mass organizations in the state is about ten million. Besides, there is a vast net work of cooperative organizations of the library and literary movements. I am aware that there are some people who consider all these to be the bane of Kerala society. I have devoted my life to mobilizing the people for radical transformation of our society, and I cannot but disagree with such perceptions. I feel that one big question that we face is whether the organized strength and political consciousness of our people can be used to increase production and productivity. I would like to answer in the affirmative" (EMS 1994 as quoted by Thomas Isaac, 200:26). We have reproduced the excerpts from the writings and speeches of EMS Namboodiripad as quoted by Thomas Isaac to substantiate that the theoretical base of the campaign had been provided by no less a person than EMS, the veteran theoretician and tactician. From the extracts cited above we could see the following. Firstly, EMS in unequivocal terms underlined the importance of production and productivity for sustaining the achievements in social sector. Secondly, we should do all possible to overcome the challenges of economic growth and past mistakes had to be corrected. Thirdly,

he articulated the view that the organized strength of mass movements should be used for increasing production and productivity.

Marxist In-house Dialogue

CPI (M) continued the development debate initiated by EMS on its own platform. A Round Table was organized under the auspices of the theoretical of journal of CPM in Kerala. Left political party leaders and academics participated in it. A discussion document was prepared and submitted to the party for further debate and action.

The starting point of the discussion document was reference to the Kerala model of development with its social sector achievements and underlined the following:

> Kerala has been successful in providing the basic needs of the people. Kerala's achievements have resulted from redistributive strategies in response to mass pressure from below. The left carries forward the progressive legacy of earlier social reform movements. The struggle of the left has not been only for land reforms and wage increases, but for the right to shelter, education, health care, safe drinking water and other basic needs. The social sector achievements did not have a complementary positive impact on economic growth. Despite land reforms there was no remarkable improvement in agricultural productivity. Despite educational expansion industrial modernization and diversification remained retarded. As a result unemployment was three times the national average. The quality of the social infrastructure was deteriorating. The fiscal crisis of the state was rendering it incapable of intervening in the crisis. In the absence of economic growth it would not be possible to sustain redistribution strategies. The economic stagnation had serious political implications – unemployment, growth of caste based movements etc. Right wing ideologies were attacking the left that the left had no programme for increasing production. They said

stagnation resulted from the redistribution strategies of the left. The critics said that (1) the left had fulfilled its historic role in bringing about more equitable distribution and 2) now it should make way for market forces in order to achieve rapid growth.

On the basis of the debate initiated by EMS an International Congress on Kerala Studies was organized in August 1994 under the auspices of AKG Centre for Research and Studies. According to Thomas Isaac and other organizers of the conference the International Congress on Kerala studies was "an important landmark in the move towards a broad social consensus on the development of the state". As a result of continuous discussions and debates a coherent strategy with two pillars was evolved by 1996 to address the development crisis of the state. The first pillar is "resolute state intervention" in power sector and inviting private capital in electronics, light engineering and other industries, where the state had comparative advantage. The second pillar which is considered as the "centre piece" of the strategy was decentralization with the involvement of the masses for increasing productivity in small scale sectors and to improve the quality of life in public services.

Thus, the People's plan Campaign is a product of a dialogue among the left intellectuals in Kerala about the crisis that gripped the much publicized Kerala Model of Development. The state has achieved high quality of life without proportionate increase in economic growth. This is an outcome of mobilization of masses by left forces for redistribution of wealth and appropriate Government intervention. But by the end of the eighties this development model had fallen into a severe crisis because of stagnation in production sectors and quality erosion in service sectors. As has already been noted following are the problems identified in productive sector (I) the virtual stagnation of the agricultural sector (ii) the deplorably lower level of productivity of important crops (iii) growing apathy among cultivators (iv) structural decay of the industrial sector dominated by ailing traditional industries (v) rapid deterioration of power situation and (vi) overburdening of fragile ecosystem etc.

Krishnaji observes, "the efforts culminated in a massive 'people's campaign for decentralized planning', and later to the implementation itself, following an LDF victory in 1996..... EMS repeatedly emphasized his faith in decentralization as a means for helping the poor in their day-to-day struggles against oppression and exploitation. He also talked about and wrote about amicable solutions to be found through collective bargaining and discussions. The ideology formulated new during the 1990s had thus elements of pragmatic compromise, tinged by voluntarism: hopes about whole communities participating in a planned economic betterment of the poor. The implementation of the scheme in 1996, with the devolution of substantial part of plan funds to the local village bodies, was an act of rare political daring" (Krishnaji 2007).Krishnaji has ,in fact, captured the meaning and content of the decentralized planning movement when he had written that it was a pragmatic compromise tinged with voluntarism.

Contributions of Younger Marxists of Kerala

As has rightly been observed by Krishnaji, the programme formulated in 1990s is a pragmatic compromise and an act of rare political daring due to domestic compulsions that it is partly a creation of setbacks for Communist movements the world over in the context of demise of Soviet Union. No doubt EMS laid the foundation for it. However, the whole complex edifice of people's plan campaign has been built brick by brick by the comparatively younger generation of Marxists of Kerala. About this Richard Franke raises two questions. "Can we go beyond the earlier Kerala model of public action to generate a high material quality of life through redistribution by adding to that model a mechanism for an egalitarian strategy of growth? And if we wanted to do that what would be the fuel?" Franke himself answers these questions thus. He is of the opinion that the new generation activists of Kerala had come to realize by 1980s certain facts about the new world. While maintaining intense respect for the sacrifice and idealism of the older activists for their fight for land reforms and higher wages and benefits for the poor, they found immense potentialities offered by non violent action for social change. They have been inspired by Gramsci's thinking rather than by the long march of Mao's army. Also they have realized that time has come to move beyond traditional activism of the left in the spheres of land reforms ,wage increase ,improving working conditions and overcoming caste discriminations to newer frontiers of gender equity, environmental protection and expanding democracy through building community. They felt that struggles would have to become less mechanical and more democratic and participatory. Here Franke raises another question. Why did they arrive at this historically significant breakthrough? He answers: "I can only tell you at this time that the US movements of the 1960s had a profound effect on their thinking. And the evolution of the Italian communists with their emphasis on cooperatives and local government accountability struck strong chords in Kerala. The collapse of the Soviet Union in turn welcomed the position of the old left forces and created an opening for the younger activists who were reading green and feminist literature. And looming behind all these intellectual developments was Mahatma Gandhi, whose teachings on village self-sufficiency, exemplary simple life style, and economic growth as a means to benefit the most needy have continued to inspire each new generation of activists in Kerala".(Franke 2001).

According to Franke the new generation Marxists of Kerala has been influenced by green and feminist literature as also by the writing of Gramsci and teachings of Mahatma Gandhi. Richard Franke is the academic collaborator of Thomas Isaac. Therefore his narrative about the orientation of the younger generation of the Marxists bears the authenticity of an insider. The new role of the younger generation Marxists of Kerala has been succinctly summarized by Patrick Heller as an attempt to 'de-Leninize' CPI (M) in Kerala. Heller writes that historically CPI (M) does not have any intense affinity for democratic decentralization and the organizing principle of that party is democratic centralism. Then why the key elements in CPI (M) embraced decentralization?

To answer this question two developments have to be singled out, according to Heller. "First, the party has come to recognize the limits of its electoral appeal and in a context of competitive party politics has identified decentralization as encompassing a set of interests and issues that can appeal to new post-class struggle constituencies. Second, the embrace of decentralization marks a tacit recognition of that the redistributive capacities of the developmental state have exhausted themselves. If a strong, centralized and interventionist state did secure many of the benefits associated with the Kerala model, the second generation social development challenges Kerala faces call for a fundamentally different mode of governance" (Heller2000).

Thus the launching of the campaign for decentralized democracy and participatory planning is an outcome of the burning desire of the younger activists within the CPI (M) with the blessings of EMS to create newer institutions, on the solid foundations of achievements of yester years, that could address the challenges of environmental degradation, gender equity and above all economic growth.

PCDP and Economic Growth

Over a period of ten years, by utilizing the funds devolved to the local bodies, several kilometers of new roads in rural areas have been constructed. Houses for homeless have been constructed, drinking water projects implemented with community participation. Krishnaji observes, "the results of Kerala's democratic decentralization experience show in fact that a major part of the plan funds had gone in support of the so called social sector, through the construction and improvement of roads, move tangibly for provisions of public toilets and houses for the poor and so on" (Krishnaji2007).

When it comes to production and productivity the record of PCDP is not on par with achievements in infrastructure and allied sectors. It has been reported that the projects under taken particularly in agriculture sectors, are not sustainable. However revival of cultivation of labour intensive crops such as paddy is difficult because of land ownership pattern and because of "non availability of labour for time bound operations such as harvesting and other types of mass work. Labour in Kerala is withdrawing from manual work" (Krishnaji 2007). At the same time in several places micro-enterprises have been started by *kudumbasree* cooperatives and self help groups. These units are now successful in establishing backward and forward linkages. In certain locations marketing companies have been registered for marketing of the products of micro enterprises on common brand name (Thomas Isaac 2007). After observing the PCDP for the first three years Franke has written that thousands of new acres of land have been brought into cultivation. It recorded an increase of 5.6%. The long stagnated agriculture sector, recorded a growth in 1988-99 by 3.82% compared with an average of 1.3% in the previous 3 years. Industrial sector rose by 7.2% and more than 100,000 new jobs were created. It represents possible 5% decrease in the employment rate of Kerala (Franke 2000).

In this context it would be appropriate to have a brief mention about recent trends in economic growth of Kerala. Achin Chakraborty, K.P.Kannan, P.D Jeromi and a number of other economists have, of late, reported that Kerala economy is growing. Chakraborthy observes that "growth has not eluded Kerala after all". He says that Kerala's SDP has been growing at a rate closer between Kerala's achievements in education overseas migration of job seekers and flow of remittance at phenomenal proportions (Achin Chakraborty 2005).

Similarly, K.P.Kannan(2005) talks about a turn around in economic growth . He is of the opinion that the state which has shown high human development and low economic growth is, of late, exhibiting a new phenomenon of accelerated economic growth since the late 1980s. This is a contribution of economic reforms and massive flow of remittances. Now the challenge is addressing the issue of unemployment of its educated youth and ensuring equitable participation to women in all walks of life. P.D. Jeromi (2003) has made an analysis of the performance of Kerala in different sectors and found that, the state has recorded growth in the tertiary sector. According to him there is a revival in the growth of the state income during the 1990s from a phase of low growth during the eighties.

All these economists have noted that the growth recorded is in the tertiary sector only with the significant share of tertiary sector the state's economy has become a service oriented economy. There is persistent decline in food grain production and the state continues to be industrially backward (Jeromi 2003).

The economic growth that has been reported by leading economists coincides roughly with the period of PCDP. This is not to say that PCDP is responsible for the reported economic growth. However it has a role in bringing in certain attitudinal changes that in turn might have promoted investment in the tertiary sector. Even though the productive sector did not show impressive growth, the trends of growth recorded in tertiary sector, brings home the point that the hurdles in the way of capital development is being removed. No doubt a new entrepreneurial culture is in the making in Kerala. A new work ethics is being shaped. There are concrete evidences to show that the state is gradually making a departure from the century old agitation mode.

The Arduous Journey Through the new Development Culture

Decentralized planning campaign which has now completed ten years of its implementation is definitely a revolutionary decision and bold step in the history of planned development in India. This internationally noted programme has received both laurels and brickbats; and it is quite natural while considering the complexities and dimensions of the programme.

The most important feature that could be observed about the programme is that it deviated from the mainstream theory of people's participation and local governance as propagated by World Bank. The criticism that Thomas Isaac and other plan activists facilitated the backdoor entry of World Bank's neo-liberal agenda of development has no basis at all. In the World Bank concept of decentralized governance and participatory development NGOs got a prominent place. In the people's plan campaign NGOs did not get accommodated. Instead, the constitutionally established Local Self-Government Institutions themselves prepared their plan proposals with people's participation. To mobilize people at the local level as a support system to LSGIs, the People's Science Movement in Kerala (KSSP) took the lead role assisted by individual volunteers drawn from among school, college, university teachers and sectoral organizations of state government employees, all affiliated to CPI (M).

Here it is noteworthy that the teachers and government employees who took part in People's Plan activities were not officially representing their sectoral organizations; they participated in PCDP activities as members of KSSP. It is very significant to note that the sectoral organizations of CPI (M) did not cooperate with PCDP as it was desired by EMS.

The mass organizations have been given training to work on the basis of their understanding of the economic, social and cultural issues in the sector they are operating. For instance a union in the industrial sector would be organizing agitations to get their demands accepted. Similarly agricultural workers union, students union, teachers' organizations, women's associations etc. would be organizing and articulating their demands through agitation methods. In other words the methods of all mass organizations are that of agitation.

All on a sudden putting agitation on backburner and involving in development work was unthinkable for a sizeable section of the organized masses, if not all. The important aspect of Kerala's development experience has been the intervention of the state to bring about distributive justice. The compelling factor in this kind of state intervention is that it is the response of the state to the pressures and demands of common people articulated through mass movements.

The CPI (M) can take the credit for organizing all sections of the people in Kerala. The organizations of government employees, teachers, students and labourers are very vocal in articulating their sectarian demands. These organizations controlled mainly by CPI (M), till the initiation of People's Plan, were not ready to make minor sacrifices for overall growth and welfare of the state as a whole. This has created a situation where the political society in Kerala has become an arena for pressurizing the government for the attainment of sectarian demand; no concern for production and productivity.

EMS in the last few years of his life devoted his intellectual prowess to re-canalize the organized strength and political consciousness of mass organizations to increase production and productivity.

Even though the mass organizations of CPI (M) did not participate in PCDP programmes officially, the involvement of several members of various organizations through the KSSP route did have a "de-schooling" effect on mass organizations in Kerala. This is evident from the slow percolation of changes in the nature of production relations in Kerala. The trade union militancy for which Kerala was known till the eighties is waning rapidly. The state is now encouraging private investment. The *Bandh/Harthal* culture etched in Malayalee psyche over several decades shows a trend of getting erased. It is very clear that the campaign for democratic decentralization and participatory planning succeeded in ushering in an attitudinal change of long-term import in the organized sector of Kerala. A gradual transition from agitation mode to a kind of politics of community integration is in the making.

This is in fact a major departure from the past. From the social history of Kerala roughly from 15th century onwards one could glean the way that the typical Malayalee work culture got shaped and got transmitted through generations. Even though protestant Christianity embarked on Kerala shores around fourteenth century the protestant work ethics failed to percolate into the *Keralam* of that age because caste system controlled the relations of production.

The colonial capitalism did have a chain effect on production relations in Travancore and Cochin. About that Geneveve Lemercinier writes: "our empirical analysis also revealed diversity in the reaction of the social actors to the changes brought about in the traditional economic order by the particular form of colonialism that developed in Travancore. Now this diversity was not unrelated to caste belonging. Without wishing to generalize these observations so as to include all their members, it would appear that certain castes and similar groups entered more easily than others into this process of change. We have already noted, indeed, that some Syrian Christians had readily involved themselves in big agricultural and commercial projects.... A rather similar attitude could be observed among the Ezhavas who very quickly oriented their cultivation towards export crops, and developed small manufacturing industries for the process of coconut fibers and the production of coir" (Lemercinier 1974:179).

It is significant to note that on the plane of social relations of production massive changes had been introduced by colonial capitalism. It had helped the emergence of local entrepreneurs particularly among Syrian Christians. But this trend did not sustain. The new education system, that was emerging, did not help the development of productive forces in the rural milieu because the objective was oriented towards serving the interests of colonial capitalism. Secondly, "the cultural models involved in the production of kinship relation were not damaged....so that the persistence of rural dominance in the economy created conditions favourable to the reproduction of a culture supporting the stability of practices of traditional type" (ibid p.185).

In short the feudal values had reproduced it whatever be the mode of production. This in turn had shaped very much the nature of social reform movements also. The social psyche of the right (over)conscious Malayalee whose life ambition had been to enter into the government bureaucracy irrespective of the size of pay packet had thus been formed. Employment in the bureaucratic structure of the government had become the criterion of social status. This had had twin effect. Firstly, the entrepreneurial talent started sprouting during the initial period of introduction of colonial capitalism did not flourish. The economic behaviour of the Syrian Christians and Ezhavas stand testimony to it. The Syrian Christians had entered into money lending business rather than taking the risk of investing in production sector. If at all they had invested in production sector it was outside the territorial boundary of Kerala. Secondly, the new education system introduced by the colonial power grew in such a way that it produced only stenographers, typists, clerks and teachers (PM Mathew2005). No concerted effort during the colonial period or even after the attainment of freedom towards entrepreneurial talent development.

The left in Kerala used to boast that they are the inheritors of the progressive legacy of the social reform movements of the pre -independent period. They are, in fact, the inheritors of not only the positive legacy of social reform movements but the negative legacy also. We have noticed that Protestant Christianity had failed to induct protestant work culture into Kerala society. Similarly, the Marxists of Kerala mobilized the masses for redistribution of wealth, without touching the dominant values of the caste system; and it is to be reiterated that they have been successful in the re-distribution of wealth. As the way Protestant Christianity failed to bring in protestant ethics, the communist movement has, by and large, failed to utilize the collective strength of their mass organizations for increasing production and productivity side by side with the agitations for maximizing the welfare of the working class.

In the context of far reaching changes at the global level as also the compulsions of the domestic situation, including the political demography of the state, the CPI (M) was forced to come out with a strategy that could ensure a complete break with the historical legacy of negative attitude towards production and productivity.

Concluding Observations

From the foregoing, it is quite clear that the politics of democratic decentralization and campaign for people's planning initiated in Kerala is the outcome of the quest for a new agenda for action in response to the development challenges of the state political demography and the contextual compulsions. It evolved through the writings of EMS, specifically between 1989 and 1994. In fact democratic decentralisation was a pet theme of EMS from the early fifties. However, the people's plan phase of communists' engagement with decentralization is radically different from ideas and strategies of the earlier period. Apart from EMS' appeal for utilizing the collective strength of mass organizations for production and productivity, the new generation Marxists of Kerala has contributed substantially to the operationalisation of the new politics of democracy at the grassroots level with the objective of breaking the limits and limitations imposed by the political demography. The attempts of the younger activists of the party has been to rescue the party becoming redundant in the context of new challenges to socialist movements the world over as also further advancement of the left in the state by befriending the social formations that are historically hostile to communism in the state.

It is clear that more than anything else circumstances within the state compelled EMS to formulate a new strategy with the active assistance of the new generation activists to replace partly the orthodox lines of class struggles on behalf of masses marked by agitation and resultant violence. PCDP did not bring massive increases in economic productivity. However, Kerala society's attitude towards economic production and productivity has changed tremendously after the implementation of PCDP. Previously there was organized resistance against private investment. In other words, the focus of the state has all along been on distribution rather than growth of income and therefore the society developed a kind of negative attitude towards private sector investment. The general perception has been that private investment is a means of exploitation of workers. Now attitudinal changes are on the horizon of Kerala society. Private investment is being promoted. The global investors meet during LDF regime and the singing of smart city agreement for investment in information technology between the LDF Government and the Dubai based company vouch for the changing attitude towards private investment. Kerala society, of late, is not patronizing trade union militancy. The state is no longer investor unfriendly. On the whole, the Kerala's political culture of inflated consciousness about one's own rights that got shaped through a hundred years social history and that stood in the way of economic growth started showing signs of melting out. Thus a new culture of development rooted very well in the dynamics of parliamentary democracy is in the making, thanks to democratic decentralization initiative. For the new generation Marxists of Kerala Gramsci as also Mahatma Gandhi are equally important for developing strategies for overcoming the demographic limitations of the left in Kerala.

The mainstream print media of Kerala who sensationalized the campaign, it seems, have failed to grasp the meaning of parliamentary road to socialism and it's far reaching implications, for the society and polity of Kerala, by way of the 'de-leninizing' process in the programme of CPI (M).

References

Achin Chakraborty (2005) "Kerala's Changing Development Narratives", *Economic& Political weekly*, Vol XL No.6 Feb.5, 2005, pp. 541-47.

Franke, Richard W. (1996): *Life is a little better: redistribution as a development strategy in Nadhur Village, Kerala,* New Delhi: Promilla and Company Publishers.

Franke, Richard W., and Barbara H. Chasin. (1994): *Kerala: radical reform as development in an Indian state*. Oakland, C A: Food First. Second edition. Also New Delhi: Promilla and Company Publishers.

____________ (1997): "Power to the Malayalee people". *Economic and Political Weekly* Vol32, No. 48, pp. 3061-68.

__________________(2001) "Fueling Economic Growth Through Democratic Participation" http://chss.montclair.edu/anthro/fuelinggrowth.htm.

Genevieve Lemercinier(!994): *Religion and Ideology in Kerala*, ISDA Trivandrum

Government of Kerala,State Planning Board (1996): *Janakeeyaasootrana Prasthanan:A handbook* (Malayalam)

Kannan K P (2005): "Kerala'sTurn around in Economic Growth" *EPW,* Vol. XL No. 6 2005, pp. 548-53.

Krishnaji N (2007): "Kerala Milestones: On parliamentary Road to Socialism", *Economic and Political Weekly,* Vol. XLII No. 23, pp. 2169-76.

Mohanan, B. (1998): 'Controlling Corruption at the Grassroots: Lessons from a Decentralized Participatory Development Administration', *ISDA Journal*, Vol. 8, No. 2, 3 & 4, April-December, pp. 245-65

____________(2002):'Pradeshika Jenadhipathyavum Keraleeya Civil Samooham', *Bharanachakram*, (Malayalam) Book 27, Vol.12, December, pp. 8-11.

__________ (2003): 'Decentralized Governance and Development in the context of Globalization: Lessons from Kerala', *ISDA Journal*, Vol.13, No.2, April-June, pp. 417-55.

__________(2003): 'Decentralised Planning and development in the Context of Globalization: Lessons from Kerala', *South Asia Politics*, July, pp. 36-42.

__________ (2005): *Decentralised Governance and Participatory Development: Issues, Constraints and Prospects*, Concept Publishing Company, New Delhi .

Mohana Kumar S(2002): "From People's Plan to Plan sans People", *Economic and Political Weekly*,Vol.36,No.16,pp 1492-7.

Nair, Rajendran V(1999): "Political Socialisation and empowerment of women:Experience from the People's Plan Campaign",*ISDA JOURNAL,*Vol9, No.4, October-December, pp. 263-94.

Nayar,Sukumaran V K(1992): "Decentralisation should start with political parties", *ISDA JOURNAL*,Vol. 2, No. 4, October-December, pp. 267-72.

Namboodiripad EMS(19992): "Democratic Decentralisation in Kerala Today",*ISDA JOURNAL*, Vol. 2, No. 4, Oct-Dec, pp. 263-65.

Patric Heller(2001) "The politics of Decentralisation in Kerala ,South Africa And Porto Alegre", http://localgovkerala.net/LSGD Links?Research/Books 12.asp

Thomas Issac, T.M.(2000): *Local democracy and local development: the people,s campaign for decentralized planning in Kerala*. New Delhi: Leftword Books.

Thomas Issac, T.M., Richard W. Franke, and M.P. Parameswaran. (1997:." From antifeudalism to sustainable development: the Kerala Peoples Science Movement", *Bulletin of Concerned Asian Scholars* 29(3): 34-44.

Thomas Isaac,(2005), The politics of Democratic Decentralisation (Malayalam) DC Books, Kottayam.

World Bank, (1999a): *Entering the 21st century: world development report 1999/2000.* New York: Oxford University Press.

_____________(1999b): Beyond the center: decentralizing the state. Washington, D.C.: The World Bank.

______________(1991): *World development report: the challenge of development.*, New York: Oxford University Press.

13

The Changing Paradigm of Rural Governance : A Case from Kerala

T.M. Joseph

The advent of the new economic order, manifested in the form of globalization, liberalization, and privatization has brought in a new governance paradigm prescriptively being referred to as good governance. The new system of governance is making the state to loose its pre-eminence as an agent for development. The government has started receding to the background from many of its traditional areas of operation and the non-governmental organizations, community based groups and multinational development agencies have stepped in to fill that void. The thrust of the new approach appears to be one of maximising the growth potential by unleashing outward looking and market driven forces by making necessary adjustments in the structure of the economy and the manner of exercise of control over power and resources (Government of India 2002).

Basic Principles of Good Governance

The concept of good governance became prominent in the late 1980's simultaneously with the end of cold war. The idea is propelled and propagated by the Bretton Woods institutions- the World Bank, the IMF and the WTO. The notion of good governance is a logical extension of the Structural Adjustment Programme (SAP), proposed by these institutions. Its aim is to complement SAP by political reforms to achieve greater accountability, transparency and efficiency in public service along with the protection of civil and human rights, and to ensure the rule of law through an independent judiciary (Oommen 2003:128).

It appeared when Structural Adjustment Programmes experienced serious implementation difficulties which were then diagnosed as failures of public management owing to unaccountable, patrimonial, and non-transparent governments. Consequently, World Bank (1992:3) defined governance "as the manner in which power is exercised in the management of a country's economic and social resources for development". Good governance, for the World Bank, appeared to be synonymous with sound economic management. In answering to widespread criticism of the international development community that top-down institutional structural reforms lead to institutional vacuum rather than a mobilisation of the societal self-help potentials, the Development Assistance Committee of the OECD formed a Working Group on Participatory Development and Good Governance. It linked good governance to participatory development, human rights and democratisation, and identified the rule of law, public sector management, controlling corruption and reducing excessive military expenditure as important dimensions of good governance (OECD 1995:14).

The new system of governance is making the state to loose its pre-eminence as an agent for development. The government has started receding to the background from many of its traditional areas of operation and the non-governmental organizations, community based groups and multinational development agencies have stepped in to fill that void. The thrust of the new approach appears to be one of maximising the growth potential by unleashing outward looking and market driven forces by making necessary adjustments in the structure of the economy and the manner of exercise of control over power and resources (Government of India 2002).

UNDP's (1997:4) understanding of the concept of good governance reflects this changing awareness about the relative role of the state:

> Governance can be seen as the exercise of economic, political and administrative authority to manage a country's affairs at all levels. It comprises the mechanisms, processes and institutions through which citizens and groups articulate their interests, exercise their legal rights, meet their obligations and mediate their differences. Good governance is, among other things, participatory, transparent and accountable. It is also effective and equitable. And it promotes the rule of law.......Governance has three legs: economic, political and administrative.... Governance encompasses the state, but it transcends the state by including the private sector and civil society organisations.

The good governance agenda underlines the curbing of the role of state and expanding the space for market and competition. It further places emphasis on civil society institutions to strengthen democracy and in constructing an informal sector that can harness people's entrepreneurship through community institutions and inter-personal relationships. That is, governance encapsulates government but it also encompasses non-governmental mechanisms to meet the demands, and aspirations of citizens. In this way, the state and civil society are co-responsible for citizen welfare (Oommen 2003:128-9). In the good governance discourse, democracy emerges as the necessary political framework for successful economic development, and within this discourse democracy and economic liberalism are conceptually linked: bad governance equals state intervention; good governance equals democracy and economic liberalism. (Abrahamsen 2000:51)

In its current usage 'good governance' always includes the following core elements: people-centered, equity, accountability, transparency, participation and consultation in planning and decision-making, effective and efficient public sector management, and civil society involvement. In other words, good governance is pro poor and gender-conscious, is legitimized by participatory processes, undertakes anti-corruption efforts, is bureaucratically accountable, is efficient and effective in the use of resources, and promotes the active involvement of the private sector and the civil society to counteract vested interests. Box 1 provides a full list of properties which have been associated with good governance developed by a UNDP Workshop on Good Governance for Sustainable Development in 1996.

Box 1: Characteristics of Good Governance

- Participatory
- Sustainable
- Legitimate and acceptable to the people
- Transparent: Promotes equity and equality
- Able to develop the resources and methods of governance
- Promotes gender balance
- Tolerates and accepts diverse perspectives
- Able to mobilize resources for social purposes
- Strengthens indigenous mechanisms
- Operates by rule of law
- Efficient and effective in the use of resources
- Engenders and command respect and trust
- Accountable
- Able to define and take ownership of national solutions
- Enabling and facilitative
- Regulatory rather than controlling
- Able to deal with temporal issues
- Service-oriented

The style of governance has far reaching consequences for people's behaviour. Participatory governance gradually leads to more egalitarian institutions which will substitute the rigid hierarchical institutions which captured the thinking and behaviour of people.

Though the essence of the new paradigm could be seen in the efforts made in the west to dismantle the welfare state in the 1980's, the clear conceptualization and articulation of the paradigm emerged only at the end of 1990's. The emergence of this new paradigm of governance has serious implications for both developed and developing nations (Chandhoke 2003). In the developed countries of the west, the role of welfare state has been declining under the influence of the neo-liberal Reagan Thatcher ideology, which advocates a drastic cut in the public spending on welfare activities. In the developing countries, the state is being forced to give more scope for other actors in development with the introduction of globalization and structural adjustment programmes. As a result, there is a growing pluralisation of state with multiple actors or agencies spread over from local to global level trying to both supplement and supplant the conventional state in its basic role of development.

Good Governance, according to World Bank, is characterized by 'predictable, open and enlightened policy making; a bureaucracy imbued with a professional ethos; an executive arm of government accountable for its actions and a strong civil society participating in public affairs; and all behaving under the rule of law'. The four major areas of concern, identified by the World Bank to be achieved in good governance are: (i) improving the public sector management; (ii) ensuring accountability of public and private sectors, (iii) creating appropriate legal framework for development, and (iv) promoting transparency and information (World Bank 1994). All these four dimensions are to work in a mutually reinforcing way leading to establishment of good governance.

The concept of good or effective governance as advocated by World Bank is broadened and adapted to suit the development demands of developing countries with a view to address the vexed problem of poverty. This has been done by integrating political dimensions into the World Bank's concept of good governance. This assumes that good governance goes along with participatory development and democracy. Democratic system which encourages inclusive and participatory institutions and promotes transparent and accountable societies is a major requirement for good governance (Shylendra 2004). It is in this framework, Government of India has outlined its approach to governance for the implementation of the Tenth Five Year Plan (2002-07) in the country.

The Government of India acknowledges the universally accepted features of good governance like the legitimate exercise of political power along with creating administration which is transparent, equitable, participatory and accountable. But the thrust is made on contextualising them to the emerging needs of the country. 'Governance', to Government of India, 'relates to the management of all such processes that in any society, define the environment which permits and enables individuals to raise their capability levels, on the one hand, and to provide to realise their potential and enlarge the set of available choices, on the other' (Government of India 2002:177). Thus, the proclaimed goal of governance is to bring about human development. The processes of governance are managed by multiple institutions or agencies consisting of the state, market and the civil society; each playing a specific and a critical role in a harmonious manner.

In contextualising governance, the Government of India goes further and has identified specific operational strategies that are to be implemented for realising good governance for development. These strategies include: improved people's participation by way of effective decentralisation through local self governments and involving civil society and voluntary organisations to accelerate socio-economic development; ensuring right to information for transparency; reforming civil service to improve accountability and efficiency; administrative procedural reforms for a hassle free public-government interface; improving the fiscal health of government by improving the resource mobilisation through a transparent and equitable tax-administration and by correcting the subsidy and pricing system of various public services; reforming the judicial system for a speedy delivery of justice; improving the co-ordination between different public agencies and departments involved in development for a better synergy and efficiency; systematic and professional programme/project formulation, implementation and monitoring; empowering the marginal and the excluded to equip them to act as pressure groups to resist bad governance and exploitation by vested interests; and using information technology for a transparent and efficient administration (Government of India 2002).

Taking into consideration various dimensions of governance as well as its contextualisation, the following key elements emerge which are also summarised in Table 1 (Shylendra 2004).

(i) The role and responsibilities of the state for development are to be handled by multiple actors like state, civil society, and market institutions whose reach may extend from global to local level, and who may interact with each other more in a non-hierarchical way. Development is no longer the sole prerogative of the state.

(ii) The ultimate goal of governance paradigm is to bring about human development which is to be achieved through the contribution of multiple actors. Efficiency, equity and accountability are the major ways for attaining the goal. While efficiency is to be attained through market mechanisms and administrative reforms; equity is to be ensured through growth and by enlarging choice and opportunities for all sections. Accountability for delivering development is to be brought about through democratic, transparent and participatory decision-making processes.

Table 1. Comparative Features of the Existing and New Governance Paradigm

Features	Existing Paradigm	New Paradigm
Goal	Economic Development	Human Development
Political System	Democratic or non-democratic	Democratic and Participatory
Actors in Development	State or Market with or without Civil Society	State, Market and Civil Society
Legal framework	Favouring State or Market	Suitable for the co-existence of all three actors
Outcome of various transactions	Non-predictable	Predictable
Reach/Jurisdiction of Actors	National / Local	Global, National and Local
Source of Mandate for Actors	National / Local	Global, National and Local
Relationship between Actors	Bureaucratic & Hierarchical	Horizontal/ Non-bureaucratic
Purpose of Relationship	Control by State or Market	Co-ordination/ Networking
Delivery Mechanism	Government agencies and / or Private firms, and / or NGOs	Government agencies, Private firms and NGOs

(iii) Harmonising the relations between multiple actors is the major essence of the new governance paradigm. Different actors and elements of governance are to adapt to the scenario of plurality in order to evolve a system with harmonious interactions. Making the system more predictable and stable through suitable institutional and legal arrangements is the key for such a harmony.

Development is thus perceived to be delivered by multiple agencies including the state. This realisation has been necessitated as the state alone cannot respond to the diverse needs of development. The different actors who come into picture for development include state agencies like local, state and national governments, and multilateral agencies; market agencies like local traders, national and multinational companies; and civil society institutions like community based organisations (CBOs), and national and international NGOs (Table 2). Thus, governance as a paradigm includes real multiplicity or plurality of institutions which are supposed to be acting in unison to influence development at and from different levels. All these actors are to co-ordinate and network with each other more through horizontal linkages which are both non-hierarchical and non-bureaucratic (Chandhoke 2003). Through such a linkage, the sharp difference between the state and non-state is to be blurred or rendered irrelevant for development.

Table 2: Actors in development under governance paradigm

Reach/ Jurisdiction	State	Market	Civil Society
Global	Multilateral Agencies (UN, WB, WTO etc.)	Multi-National Companies (MNCs)	International NGOs
National	National/ Regional Governments	Domestic Companies/ MNC Branches	National/ Regional NGOs
Local	Local self government	Local Traders/ Businessmen	Local NGOs/ CBOs/ Citizens

Source: H.S. Shylendra (2004):'The Emerging Governance Paradigm and its Implications for Poverty Alleviation and Equity', Working Paper 182, Institute of Rural Management, Anand.

This new paradigm of governance has got special significance in the state of Kerala which has demonstrated a high degree of social and political development. The institution of State has been, traditionally, held in high esteem by the people of Kerala. This, in turn, had the effect of keeping private initiative and volunteerism at a reasonable distance from the public realm. The people, by and large, looked towards the intervention of the government for the betterment of their living conditions and infrastructural development. This is evident from the fact that the private sector undertakings and large scale business establishments were not given a prominent place in the Kerala society till recently. The delivery of welfare measures was considered to be the exclusive domain of the state.

But with the advent of the new economic order, it is being increasingly realised that the state, though still dominated by the leftist ideology, cannot withstand the global current towards economic integration. As a result, the government has started receding to the background from many of its traditional areas of operation and the non-governmental organizations, community based groups and multinational development agencies have stepped in to fill that void.

It is the purpose of this paper to examine what kind of synergy and harmony is achieved among these multiple players. It also looks into the impact this new paradigm has created in solving the problems of the rural people. The paper concludes by making some suggestions for making these multiple players to become more active and accountable.

One of the reasons for the increased role of these multiple players in development process, in fact, is the decentralization drive that was unleashed in the country for the last one decade. The historic 73rd Constitutional Amendment Act 1992 which came into being on April 20, 1993, was intended to improve participation of people in the process of development and to transform Panchayati Raj institutions into institutions of self government for rural areas. The PRIs are provided with new opportunities for planning based on local needs and priorities, empowerment of women, SC/ST development, mobilization of local resources, generation of demand for services, participation of women in decision making etc. The Kerala Legislature in follow -up to the 73rd amendment enacted the Kerala Panchayati Raj Act in 1994 which provides for a three tier Panchayati Raj system in the state. The Panchayati Raj Institutions are Grama (village) panchayat, Block panchayat and District panchayat. The basic unit of Panchayati Raj system in Kerala as stipulated by the Kerala Act is a general body of all persons registered as voters in each of the wards (constituencies) of a Grama panchayat termed as "Gramasabha" (Village Assembly). The Gramasabha is a fundamental participatory unit of PRIs in Kerala, constituted at the ward level and there are a total of 13,259 wards. There are 991 Grama panchayats with an average population of 21,600, 152 Block panchayats with an average population of 1,80,900 and 14 District Panchayats with a population of 15,24,000.

The focus of this paper is further limited to the emerging pattern of governance in Kerala with special attention on the drinking water sector. It has now been experimented in Kerala to address the drinking water problem with an increased involvement of the people and civil society organizations. The experiment is called *Jalanidhi*, a project implemented with the support of the World Bank, Village Panchayat, Beneficiary Groups and NGOs.

Background of the Project

Kerala is one of the smallest states in India-covering only 1.3% of the total area of the country. However, it has a total population of over 29 million. The population density, at 747 per sq. km, is much higher than the national average of 267 per sq. km. Geographically, Kerala can be divided into three distinct natural divisions- viz., Sandy Coastal Region (<7.6 m above MSL), Midland region (7.5 - 75 m above MSL) and the Western Ghats (> 75m above MSL). Kerala gets on an average of 307 cms rainfall, the bulk of which (70%) is received during the South-West monsoon which sets in by June and extends upto September. The state also gets rains from the North-East monsoons during October to December. Blessed with an abundance of rainfall of about 3000 mm annually, Kerala has 44 monsoon- fed rivers with a minimum length of 15 kms. However, given the terrain conditions, run-off is also quite high. The state experiences severe summer from January to May when the rainfall is minimal. Thus, it is an irony of sorts that a green, verdant state like Kerala has a lesser than average per capita availability of potable water, even lesser than that of Rajasthan.

Most of the families depend on private water sources, which are usually open wells. Most of these wells dry up by early March and remain so till the monsoons, which start by May end. Sanitation coverage is only 51.36% in the urban areas and 44% in the rural areas. Only 32% of families below poverty line have latrines.

It is estimated that the Government of Kerala has already invested Rs.50000 crores in the drinking water sector. Despite the more than adequate investment made by the Government on the water and sanitation sector over the years, only one third of its population is having access to safe drinking water. Some of the reasons cited for this dismal performance were: an unacceptable top down approach to planning, non- involvement of the users, highly inadequate levels of cost recovery, depletion of sources due to overdrawal, frequent breakdowns due to poor operation & maintenance, etc.

In this context, the policy makers in the state have been influenced by the success of a drinking water scheme that was going on in the *Olavanna Panchayat* in *Kozhikode* district. Popularly known as the *Olavanna* model, this single project stands testimony to the success of a programme that is carried out with people's participation. Taking cue from the *Olavanna* model, The Kerala Rural Water Supply and Sanitation Project (*Jalanidhi*) is designed and implemented by the users themselves as against the "top-down approach". This will be owned, operated and maintained by the users themselves on a total cost- recovery basis. The major objective of the organisation being the sustained provision of adequate quantities of safe, drinking water to the rural poor, the focus on ensuring sustainability of source, sustainability of operations, adequacy of water and quality of water are equally important and are designed into components within the project design.

Jalanidhi

The Kerala Rural Water Supply and Sanitation Project (*Jalanidhi*) is supported by the World Bank and is being initially implemented in four districts: *Kozhikode, Palakkad, Malappuram and Thrissur,* but later extended to all districts. The Government has also created an autonomous institution "Kerala Rural Water Supply and Sanitation Agency" to implement this project. The project is implemented through village Panchayats. The total outlay of the project is Rs.450 crores out of which Rs.350 crores are to be repaid to the World Bank within 35 years. The original project is implemented in six years (2001-2006) and expected to cover three lakh households, benefiting a population of over 15 lakhs in 4 districts through 2500 piped water supply schemes.

Philosophy of the *Jalanidhi* Project

Demand driven approach - Unlike the supply driven approach hitherto followed, this project is based on the need of the people. The Project will be introduced only in areas where interested groups of people show their willingness to participate in the project and abide by the conditions of cost-sharing. The group then gets a legal entity by registering themselves and only then proceeds with the rest of the planning. The source selection, technology selection, purchase, contracting and implementation is done by this registered body, the beneficiary group, with technical help from Support Organisations. This inculcates a sense of ownership in the people.

Cost sharing - To ensure stake holding of the project, 15% of the capital costs is borne by the beneficiary community. Of the remaining, the *Grama Panchayat* bear 10% and 75% is the share of the Government.

Cost Recovery - The Beneficiary Groups themselves meet 100% of the recurring costs of operations and maintenance. This lightens the burden on the state exchequer, thereby helping the Government to utilise this money for other priority needs.

Integrated Approach - The objective of the Project being sustainable supply of safe drinking water, sustainability of source, sustainability of operations, regularity and adequacy of supply and quality of water needs to be ensured. This is being met through other well-integrated components. Sustainability of source is ensured through Point- Source recharge measures. Quality is ascertained through a mix of Sanitation & Hygiene promotion and provision of infrastructure like latrines, compost pits etc. Sustainability of system is ensured through community empowerment, capacity building, women empowerment and social mobilisation.

Pro-Poor Approach - Special efforts have been taken in the project design to include the poor and vulnerable while selecting the user groups. The project has been so designed to incorporate the beneficiary contribution of 15% of capital costs either through cash or in kind, as labour. Intra-group subsidisation and even inter- group subsidisation is permitted at the behest of and under the total responsibility of the beneficiary groups. Thrift & Credit schemes are promoted in the Beneficiary Groups as "Self Help Groups" which are operated by the women of that group.

Women Development Initiatives - Women are the most affected both directly and indirectly, during water shortages. The project makes conscious efforts to mainstream the women users in the planning and decision-making activities. Apart from this, they are also encouraged to form "Thrift & Credit Groups" to help them make the payments towards the recurring expenditures of the water supply system. Income generation activities are also designed in the project where groups of women are given financial assistance and skill development training to start viable micro- enterprises of their choice.

Community Empowerment - Capacity building and equipping the community to operate the project is a major thrust area of this project as this is planned, designed, implemented, owned, and operated by the users themselves. This will not only ensure the involvement of the people but will also chart a new path to community- based approach for meeting any local needs.

Community Contracting - The users themselves are fully involved in all the activities right from identifying their sources, deciding on the technology to be utilised, community contracting and implementation till the operations and maintenance aspects of the schemes. All contracting of goods, works, and services will be done at the user level itself for which adequate training will be provided and guidelines made available.

Utilization of available resources - The Schemes already operational in these project areas, will also be rehabilitated, and handed over to the User groups. This will ensure efficient utilization of investments made.

Dovetail with Decentralised Planning - This project will be operationalised through the Grama Panchayats and the beneficiary groups, thereby acknowledging and strengthening the efforts of decentralised planning in Kerala.

Implementation

Government of Kerala has overall responsibility for implementing the state project and the national component with the Government of India's Rajiv Gandhi National Drinking Water Mission (RGNDWM). The main implementing agencies are shown in the following table.

Table 3: Division of Responsibilities under the *Jalanidhi* Scheme

Activity	Implementing Agency
Component A (Institution Building)	KRWSA on behalf of its General Body
Component B (Community Development & Infrastructure Building)	Beneficiary Groups, Grama Panchayats, Support Organisations, and KRWSA
Component C (State-wide Sector Development)	Secretary (Irrigation and Water Supply), Govt. of Kerala and KRWSA
Component D (National Sector Development)	Govt. of India's Rajiv Gandhi National Drinking Water Mission

The Project will be implemented in 80 Grama Panchayats (GPs) in 5 successive but overlapping batches consisting of 5, 15, 20, 25 and 15 GPs respectively. Each Batch will follow a 27 month scheme cycle consisting of four distinct phases.

Table 4: Plan of Implementation under the *Jalanidhi* Scheme

1	Pre- Planning Phase	-	3 months
2	Panning Phase	-	12 months
3	Implementation Phase	-	8 months
4	Post- Implementation phase	-	4 months

The main activities and outputs of each phase are as summarised below:

1. **Pre-Planning Phase:** The main activities during this phase are GP selection, Pre-qualification of Support Organisations and signing of a Planning Phase Tripartite Agreement between the KRWSA, GP and SO.

2. **Planning Phase:** The main outputs during this phase will be orientation & capacity building of GPs and SOs, BG registration, formation of Beneficiary committees, resource mapping and pre- feasibility studies. These will be done in the first four months of this phase. Subsequent activities are technology selection, preparation of engineering designs and community empowerment plans and finally a GP level Implementation Phase Proposal. The GP, BG and BC capacity building, sanitation & hygiene promotion and women's development programmes are held as parallel activities during the planning phase. The planning phase concludes with the signing of the Implementation Phase Quadrilateral Agreement (IPQA) between the KRWSA, GP, BG and the SO. There is one IPQA per BG. A separate Implementation Phase Tripartite agreement (IPTA) is signed between the KRWSA, GP and the SO for managing SO contracts.

3. **Implementation Phase:** The main activities during this phase deal with the actual implementation. They are procurement of materials, construction of schemes as per agreed plans and procedures and management of project funds.

4. **Post-Implementation Phase:** During this phase, the GPs will provide advisory support to the communities in efficient operation and maintenance of services, on collection of water tariff and book- keeping. The signing of the Implementation Completion Reports (ICRs) in public gathering by KRWSA, GP and BCs mark the formal exit of KRWSA from a project GP. Sustainability monitoring and Impact assessments will be conducted by the KRWSA to assess the project outcome.

FUND FLOW

WB
↓
GOI
↓
GOK
↓
KRWSA
↓
DPMU
↓
GP
↓
SO BG

The Multiple Actors involved in the Project

A. *Grama Panchayat*

The Grama Panchayat (GP) will be the focal point for project activities in the GP area. GPs will be mainly responsible for seeking project assistance following a self-selection process, preparing the implementation phase proposal during the planning phase, and for facilitating project implementation by BGs during implementation phase. GPs will provide counterpart funding to BGs as a percentage of infrastructures building costs. During the post-implementation phase, the GPs will monitor the sustainability of scheme operations and ensure that the BGs satisfactorily discharge their O&M management function including levying and collecting user charges from the beneficiaries to fully recover the recurrent O& M costs.

B. Beneficiary Groups

The Beneficiary Groups (BGs) will be responsible for planning, technology selection, and constructing their RWSS facilities, providing their part of the capital cost contribution, managing O&M of the improved facilities, and levying and collecting sufficient user charges. Representative beneficiary committees (BCs) will be set up by each of the participating BGs. Their composition, functions, method of selecting members and relationship with the GP and KRWSA have been agreed. The project would make vigorous efforts to maximize women's representation and management role in the BCs. The project rules require that membership of BCs would be at least 50% women, and 20% from socially disadvantaged groups. At least one of the top management position of the BC (President or Treasurer) will be held by a woman.

C. Support Organisation

The NGOs and private sector consultants will play an important role in the projects. There will be three categories of Support Organisations (SOs). The first will support the GPs, BGs and Beneficiary Committees on a day-to-day basis in planning and implementing the project's activities, and provide brief support to BGs during post-implementation stage to stabilize scheme operations.

The second will be a range of programmes or providing specialized assistance- such as in the preparation of ground water recharge schemes, water quality monitoring, or in developing strategy and materials for sanitation and hygiene promotion programmes.

The third category will be private sector consulting firms which would provide assistance in computerized financial management systems, audits and accounts, design engineering of multi-panchayat water supply schemes, independent construction quality monitoring, and management of information systems.

D. DPMU

The District Project Management Unit (DPMU) is set up as the district office for the KRWSA project. The main activities of the DPMU are:

- Capacity building of the SO through appropriate training and guidelines

- Capacity building of the BGs through training organised in support with the respective SO.
- Orientation to the GP, members and staff.
- Confidence building of the BGs through field visit and attending BG meetings by DPMU officials.
- Monitoring of the project activities of SOs and BGs.
- Liaison with the other agencies for effective convergence of various govt. programmes for the benefit of the BGs.

The Setting of the Study

The study is conducted in the *Mundathicode Panchayat* in *Trissur* District of Kerala. The importance of Mundathicode is that it is the panchayat in which the *Jalanidhi* project is first launched. Severely affected by the drinking water shortage, the *Panchayat* received this project with lot of enthusiasm and expectations. As many as 28 beneficiary groups (BGs) were formed in the panchayat and efforts were made to implement the project. All the BGs were studied in detail. Profiles of the BGs were given in table 5.

The field level data were collected at two levels. First is at the leadership level and then at the beneficiaries' level. The leadership level information was collected from the leaders of *Panchayat*, Beneficiary groups, Support Organisation and the KRWSSA. The beneficiary level information is collected through an intensive field work done among 230 beneficiaries of all the 28 BGs.

Table 5. Beneficiary Groups under the *Jalanidhi* Scheme in *Mundathikode* Panchayat

Sl.No.	*Name of the Beneficiary Group*	*Total No. of Households in the B.G.*	*No. of households surveyed*
1.	Aiswarya	52	05
2.	Anugraha	47	04

Sl.No.	*Name of the Beneficiary Group*	*Total No. of Households in the B.G.*	*No. of households surveyed*
3.	Athani Medical College Development	163	1
4.	Bageeratha	98	10
5.	Gandhinagar	38	04
6.	Gramasira	105	10
7.	Gramasree	94	10
8.	Irunnamkallu	41	04
9.	Jawahar	147	15
10.	Kallidathuchira	57	06
11.	Kiliathuchira	64	06
12.	Kottakunnu	49	05
13.	Manakulam	68	07
14.	MKKVS	43	37
15.	Navajyothi	51	05
16.	Peringandoor	87	09
17.	Pheonix	70	07
18.	Pratheeksha	65	07
19.	Puthuruthy Sudhajalam	74	07
20.	Puthuruthy Vadakkummury	48	04
21.	Safron	53	04
22.	Samrudha	148	14
23.	Sangamam	58	06
24.	Sanjeevani	94	09
25.	Souhrudha Nagar	37	03
26.	Subiksha	87	09
27.	Theerthadhara	56	05
28.	Yuvajana Sangam	34	03
	Total	2115	230

It has been found that the water use patterns of the villagers have changed after the launching of the *Jalanidhi* programme. Though the number of people who used to take less water before the implementation of the scheme has reduced after the programme, the number of those who take more water has increased. This indicates that the people have got more access to drinking water after the introduction of the scheme.

Table 6. Water use patterns before and after the launching of the *Jalanidhi* scheme

Usage of water (in litres)	*Before Jalanidhi*		*After Jalanidhi*	
	No.	*%*	*No.*	*%*
100-300	67	29.13	57	24.78
301-500	132	57.39	121	52.60
501-750	31	13.48	52	22.61
Total	230	100	230	100

Though the water intake has changed, majority of the respondents were not happy with the volume of water they got. As many as 157 people said that they did not get the volume of water that they expected at the launching of the programme. 123 people have opined that there was no sufficient water at the source, while others have attributed certain technical problems like insufficient tank, lesser width of pipe etc. for the inadequate supply of water.

The technical aspects of the project implementation were supposed to be looked after by the Support Organisation (SO). In the case under study, the S.O. involved is Centre of Science and Technology for Rural Development (COSTFORD), an organization which is widely acclaimed for its commitment to the cause of Rural Development. Established in 1985 by a group of Scientists, Technologists, Educationists, Professionals and Social Workers under the leadership of late Shri. C. Achuta Menon, COSTFORD strives to change the social, economic and political position of the poor, the deprived, the oppressed and the weak. COSTFORD is involved in sustainable development based on Gandhi's and Laurie Baker's vision through field application of the philosophy, by leading an example

As it is the purpose of the study to examine the synergy between various state and non-state actors in pursuit of rural development, the performance of the Support Organisation is brought under close scrutiny. The degree of acceptance of the SO among the beneficiaries is taken as one of the indicators in this regard.

A question was posed to all the sample beneficiaries that "are you aware about the existence of a support organization in this project?" It is surprising to note that only 28.70% beneficiaries are aware that a support organization does exist at all. This is supplemented by another answer which revealed that only 30.87% beneficiaries have positive opinion about the job done by the COSTFORD. It has been made clear in the survey that the SO could not effectively integrate with the society in which it is put to work. On a specific question whether the SO has made its presence felt in the Panchayat, only seven percent of the beneficiaries replied in the affirmative. No wonder in 76% of the beneficiaries saying that there is no need for any support organization in this kind of a project.

The apparent problem with the SO is that they did not trust the villagers. On many aspects of the project, the common people had their own ideas about the implementation process. But the staff of the COSTFORD strictly went by the text of their technical knowledge. The local circumstances and wisdom were completely ignored. Shri. Ajith Kumar, a member of Gram Panchayat, for instance, said that the COSTFORD actually worsened the situation. They have constructed the water tank at a much lower terrain, ignoring the views of the Beneficiary Groups. The common men knew that the tank should be kept at a higher plane, to make water available in the remote areas. But since such local wisdom was not heeded to, most of the beneficiaries do not get water at all. Shri Ajith Kumar even suspected financial irregularities in the project. He said that Rs. 35 lakhs were given to the SO in the Mundathikode Panchayat itself. He is of the opinion that the entire project could be completed with half of this amount.

It is made known in the study that the Village Panchayat, another actor involved in the project was not given the due role in the project implementation other than contributing 10% of the total project expenditure. It did not have any regulatory authority over the SO in designing and implementing the project. But the beneficiaries always view the Panchayat as their sole authority in terms of rural development. It has become evident from the high degree of acceptance that the Panchayat as an institution has got among the beneficiaries.

As many as 208 people (90%) said that they got good support and encouragement from the village panchayat. In fact, none of the beneficiaries had even a minute complaint against the Panchayat. It was an irony that when people put their trust in the Panchayat, it was found itself in a helpless situation. One Panchayat member who does not want to reveal his identity said that the Panchayat has no control over the SO. "In fact, the Panchayat and the SO work at parallel levels. The SO is just a temporary installation of people with no practical experience. They are not competent to carry out this kind of work. They were giving just 1000 rupees to those girls who supervised the work. How much sincerity and commitment can we expect from a diploma holder in civil engineering with such a meagre amount of salary", he asked.

One of the indirect aims of this kind of a project is to generate the right kind of trust and cohesiveness among the beneficiaries. Therefore, more attention was given in the study to ascertain the level of social capital that has been created as a result of this *jalanidhi* project. The major idea emerged from the study is that the objective is not met. In fact, some of the ideas shared by the leaders of beneficiary groups reveal that the social capital generated was of negative nature.

Shri. Gopi (a traditional Ayurvedic physician by profession), the president of the *Bhagiratha* Beneficiary Group, for instance, said that this project actually cheats the people. It could not solve the water needs of the people. The people were not giving the user fee regularly. He had to spend money from his pocket. He lost his public acceptance even as he took up this responsibility.

The leaders of beneficiary groups were, by and large, not satisfied with the degree of co-operation they got from the beneficiaries. It was difficult for them to collect the users' fee in time. In case someone doesn't get water he/she used to rush to the houses of the president or secretary of the BG with complaints. It becomes a headache for the BG leaders to address these issues. Sheela, an unmarried girl of 22 years who heads the *Puthuruthi Sudh Jal,* said that she had to suffer a lot of humiliation on account of these complaints. Her parents were not happy with creating such unruly scenes in the house. Even good marriage proposals were called off as this girl is 'a public figure'. She wants to get rid of this responsibility at the earliest. But nobody seems to be willing to take over.

Most of the complaints were due to the forcible opening of locks that regulate the water flow to various outlets. The beneficiaries have a tendency to break open these locks to access more water. The beneficiaries have an understanding among themselves that they should not indulge in such malpractices. But the frequent violations of such understanding indicate the lack of trust that exists among the beneficiaries.

One general trend that has been seen in the survey is that those who are in the leadership positions do not want to continue any longer. On the other hand, nobody seems to be interested in taking over. This has been made clear from the data collected. In most of the BGs, the leadership positions were not changed since the launching of the scheme. Voting has not been taken place in any of the BGs to choose the office bearers. It indicates the BGs have not yet become vibrant associations.

The general body meetings of the beneficiaries were held rarely. Only seven respondents have said that the general body is held 2-4 times so far. 23 respondents have said that it has been held once. The remaining 200 respondents said that the general body is either not held or they have no idea about it. As many as 226 respondents do not know anything about the executive committee meetings of their BGs. They have no idea of what they are discussing in the executive committee meetings.

One interesting thing noticed in the survey is that the political identification of beneficiaries does not affect the smooth functioning of the scheme. As many as 219 respondents were identified with one political party or the other. But only two respondents have said that political identification adversely affected the scheme. Majority of the respondents have said that the problems emerged in the beneficiary groups are settled within the group amicably. All problems are related to the inadequate availability of water. In any case, the internal disputes and quarrels have not disturbed the implementation of the scheme.

Beneficiaries' identification with the project has been another concern of the study. To ascertain this aspect, questions were asked to test their knowledge about the source of funding for the project. It is noted that 56 respondents had no idea about the sources of funding. Of the total 230 respondents, 174 knew that money comes from the World Bank. But only 82 respondents knew that this money has to be refunded. Even among them only 30 people know that it is the government which should refund this money.

But nobody knows the period of repayment and the rate of interest. As many as 217 beneficiaries justified the act of seeking foreign money, since it is a problem of drinking water. The low level of knowledge about the project among the beneficiaries again indicates that the project could achieve only limited success in activating the rural community.

The *jalanidhi* project in Kerala has to be seen as an attempt to achieve rural development through an interface between state government, panchayats, community based organizations (CBOs) and non governmental organizations (NGOs). Among these, government and panchayats are state actors and CBOs and NGOs are non-state actors. The study has been focused on ascertaining the effectiveness of the synergy between the state and non-state actors as it is an emerging pattern of development governance.

The inference drawn from the study is that there is no proper coordination between panchayat, CBO and the NGO. While the CBO believes that the panchayat is the main actor, the panchayat takes NGO as the main actor. In fact, as per the script, it is the NGO which has to supervise and implement the project. Therefore, the panchayat is not supposed to interfere in the day-to-day administration of the project. But the people do not know this. There is a wide divergence between the perception of the beneficiaries about the role of the panchayat and its assigned role. On many occasions when the beneficiaries do not get water, the beneficiaries rush to the houses of panchayat members with complaints. But the panchayat members were helpless as they were not given any meaningful role in the design of the scheme. The designing of the scheme is left exclusively with the SO. But the SO is neither accountable to the panchayat nor to the people. After the completion of the project, the SO withdraws from the scene and the project is to be then managed by the beneficiary groups themselves. At this stage the people look towards the panchayat as the sole saviour of all their problems.

One of the implications is that there is a gross sidelining of the panchayat in the whole process, though the people lend legitimacy and credibility to the institution. The panchayat's role is limited just to select the SO from the list of SOs approved by the state government and provide 10% financial assistance to the project. It has no control over the SO in the process of designing and implementing the project. At the same time, all complaints against the SO are to be settled by the panchayat. This dichotomy is not visualized in the jalanidhi project.

The SO on the other hand, takes this opportunity to exert their authority over the beneficiaries. Having bestowed with technical knowledge and expertise, they tend to ignore the indigenous knowledge and wisdom of the local people. On many occasions, the local people have convincingly argued for a different design and method of implementation. But they, in turn, were cajoled for their lack of modern knowledge and experience. This had the effect of lessening the credibility of the SO in the eyes of the public.

The beneficiary groups have the good intention of running the project effectively, and thereby solve their water problems. But they were found without proper guidance and discipline. Driven with their self-interests, they had least concern for the interests of their fellow users. This caused unnecessary tension and non-cooperation within the beneficiary group, defeating the much desired objective of generating social capital within the society. The study reveals that the already existing amount of social capital is at a loss as they got a new space to quarrel over sharing the facility offered by the project. This makes one to conclude that any good intended programme may result in generating 'negative social capital' if it is poorly designed and implemented.

References

Abrahamsen, Rita (2000): *Disciplining Democracy: Development Discourse and Good Governance in Africa*, Zed Books, London

Chandhoke, Neera (2003): 'Governance and the Pluralisation of the State: Implications for Democratic Citizenship,' *Economic and Political Weekly,* 38(28): 2957-68.

Government of India (2002): Tenth Five Year Plan (2002-2007): Dimensions and Strategies, Vol. I., Planning Commission, New Delhi.

OECD (1995): *Participatory Development and Good Governance,* Development Co-operation Guidelines Series, Paris.

Oommen T K (2003): 'Civil Society and the Goal of Good Governance' in Rajesh Tandon and Ranjita Mohanty ed. *Does Civil Society Matter?* Sage, New Delhi, pp125-144.

Rajasekher, D and R.R. Biradar (2002): People, Government and the NGOs, Working Paper 114, Institute for Social and Economic Change, Bangalore.

Riley, John M (2002): Stakeholders' Participation for Rural Development: Critical Collaboration in State NGO Partnerships, Sage, New Delhi.

Shylendra, H.S. (2004): 'The Emerging Governance Paradigm and its Implications for Poverty Alleviation and Equity', Working Paper 182, Institute of Rural Management, Anand.

UNDP (1997), *Governance for sustainable development,* A UNDP policy document, New York.

World Bank (1992): *Governance and Development,* Washington DC.

World Bank (1994): *Governance: The World Banks's Experience,* World Bank, Washington D.C.

14

Political Economy of Pre-Launch Preparedness of NREGA in Kerala

Jos Chathukulam and
K. Gireesan

Background

The Government of India have passed the National Rural Employment Guarantee Act (NREGA) in September 2005, with a broad 'national consensus'. This was hailed as a 'historic piece of legislation' and 'People's Act' by several thinkers and writers on Panchayat Raj and Rural Development. The Act provides for the enhancement of livelihood security of the households in the rural areas by providing at least one hundred days of guaranteed wage employment in every financial year to every household whose adult members volunteer to do unskilled manual labour. The Act came into force initially in 200 districts, and will be extended gradually to other areas notified by the Central Government. It is expected to cover the whole country within five years.

NREGA has come into force from February 2, 2006 in the rural areas of two Districts in Kerala - Palakkad and Wayanad. NREGA calls for the formulation of a Rural Employment Guarantee Scheme (REGS) by each State Government within six months of the date of commencement of the Act. It is noted that NREGA envisaged a paradigm shift 'From Programme to Act', compared to the different Wage Employment Programmes (WEP) operating in the country since 1980. At this juncture, it would be pertinent to understand and analyse the implementation of different WEPs in the State of Kerala and various other aspects connected with it, before taking up the REGS in the State.

Different WEPs were implemented in the State starting from National Rural Employment Programme (NREP) in the 80's. Rural Landless Employment Guarantee Programme (RLEGP), Jawahar Rozgar Yojana (JRY), Employment Assurance Scheme (EAS) and Jawahar Gram Samridhi Yojana (JGSY) were executed in the State. The Sampoorna Grameen Rozgar Yojana (SGRY) has been implemented in the State since 2001. Wayanad was selected to launch the National Food for Work Programme (NFFWP) in 2004, and implementation of SGRY carried on in other Districts. It is noted that any form of market mechanism under capitalism cannot provide the required job to the needy and able-bodied persons, which makes it imperative for the Government to intervene (Wray, 2006). The present intervention by the Government of India is, therefore, a welcome step.

In this paper, an attempt has been made to assess the pre-launch preparedness of the scheme in Palakkad District. We have made the assessment of the scheme in the following seven parts, in addition to background. Collection of data from the field was carried out from May 8 to June 17, 2006. The data was collected from all the Blocks and Grama Panchayats in the district that constitutes the universe of the study.

PART - I

LESSONS FROM IMPLEMENTATION OF WEPS IN KERALA

As in other parts of the country, implementation of WEPs in the State of Kerala was also not devoid of problems. Presence of contractors and attached labourers, use of machines, manipulation of muster rolls, fabrication of details regarding labour and materials, non-procurement and supply of food grains to the workers, etc. have been prominent among them in the State.

It is noted that the food grains intended for workers as payment in kind have not reached them, in majority of the cases. The food grains appear to have been diverted to the open market, depriving the poor of the food security envisaged in the programme. The sale proceeds of food grains appear to have been utilised for making payment of wages in cash and invested in building community assets in the rural areas. Workers who took advantage of the employment opportunities were mostly men. Women who need work not far from their houses were given a short shrift. Various facilities offered at the worksites like drinking water, toilet, rest shed, crèche, etc. were rarely found.

It is observed that implementation of WEPs in Kerala is showing all signs of becoming less of an employment generation programme, and it is being carried out just like other public works programme. It is found that the thrust was more on creation of community assets, which is the secondary objective, while the primary objective of employment generation was largely sidelined during the programmes.[1] To put it bluntly, a distinctly 'Kerala pattern for implementation of the WEPs' has come into vogue.

However, this cannot be viewed merely as a technical and administrative issue. Larger questions of political economy including the capability of the political executive, their class background and approach, issues related to governance, clientelism and populism are involved here. This results in non-meeting of the expected targets in a potentially sound programme to benefit the marginalized and weaker sections of the society.

The lack of ownership by the State Government, local bodies, political parties and by the third sector organisations also had adversely affected the implementation of the WEPs. Quite interestingly, an impression was created in the Kerala society in general and the administrative circles in particular that such programmes are not suited to the State as they were designed primarily keeping in view the interests and requirements of North Indian states. Not being challenged by the activists and academicians focussing on rural development, this impression came to be reinforced in the Kerala polity. Double standards were observed in the public pronouncements made by the rural development officials in their dealings with their counterparts at the centre and in their private talks. In all representations to the external agencies, the acuteness of poverty, unemployment, shortage of food grains, etc. were highlighted by the state and need for such programmes were emphasised. But in private, the futility of such programmes was acknowledged.

As indicated earlier, the distinctly 'Kerala pattern' could be observed during the implementation of WEPs in the state. Majority of the records are maintained as per the guidelines, but in actual implementation, guidelines have been flouted as per the convenience. This aspect is crucial. The NREGA and the Kerala Rural Employment Guarantee Scheme (KREGS) inherits all the hangovers of the previous WEPs in the State. The introduction of decentralised planning in 1996, amendments to the Kerala Panchayat Raj Act in 1999 and various other measures have not made any significant difference in the implementation of WEPs in the State (Chathukulam, 2006).

PART - II

FROM ACT TO PROGRAMME - KREGS

The NREGA calls for the formulation of a Rural Employment Guarantee Scheme (REGS) by each State Government within six months from the date of commencement of the Act. The State Government formulated the Kerala Rural Employment Guarantee Scheme (KREGS) which is notified as a Government Order on January 31, 2006 for implementation in two districts (Palakkad and Wayanad) of Kerala. It is noted that the salient provisions of the State scheme were drawn up in line with the Central Act. Subsequently, the Commissionerate of Rural Development (CRD) has issued certain working instructions on March 14, 2006 to facilitate the implementation of the scheme in the districts.

Most of the design features of KREGS were prepared in conformity with the NREGA. Some of the typical features of KREGS are given below.

(a) Preparation of a Perspective Plan

The Perspective Plan (PP) is intended to facilitate advance planning and to provide a development perspective for the area of jurisdiction. It points to the need of a PP of five years, so that working plans based on annual budgets can be derived accordingly. It aims at identifying the types of works that should be encouraged, and seeks to develop potential linkages between these works and long-term employment generation. Each Grama Panchayat (GP) should develop its Perspective Plan, which includes the demand for work and the nature and timing of work preferred by the potential beneficiaries. It is suggested that, 'as far as possible', the Block Panchayat (BP) shall propose works that may involve more than one GP, and the District Panchayat (DP) may take up the works that may cover two or more BPs.

(b) Identification and Prioritization of works

The different types and priority of works which can be included under the programme on a priority basis are: Water conservation and harvesting, drought proofing, micro and minor irrigation works, provision of irrigation facility to land owned by SCs/STs/beneficiaries of land reforms/beneficiaries of Indira Awaas Yojana (IAY), renovation of traditional water bodies, land development, flood control and protection works and rural connectivity. Rural connectivity works can be taken up as the last priority and should not exceed 10 per cent value of all types of works. It is suggested that a shelf of works should be maintained by the Panchayat Raj Institutions (PRI) that includes their priority as well. It is also mentioned that the GP shall facilitate the conduct of Grama Sabha for identifying priority works to be taken up.

(c) Labour Budget

KREGS talks about the preparation of a labour budget for the ensuing financial year, keeping the District Perspective Plan in view. The task for preparation of a labour budget has been assigned to the Joint Programme Co-ordinator (JPC), which includes the details of the anticipated labour demand for unskilled manual work in the district to facilitate the planning exercises.

(d) Wage Rate

The wages shall be subjected to the Public Works Department (PWD) schedule of rates till the finalisation of Schedule of Rural Rates (SRR). It suggests that the payment of wages to the workers shall be made through banks and shall be credited to the individual account of each job cardholder once in a week/fortnight.

(e) The Proposed Nature for the Execution of Works

The execution of works by GP, BP and DP shall be in the ratio of 50 : 30 : 20 in cost terms as communicated by the District Programme Co-ordinator (DPC). The administrative sanction for the works will be issued by the concerned PRIs. The Engineers of Rural Development Department (RDD), Local Self Government Department (LSGD) and engineers appointed on contract basis, shall issue the technical sanction. It suggests that the GP may execute the work through Area Development Society/ Community Development Society (ADS/CDS) of Kudumbasree, Self-Help Groups (SHG), Group formed by the workers themselves and Beneficiary Committees.

In this paper, an attempt is made to understand and analyse the preparedness and status at the launching of the NREGA/KREGS in Palakkad District. During the analysis, delineation of different aspects connected with the preparedness and launching of the scheme in the district will be taken up.

Collection of data from the field was carried out from May 8 to June 17, 2006. The researchers collected the data from all the Blocks and Gram Panchayats in the district, which constitutes the universe of the study.

PART - III

STUDY AREA

Palakkad District consists of 13 Block Panchayats and 91 Gram Panchayats. There are five Municipalities in the District. The District has a population of 26,17,482 spread over 4480 square kilometres. Women outnumber men in the District, the sex ratio being 1066, that is, slightly higher than the State average (1058). The population density is 584 persons per square kilometre of land, which is much lower than the State average (819). It may be noted that 86.38 per cent of the population in the District live in rural areas. The District has as many as 3,90,144 people belonging to the SC community living in its rural areas. The corresponding number of STs living in the District as per Census 2001 is 39,236. Considering the percentage of SC population to the total population in the District, Palakkad is at the top (16.53 %) and it is higher than the State average (9.81 %). The percentage of ST population to total population in the District is 1.52 per cent, which is also higher than the State average (1.14 %). Literacy rate in the District is the lowest in the State - 84.35 per cent. It is observed that female literacy rate in the District is lesser than male by 10 per cent. (Census 2001).

Regarding land utilisation, it is found that just less than half of the land (48.9 %) is under cultivation. The net sown area in the district is 214456 hectares. The District is predominantly agrarian in nature, with paddy, coconut, groundnut, tapioca and cotton being the major crops. Characteristic of agrarian economies, participation in the labour force is quite high among both men and women, which is higher than the State figures. Majority of the working class in the district are cultivators and agricultural labourers. Some residual forms of feudal relations are also visible in the agrarian structure.

The region has an active presence of all major political parties and class and mass organisations affiliated to them. The Communist Party of India – Marxist [CPI (M)] of Left Democratic Front (LDF) and the Indian National Congress (INC) of United Democratic Front (UDF) are the dominant parties in the District, with the Bharatiya Janata Party (BJP) also having a marginal presence. However, 70 of the 91 GPs in the district have Presidents from CPI (M) led LDF, and the remaining 21 GPs have Presidents from INC led UDF; most of the BPs have Presidents from the LDF. The District Panchayat President also belongs to CPI (M). Out of 11 MLAs from the District, nine are from LDF. Two MPs representing Palakkad region also belong to CPI (M). Majority of the Primary Co-operative Societies in the District are controlled by CPI (M) led LDF. The present Chief Minister of the State also represents an Assembly constituency from the district. Traditionally, the district is a strong bastion of CPI (M) in terms of both electoral representation and organisational structures. The results of recent elections to the Panchayats and the State Legislative Assembly only reinforced the same party equations in the district.

The region has a good number of traditional and modern associations. Vertical associational life is stronger in the District compared to horizontal. Women's associational life has been strengthened in the District through the intervention of SHGs, initiated by the Kudumbasree Mission of the Government of Kerala.

The District has a larger concentration of registered small factories and small-scale industrial units, which is on the higher side when compared to the State as a whole. Barring this, the district lags behind in most other aspects of development, compared to the State average.

The District is particularly known for its predominantly agrarian background. Paddy cultivation makes up most of the cultivable area in the District. The low agricultural wage rate, decline in the area under paddy cultivation, rising operational cost of farming, fall in yield per acre, issues related to collection and storage of paddy, uneconomical returns, mechanisation of operations, etc. prevailing in the District need a closer look in the context of the launching the scheme.

Interactions in the field revealed that the farm wages prevailing in the District is in the order of Rs.125 - Rs.135 for men and Rs.60 – Rs.70 for women. It is found that 88 per cent of the activities in the paddy fields are being performed by women[2]. This may be the result of partial mechanisation of the farming activity like ploughing, prevalence of higher wage rate for men, and alternative avenues for employment like construction activities.

It would be worthwhile to analyse the possible effect of KREGS in the agriculture sector in the District. The scheme provides equal wages to men and women, and it is mandatory to provide at least one-third of the job opportunities for women. This may lead to an exodus of women workers to work in KREGS projects, which may have a negative impact on agriculture[3]. In addition, there is temporary migration of labourers to spinning industries in Coimbatore, Tirupur and Erode in Tamil Nadu. All these point to the need for preparation of a calendar that does not infringe on women's job opportunities in the agriculture sector and spinning industries. It would be interesting to analyse the nature and extent of prevalence of poverty among the poor in the district and the possible effect of this scheme on their life in a 'before - after' format.

PART - IV

PREPAREDNESS AND STATUS OF THE SCHEME IN KERALA

During the assessment of preparedness and status of the

scheme in the District, eight steps have been identified and the present status of each step has been examined here.

(a) Registration – related aspects

In Palakkad District, registration of employment seekers who intended to participate in the scheme was closed in 81 GPs. The remaining Panchayats kept the registration open. Out of 91 GPs in the district, 86 GPs made registration of both households and individuals, and have as many as 2,25,691 persons including 1,23,799 females on their rolls. Only households were registered in 5 GPs, which make up 5868 households including 3350 female-headed ones. From the data collected from the GPs and BPs during the field visits, it is found that a total of 2,55,031 persons were registered, which makes up 11.28 per cent of the rural population in the district.

Regarding the registration of SC communities, 64 GPs maintained separate records for registering SC households, which came to 23,407 and 16 GPs kept records for registering individuals, whose number came to 8662. It is ascertained that a total of 1,25,697 persons from the SC community were registered, which makes up 32.21 per cent of the rural SC population in the district. However, it is noted that no separate records for registration of SC individuals/households were maintained at 11 GPs.

A good number of persons belonging to ST communities were registered. A total of 5092 ST families from 15 GPs were registered which make up 25,460 persons in the district or 64.88 per cent of the ST population in the district (Rural areas only). It is observed that the remaining 76 GPs did not have any registration of ST community.

(b) Verification of registration and Data entry

Verification of applications for registration is an important element of the scheme. There is a need to verify and find out whether those registered are residents of the GP, and are adult members of the household. However, after going through the details relating to the registration in 91 GPs of Palakkad District, it is found that no verification of registration was made. It is seen that the process of entering data relating to registration was going on in 50 GPs, and was yet to be initiated in the remaining 41 GPs. Data entry activities were going on at four different places – District Rural Development Agency (DRDA), Palakkad and Block Development Offices at Alathur, Mannarkkad and Ottappalam - in the District.

(c) Administrative Set-up

In the District, an official in the rank of a Deputy Development Commissioner (DDC) from the Rural Development Department (RDD) is appointed as the Joint Programme Co-ordinator (JPC). JPC functions in a separate office, near that of the District Rural Development Agency (DRDA). The District office of KREGS has an Accountant-cum-Computer Operator (ACO), and secretarial and ministerial support is provided by the DRDA.

At Block level, a Block Programme Officer (BPO), in the rank of Block Development Officer (BDO), is responsible for the implementation of the scheme. During the field visits, it has been found that BPOs were posted in 12 out of the 13 Blocks. In Pattambi Block, Extension Officer (Housing) is given the additional charge of BPO. The BPO is supported by an Assistant Engineer (AE) to look after the technical aspects and an ACO for the accounts and ministerial works. Though the scheme was launched on the 2nd of February 2006, selection of supporting staff on contract basis and their deployment at Block offices was not completed. It is known that interviews for the selection of staff were scheduled, but no one turned up.[4] Details of supporting staff available at the Block offices are given in Table 1.

Table 1. Deployment of NREGA staff at BPs

Availability of staff	*Number of BPs*
Both AE and ACO	8
ACO only	2
None available	3
Total	13

Source: Field survey

At the Grama Panchayat level, the Grama Panchayat Secretary is responsible for implementation of the scheme. The Secretary is assisted by an Engineer/Overseer to look after the technical matters and an ACO for accounts and ministerial works. Details of supporting staff available at GPs are given in Table 2.

Table 2. Deployment of NREGA staff at GPs

Availability of staff	*Number of GPs*
Both Overseer and ACO	47
Both AE and ACO	4
ACO only	4
Overseer only	1
None available	35
Total	91

Source: Field survey

At the time of data collection, it was noted that the required staff for technical and administrative support were deployed in 62 per cent of the BPs and 52 per cent of the GPs only. Even after the lapse of four months, no staff was in place in 23 per cent of the BPs and 38 per cent of the GPs in the district. It is known that interviews were conducted in 24 GPs, but no appointment was made, and in two GPs, none turned up for the interview. No initiative for the selection of staff was taken in nine GPs. A notable feature is that 76 percent of supporting staff appointed in the GPs are women.

(d) Training

A number of training sessions were held in the District, during the preparatory phase. A one-day training for the Presidents and Secretaries of GP was organised on January 19, 2006 in Thiruvananthapuram. Subsequently, a one-day training session for DP members, BP members, President of GPs, Vice-President of GPs, Chairpersons of Standing Committee (Welfare) and GP Secretaries was held at Palakkad.[5] Another one-day training session for the Presidents and Secretaries of GPs in the district was held at Palakkad on March 7 and 8, 2006 (two batches). A session for BDOs and BPOs was conducted at Palakkad on February 18, 2006.

The Kerala Institute of Local Administration (KILA)[6] and Capacity Development for Decentralisation in Kerala (CapDecK)[7] also organised a workshop for selected GP Presidents and NGO representatives from Palakkad and Wayanad districts in Thiruvananthapuram on May 31, 2006.[8]

It indicates that there is no dearth of training to elected members and officials during the preparatory phase of the scheme. However, most of the sessions were organised on an ad-hoc basis and did not result in removing various doubts that remained among the elected members and officials relating to the scheme.[9] It is also observed that these sessions did not result in emergence of operational guidelines of KREGS.

(e) Infrastructure facilities

Separate office rooms and associated furniture for the functioning of BPO and the supporting staff were available in eight Blocks only, though most of them were provided by the Block Panchayat on an arrangement. In five Blocks, a separate telephone connection was also provided. However, dedicated computer systems were installed at three Blocks and DRDA office for facilitating data entry operations.[10]

(f) Issue of Job Cards

Printing of job cards was going on at the time of the field visits. The print order for supply of 1.5 lakh job cards was placed with Kerala Books and Publications Society, Kakkanad, and the delivery was expected to take place by the end of May 2006.[11] Before issuing job cards to the job seekers, various other preparatory steps like verification of registration, opening of bank accounts by the job holders, pasting of photos in the job cards and attaching a face sheet with personal details of the worker in the job card are required to be carried out. However, no such activity was taken in any of the GPs in the District. Hence it is expected that even after making the job cards available, it may take some more time to start the issue as verification of registration and data entry operations were not completed. It is reported that no job cards have been issued even at mid of July (The Pioneer, 2006).

(g) Bank-related aspects

During the operational phase of the scheme, the secretaries of GPs were directed to open a joint savings bank account in favour of concerned Presidents and Secretaries of GPs. After the launching of the scheme in the District, it took eight weeks to provide intimation to the PRIs about the list of banks for opening of bank accounts.[12] Three types of bank-related issues came up in some parts of the District. Non-availability of the notified bank in the GP area is one of the issues faced.[13] The second issue relates to the difficulties to open a zero balance account by the GPs at some places.[14] Dishonouring of cheques presented by the GP for the purpose of payment of salaries to the staff is another issue noticed during the field visit.[15] It is ascertained that out of 91 GPs, only 54 GPs have opened the NREGA account in banks at the time of field visits.

(h) Preparation of Action plan

Even before the launch of the scheme in the District, the CRD notified the PRIs to prepare the Action Plan (AP).[16] During field visits, it was noted that the AP was prepared in February 2006 by all GPs and submitted to respective BPOs.

Table 3. Flow of Instructions for Preparing the AP

Sl. No.	*Date*	*Content*	*Remarks by the researchers based on field survey*
1	2	3	4
1	18 Jan 2006	Written instructions were issued to prepare AP of 2 works in each ward of a GP at an estimated cost of Rs.40,000 per work.	Instruction was issued even before the launching of the scheme.
2.	24 Feb 2006	Written instructions about list of work categories (9 categories) that can be considered while preparing AP.	As per the order, 90 GPs prepared the AP and submitted to BPO.
3.	14 Mar 2006	Issue of KREGS working instructions that says that 'Roads can be taken up as last priority not exceeding 10 % value of all types of works taken up'.	GPs were asked to revise the APs accordingly. GPs have revised the AP with 2 works per ward and kept at ready for submission. This was prepared without consulting the Grama Sabha.
4.	Apr 2006	Oral instructions were issued to prepare a shelf of 7 works in each ward at an estimated cost of Rs.40,000 per work.	AP was revised with an addition of 5 works. This was prepared without the consent of the Grama Sabha.

Source: Col.No. 1 to 3 from CRD and Col.No.4 from field visits.

As per the timeline for preparation of AP, March 13, 2006 was the end deadline for submission to the POs, followed by scrutiny and consolidation of GP plans. However, CRD brought out the working instructions for the scheme on March 14, 2006, which indicated that schemes under rural connectivity 'can be taken as the last priority not exceeding 10 percent value of all types of works taken up'. The revised instructions were communicated to all the GPs and they were asked to revise the APs accordingly. By then, the Assembly election campaign began and the whole process of preparing AP was kept in the cold storage. There was no attempt made to adhere to the time line for preparation of AP. Most of the activities planned as per the time line were shelved, citing 'the code of conduct for the assembly elections' as the reason.[17] Subsequently, there was an oral instruction to the GPs in April 2006 to prepare the AP consisting of seven works in each ward towards preparing a shelf of projects.[18] Table 3 provides a bird's eye view of the communications to the GPs regarding preparation of AP.

PART - V

POSITIVE SIGNALS FROM THE FIELD

During the assessment of the scheme in the district, five positive signals are noted from the field.

(a) Registration of marginalized sections

It is found that registration of marginalized sections like SC and ST communities in the District has been realistic and conforms to the proportion of their population. It is noted that 32.21 per cent of the SC population and 64.88 per cent of the ST population from the rural areas of the district registered their names. This shows that the scheme could draw the attention of the marginalized sections in the district. This may be the result of composite efforts by the elected members, officials and political parties. It is noted that the involvement of elected members and political parties was limited to the process of registration only, and had an element of patronage distribution, clientelism and populism inherent in it.

(b) Scope for works/activities

The geographical features, occupational preferences and employment patterns of the district offers plenty of scope for activities in the field of water conservation and water harvesting, drought proofing, irrigation canals, renovation of traditional water bodies, land development, etc. Being an agrarian district, there is a wide scope for identifying common properties like check dams, ponds, distributory canals, drains, open fields, etc. towards taking up the scheme by the PRIs. The experts comment that by strengthening the Common Property Resources (CPR), the livelihood security of the vulnerable sections can be decisively ensured (Desarda, 2006).

(c) Political environment

Traditionally, the political environment in the district is pro-LDF with CPI (M) as the main rallying force in the front. Elections to the three-tier PRIs and the recent power change in the State reinforce the existing political equations even more firmly. In addition, CPI (M) has a special interest in an agrarian district like Palakkad, more so because it has returned the present Chief Minister of the State.[19] In addition, a Minister with experience, heads the Ministry of Local Self Government.[20]

(d) Committed and experienced bureaucracy

The civil servants responsible for providing guidance and direction to the scheme are known for their commitment, professionalism, vision and rich experience.[21] Similarly, the JPC is also known for his commitment, professional integrity, managerial skills and vast experience.[22]

(e) Signals from outside

As Aruna Roy puts it, once a pattern is laid at one place, the rest of the country can follow it. Registering a success story at one place may have a cascading effect on the rest of the country. It may be a fascinating case for Palakkad too. A success story has already been documented in Dungarpur

District, Rajasthan. Here, it is worthwhile to learn the achievements from Dungarpur and to examine how it can be replicated in Palakkad, subjected to local variations. It proved that NREGA could provide a much-needed source of livelihood in rural areas, particularly for women. It also showed that the facilities at the NREGA worksites are much better than their earlier worksites (Bhatty, 2006).

PART - VI

DEFICITS

It is felt that no adequate strategy was evolved during the preparedness and launching phase of NREGA in the District, in order to overcome the limitations highlighted during the implementation of past WEPs. In the absence of a clear-cut strategy, our fear is that the execution of KREGS also may meet the same fate. We feel that the various issues identified during the implementation of WEPs in the past need to be discussed threadbare and an appropriate strategy be devised towards overcoming them. During the preparation and launch of the scheme, six major deficits are identified in the field.

(a) Administrative deficits

We have already indicated how the impact of previous WEPs in the State can work detrimentally during the initial phase. The declaration of elections to the State Legislative Assembly in March 2006 had brought every activity connected with preparedness of the scheme to a standstill in the District. This coupled with the lethargic attitude of the officials during the period of election fever, lack of proper orientation to the Rural Development Department (RDD) officials, absence of comprehensive operational guidelines, delay in providing working instructions, non-availability of perspective plan for the district and sub-district levels, etc. have virtually made the system ineffective.

In one of the initial communications from the CRD dated 18 Jan 2006, even before launch of the scheme, it was conveyed to the GPs to prepare Action Plan (AP) by taking up two works per ward at a cost of Rs.40,000 each. The PRIs have submitted the AP, by giving greater thrust on schemes for rural connectivity. After the lapse of almost two months, on 14 March 2006, working instructions were brought out by the CRD, specifying that 'roads can be taken as last priority not exceeding 10 % value of all types of works taken up'. The GPs were asked to again prepare the APs in accordance with the new instructions – preparing a list of two works per ward and works for rural connectivity not exceeding 10 per cent of the total value of works. Then again in April 2006, another instruction was given to the GPs towards submitting a list of 5 more works in each ward for preparing a shelf of works. Such piecemeal, often contradicting, instructions have generated lot of confusion during the preparation of the Action Plan. It finally resulted in evading the Grama Sabhas in the preparation of the Action Plan. The decision regarding the selection of an agency for preparing a Perspective Plan for the district as a whole was made on June 3, 2006.[23]

Non-adherence to the time line for preparation of Action Plan

Table 4 indicates the timeline set for preparation of Employment Guarantee Scheme (EGS) Action plan in the District.

Procedural issues

Most of the BPOs were appointed in the posts after being promoted from the post of Extension Officer (Integrated Rural Development) and their new pay scale had to concurred by the Accountant General (AG). Since the necessary orders were not issued, they are not able to draw their salary in the new scale of BDO, and had to be content with their previous scale for the time being. This seriously affects the morale of the BPOs, who are the key persons in the scheme implementation, and which may further get reflected in their functioning as well.[24]

Table 4. Timeline for preparation of EGS Action Plan

Sl. No.	*Task Description*	*Start Date*	*End Date*	*Remarks by the researchers based on field survey*
1	2	3	4	5
1.	Identification of works by Grama Sabha/GP/BP/DP	01.03.2006	10.03.2006	Task was completed, but not before the end date.
2.	Approval of GP level EGS Plan by GP		10.03.2006	Task was completed, but not before the end date.
3.	Submission to the Programme Officer (PO)		13.03.2006	Task was completed.
4.	Scrutiny and consolidation of EGS Plan of GPs	14.03.2006	17.03.2006	As per the KREGS working instructions dated 14 March, APs were returned to GPs.
5.	Approval of Block GP Plan		18.03.2006	Not taken up.
6.	Submission to the DPC		20.03.2006	Not taken up
7.	Completion and consolidation of Block Plan	21.03.2006	23.03.2006	Not taken up.
8.	Approval of District Panchayat Plan		24.03.2006	Not taken up.
9.	Retransmission to DPC		25.03.2006	Not taken up
10.	Retransmission to PO by DPC		28.03.2006	Not taken up.
11.	Retransmission to GP by PO		30.03.2006	Not taken up
12.	Estimate preparation, according of Administrative Sanction (AS) and Technical Sanction (TS)	30.03.2006	06.04.2006	Not taken up.

Source: Col.No. 1 to 4 from CRD and Col.5 from field visits.

Issues of hierarchy

During implementation of SGRY, some BDOs faced problems in getting the required information from the Secretaries of Special Grade Panchayats, who are also placed in the same pay scale. In such situations, the required data was collected through the Village Extension Officer (VEO), who is a staff of the RDD. Since KREGS advocates strong operational and functional linkages between the PRIs, issues relating to the relative position of officials in the hierarchy may cause impediments in the information flow and smooth implementation of the scheme, and this needs to be taken care of. [25]

Transfer & retirement of BPOs

Transfer and retirement of key personnel during the implementation of the programme has affected its functioning and hampered the progress of implementation considerably. During the reference period, BPOs from four blocks were transferred outside the district.[26] Similarly, posting of key personnel, who is on the verge of retirement, to key posts also has adverse effects. [27]

(b) Political deficits

As indicated during the execution of WEPs in the past, the political parties in the State were not very keen on understanding the full implications of the Central Act, the philosophy and operational guidelines of the KREGS. It is noted that none of the parties considered it as a serious matter to be discussed in the political meetings/committees. Being a scheme, specifically designed to address the needs of the poor and marginalized sections of the society, this scheme did not elicit the significance that it should have among the political parties in the District. There was hardly any question/submission raised in the State Legislative Assembly to know the status and issues relating to the launching of the scheme in the District. Even during the recent elections to the State Legislative Assembly, the scheme hardly figured in the manifesto, debates, discourses and campaigns of the major political parties.[28]

The Congress party organised a meeting of the Presidents of all concerned District Congress Committees

(DCC) on 26 May 2006 at New Delhi, with the intention of orienting the Congress leaders in taking political advantage out of this welfare scheme. The party functionaries from different districts gave details of problems and shortcomings of the scheme implementation in their areas (The Hindu, 2006). However, the party functionaries from Kerala did not utilise this session as an opportunity to gain political mileage for the Congress party at the hustings.

It indicates the absence of political acumen of the leaders, weak organisational structures of the parties, the class background of the leaders associated with the decision making forums at the district level, and lack of sensitisation about the poverty-related issues of marginalized sections.

Another aspect is that, being an agrarian district, Palakkad has a strong presence of politically affiliated organisations like *Karshaka Sanghom*, *Karshaka Congress*, *Kisan Sabha*, *Karshaka Thozhilazhi Union*, etc. But none of these associations and functionaries of '*Padasekhara Samithis*' [29] took any attempt to understand, discuss and analyse the different dimensions of the scheme. It is very important to note that a large number of labourers from the agrarian sectors have registered at the PRIs under the scheme. Unless managed carefully, this may result in conflicts among the potential beneficiaries of the scheme.

(c) Deficit of Third Sector and Civil Society Organisations

With the passing of the Right to Information Act (2005), the ambit of KREGS has opened up a large space for third sector and civil society organisations. It is a well-acknowledged fact that legislation alone cannot reduce the leakages in the system and the civil society organisations can play a mediating role among the communities, PRIs and the bureaucracy by providing appropriate feedbacks and suggesting corrective measures at regular intervals. The efficiency of the system largely depends on the effective functioning of civil society organisations. NGOs could act as an interface between the local bodies and the communities towards ensuring that the planning process is participatory and reflects local priorities (Iyer and Samji, 2006).

However, this has two dimensions with particular reference to the District. First, not many performing third sector organisations or Non-Government Organisations (NGO) are available in the district. Secondly, the existing NGOs have not taken due interest to know about the scheme, its philosophy and salient features. [30]

The Kerala Sastra Sahitya Parishad (KSSP), an agency that took the lead role in literacy, People's Plan and various other leading campaigns in the State, remained a mute spectator during the preparatory phase of the scheme. Mazdoor Kisan Shakti Sangathan (MKSS), an organisation more or less similar to KSSP in its capacity, commitment, activities and functioning, took a lead role at Dungarpur District in Rajasthan. It is noted that most of the third sector and civil society organisations in the district have not identified an appropriate space for themselves in the execution of the scheme.[31]

(d) Deficit of the Kerala PR system

The Grama Sabha and the three tiers of PRIs (GP, BP and DP) are the major constituents of the Kerala PR system and rural polity. 'The principle of subsidiarity' has been interpreted in the State in such a way that each tier of PRI has its independent status, position and responsibility often disregarding the other two tiers. The holistic vision, philosophy and collective responsibility expected of the PRIs have not been found in the State. The 'principle of sphere autonomy with peer group responsibility' is totally alien in the discourse of Kerala PR system.

Each PRI used to function more or less as a 'water tight compartment' in Kerala. In NREGA, a 'Peer group responsibility' is visualised with the BP over the GPs and a similar responsibility is also vested with the DP over the BPs within the framework of a 'principle of sphere autonomy'. While operationalising NREGA in the State, this may be a tough terrain requiring adequate investment in conflict-resolution.

Lack of social accountability and transparency in the functioning of PRIs in the State is another deficit visualised. The concept of 'Social Audit' is yet to be operational in the participatory forums like Grama Sabha in most of the PRIs in the State. Similar concerns are expressed by many writers.[32] Similarly the process of demand generation under the provisions of 'Right to Information' has also not picked up the required momentum in the State (Chathukulam and John, 2002).

(e) Absence of Work-Time-Motion Studies

KREGS makes a brief mention of Schedule of Rural Rates (SRR) for unskilled labourers considering that a person working for seven hours would normally earn a wage equal to the prevailing minimum wage rate. It suggests that a standard SRR shall be worked out by desegregating each task into its constituent activities and calculating the average time taken for the activity and then assessing its payment based on labour and time expended.

It is noted that certain states carried out the studies that resulted in standardising the work and wage rates, which proved a great boon to the working class. In Andhra Pradesh, 158 works were taken up for collection of data for Work-Time-Motion Studies with the required technical support (APREGS, 2006). As a result, a labourer in Andhra Pradesh has to dig 44 cubic feet to earn Rs.80, whereas in Rajasthan, in the absence of Work-Time-Motion Studies, a labourer has to dig 62 cubic feet for Rs.73 (Frontline, 2006). Such Work-Time-Motion Studies were never held in Kerala, which may adversely affect the working class. While formulating the SRR, consideration should be given to the physically challenged, mal-nourished, women and tribal workers compared to the 'able-bodied workers' as the productivity of the latter is lower than average.[33]

(f) Preparation of the AP for 2 works per ward

This is a retrograde step when we consider the arguments raised during the People's Plan Campaign (PPC) against division of allocation of funds into various wards. PPC advocated the need for treating GP as a single unit during the plan process (Issac with Franke, 2000). However, the guidelines and working instructions of KREGS suggests otherwise. This was not ideal in several ways. It resulted in sharing of funds equally among all the wards of a GP without even considering the poverty profile, geographical factors, unemployment situation, job potentials, etc. However, the suggestion of two schemes per ward have the advantage that it is convenient, easy and non-controversial in nature; but ignoring the principle of viewing the GP as a single unit and principle of spatial planning is also not desirable.

PART - VII

SUGGESTIONS AND CONCLUSION

There is an urgent need for developing appropriate linkages between agriculture sector and the EGS scheme, taking into account the work season and other aspects. Discussions between elected members of PRIs and representatives of *Padasekhara Samithis* can be organised to sort out such issues.

There is a need for wide ranging discussions between elected members of PRIs and leadership of major political parties for drawing maximum mileage by executing the scheme creditably, efficiently and transparently, thereby contributing to the reduction of poverty. Political parties can also think of setting up monitoring committees at the field level for taking corrective steps when needed.

Need for discussions and interactions between elected members of PRIs and representatives of the third sector and civil society organisations, activists, experts, etc. also exist.

Third sector and civil society organisations can play the role of a support mechanism by providing appropriate feedbacks and suggestions. They are already performing the role of a supportive system in Rajasthan, Gujarat and Andhra Pradesh, which was almost absent during the previous WEPs in the area (Frontline, 2006). They can function as 'Participatory critics' also by getting themselves involved in the whole exercise and suggesting corrective measures at regular intervals.

Implementation of KREGS should not be viewed as the exclusive responsibility of RDD and PRIs alone. There is a need for developing total synergy between different stakeholders like third sector, civil society organisations, educational institutions, academicians, etc...

There is a need for taking up Work-Time-Motion Studies with adequate weightage being given to the mal-nourished, women, tribals and physically challenged so that workers from these sections are not treated at par with the able bodied workers in their performance.

The analysis of political economy of preparedness and launching of NREGA in Palakkad gives an impression that 'Taking ownership' by the political parties is not happening in the District. It also indicates that the existing institutional mechanisms to run the programmes have been found inadequate.

The Indian National Congress has taken the lead role by launching the scheme as promised in its election manifesto and the post-election Common Minimum Programme. Though senior leaders of the party advocated its local level leaders to take political advantage of the welfare scheme, because of organisational and structural weakness of the party in the District, no forward movement was made in the desired direction. The LDF, currently in a state of complacency following the spectacular victory in the 2006 Assembly elections, does not seem to have realised the potential of the scheme so far. The composition and class background of the third sector and civil society organisations like the KSSP also may be a hindrance for taking a lead role in pushing the scheme further. The bureaucracy is almost helpless in the absence of strong political will and lack of support from the third sector and civil society organisations. There is a vacuum of 'agency role' for social engineering and mobilisation of the poor under the potentially pro-poor scheme in the District.

We feel that the various issues identified during the pre-launch preparedness of the scheme in the District need to be discussed threadbare by policy makers, administrators and all other stakeholders so that appropriate strategy could be devised for overcoming them.

Notes

1. During the field visit to Kannadi GP on May 30, 2006, the President of the GP expressed his apprehensions about the fate of the programme. "In SGRY, despite all other issues, some asset was created. I have even doubts about creation of any asset in this scheme".
2. This data was collected followed discussions with the *Krishi* Officer, Kollengode Grama Panchayat and some experienced farmers from *Nenmeni Padasekhara Samithi* of Kollengode GP area on June 8, 2006.
3. Discussions with the officials of *Krishi Bhavan* of Kollengode GP and functionaries of *Padasekhara Samithis* of the Panchayat area on June 8, 2006 indicated that it may lead to serious negative impact on agricultural sector. Similar comments were made by Ms. N.Chandrika, BPO of Ottappalam Block during the discussions with the researchers on June 16, 2006.
4. In Nemmara BP, nobody turned up for the interview for the post of AE. In Pattambi Block, though the candidate was selected, there was reluctance to join duty. It is noted that poor attractability of the post of AE may create problems in programme implementation.
5. One day session was held on January 28, 2006 for the personnel from six Blocks – Ottappalam, Thrithala,

Pattambi, Sreekrishnapuram, Mannarkkad and Attappadi. Another session was held on January 30, 2006 for the personnel from the remaining seven blocks – Alathur, Palakkad, Malampuzha, Kuzhalmannam, Nemmara, Chittur and Kollengode.

6. It is an institute set up at Mulamkunnathukavu, Thrissur under the Ministry of Local Self Government. The main objective of KILA is to provide training to elected members and officials of PRIs.
7. It is an initiative of Swiss Agency for Development and Co-operation (SDC) for accelerating the decentralisation process in the state.
8. The Principal Secretary, Andhra Pradesh was invited to share the experiences of NREGA in that State during the workshop.
9. This information was furnished to the researchers during the field visits by a number of elected members and officials who attended the training. For example, discussions with Mr. Unnikrishnan, President and Mr. Siddique, Secretary of Ongalloor GP in Pattambi Block on May 18, 2006, indicated that district level training was not useful to them.
10. Computer systems were initially installed at DRDA Office, Palakkad and Block Office, Ottappalam for facilitating data entry from 13 Blocks. After procurement of additional systems, two more centres were set up at Alathur and Mannarkkad Blocks. The JPC issued instructions to carry out the operations of designated blocks at each centre.
11. However, during the field visits conducted as late as in the third week of June 2006, the job cards were not available with the GPs.
12. Four banks – Canara Bank, Punjab National Bank, State Bank of India and State Bank of Travancore – were selected as the participating banks in Palakkad District as per intimation to the PRIs dated 27 March 2006.
13. Nelliyampathy GP of Nemmara Block and Polpulli GP of Malampuzha Block faced the issue of non-availability of any of the participating banks in their area. BPO,

Nemmara gave special instructions to open the NREGA Account in Syndicate Bank, available at Nelliyampathy. The issue of Polpulli GP is yet to be resolved on May 11, 2006, the time of field visit.

14. Keralassery GP of Palakkad Block faced the problem of opening a zero balance account at State Bank of India, Keralassery. The issue was not settled at the time of field visit to the GP on May 11, 2006.

15. A number of contract staff from several GPs faced problems in getting their salaries. For example, Mankara GP of Palakkad District faced the issue when the GP secretary presented the cheque for the purpose of payment of salaries to the contract employees in March 2006. This issue was settled after a communication from the JPC to the Banks on April 10, 2006.

16. The communication from CRD on January 18, 2006 asked the GPs to prepare the AP for two works in each ward of a GP at an estimated cost of Rs. 40,000 per work and BPs to prepare the AP for two works in each division at an estimated cost of Rs. 40,000 per work. The DP can take up works costing Rs. 1 crore.

17. In Tamil Nadu, which held elections in the same period, Perspective Plans (PP) for the districts were prepared and the process was going on despite the declaration of assembly elections. In six districts of Tamil Nadu, 581360 job cards were issued; employment has been provided to 51,883 persons and 678 works are in progress. This information was downloaded from a document titled 'Major programmes of the UPA Government – Two years of achievements in Tamil Nadu' from *www.pib.nic.in* on June 5, 2006.

18. Most of the GPs were forced to revise the AP again as per the instructions. During the field visit, it is noted that 23 GPs have revised their AP as per the latest instructions and out of them 19 have submitted the plans to BPOs.

19. Mr. VS Achuthanandan, the Chief Minister of Kerala, got elected from Malampuzha constituency in the district.

20. Mr. Paloli Muhammedkutty, the Minister of Local Self Government, was heading the same ministry during the previous tenure of LDF in the State.

21. Mr. SM Vijayanand, Principal Secretary, Ministry of Local Self-Government, spent major part of his service in the Rural Development Department and played an active role in the decentralised planning in the State. Moreover, he has field experience in the district. Mr.TK Jose, Secretary, Department of Local Self Government, played the pivotal role in initiating, institutionalising and strengthening women's association life through the Kudumbasree Mission. Ms.Sarada Muralidharan, Executive Director, Kudumbasree Mission, has experience in the capacity as Commissioner of Rural Development.

22. Mr. K Sasidharan Nair, a senior official from RDD, has rich experience in rural development as well as field experience in the district.

23. In Tamil Nadu, Perspective Plan was already made in six districts by then.

24. Officials of RDD are drawing salary from the Consolidated Fund of the State, which is subjected to Accountant General's (AG) audit. However, NREGS is a Centrally sponsored scheme, which is not subjected to AG's audit. In the absence of clear-cut orders, the BPOs are not able to draw their salary in the new scale. During informal discussions, a number of BPOs expressed their desire to move out of the post.

25. The issue was raised by Mr. Krishnan, EO (Housing) and holding additional charge of BPO in Pattambi Block during discussions on May 18, 2006.

26. BPOs of Alathur, Kollengode and Thrithala Blocks were transferred to Vyttila, Kothamangalam and Sasthamkotta Blocks and BPO of Ottappalam was transferred to Kannur as District Women Welfare Officer (The Mathrubhumi, 2006).

27. In Pattambi Block, the BPO, who took charge in the first week of February 2006, retired on 28 February, 2006. At the time of visit to the GP on 18 May 2006, Extension

Officer (Housing) from Pattambi Block was handling the additional charge of BPO.

28. Felicitations to Prakash Karat, General Secretary, CPI (M) appeared at Vadavannur GP area in the form of a banner for 'bringing the employment guarantee scheme to Palakkad', his home district.
29. Federation of farmers in a designated area under paddy cultivation.
30. Maithri, a NGO specialised in Natural Resource Management, organised a workshop on Rural Habitation with the financial support from SDC-CapDecK at Palakkad on March 4 and 5, 2006. During the workshop, a presentation was made by the JPC of the District, followed by limited discussions. It is known that Maithri prepared a draft micro plan for the implementation of the programme at Vadakarapathy and Eruthempathy GPs of Chittur Block, on their own initiative.
31. Discussions with functionaries of KSSP, People's Social Society-Palakkad (PSSP), Integrated Rural Technology Centre (IRTC), etc. were conducted by the researchers and their responses recorded in May 2006.
32. Tharakan and Chathukulam (2006), and Vijayanand (2006) also highlight the point.
33. Singh (2006) and Shah (2006) also highlighted this point.

References

Andhra Pradesh Rural Employment Guarantee Scheme – APREGS (2006): Operational Manual, Department of Rural Development, Government of Andhra Pradesh, Hyderabad.

Bhatty, Kiran (2006): 'Employment Guarantee and Child Rights', *Economic and Political Weekly*, Vol.XLI, No.20, May 20 - 26.

Census 2001, Series 33, Kerala, Final Population Totals, Paper 1 of 2001, Director of Census Operations, Thiruvananthapuram.

Chathukulam, Jos (2005): 'Concurrent Evaluation of Sampoorna Grameen Rozgar Yojana in Kerala', *Report submitted to Ministry of Rural Development, Government of India*, Centre for Rural Management, Kottayam, October.

Chathukulam, Jos and MS John (2002): Five Years of Participatory Planning in Kerala ; 'Rhetoric and Reality'. *Economic and Political Weekly*, Vol.XXXVII, No.49, December 7 - 13.

Desarda, HM (2005): 'Guaranteed Employment for the Rural Poor – A Conceptual Framework and Operational Strategy', *Gandhian Perspectives,* Vol.XII and XIII, No.2 and 1, July-December and January-June.

Frontline, May 19, 2006.

Issac, Thomas with Richard Franke (2000): *Local Democracy and Development: People's Campaign for Decentralised Planning in Kerala*, Leftword, New Delhi.

Iyer, Yamini and Salimah Samji (2006): 'Improving the effectiveness of National Rural Employment Guarantee Act', *Economic and Political Weekly*, Vol.XLI, No.4, January 28 - February 3.

Shah, Mihir (2006): 'Delivering on the Employment Guarantee', *The Hindu*, May 4.

Singh, Puran (2006): 'National Rural Employment Guarantee Scheme – A task ahead', *Kurukshetra*, Vol.54, No.7, May.

Tharakan, P.K.M. and Jos Chathukulam (2006): 'Attempts to empower People's Entitlement in Local Governance through potentially pro-poor practices of Social Audit : The evidence from Kerala', Paper prepared for the workshop of *Writers and Thinkers on Local Governance and Panchayati Raj,* Ministry of Panchayat Raj, Government of India, New Delhi, June 23 – 25.

The Hindu, Kochi, May 27, 2006.

The Mathrubhumi, Palakkad, June 21, 2006.

The Pioneer, Kochi, July 13, 2006.

Vijayanand, S.M. (2006): 'Social accountability and participatory planning – Lessons from Kerala experience', Paper prepared for the workshop of *Writers and Thinkers on Local Governance and Panchayati Raj,* Ministry of Panchayat Raj, Government of India, New Delhi, June 23 – 25.

Wray, L.Randal (2006): 'Lessons from Argentina's employment guarantee', *Economic and Political Weekly*, Vol.XLI, No.23, June 10 - 16.

15

Reforming Local Governance in India : A New Paradigm for Development

K. Rajasekharan

1. Introduction

Development in any democratic country revolves round administration. The efficiency, simplicity and goal orientation of administration determines the effectiveness of development and well- being of the people. No plans, no policies, no measures can succeed or deliver the goods without having a purposeful and capable administration. Ever continuing attempts for improvement in administrative structures, procedures and result orientation have been a key theme for solving glaring inadequacies in administration in our country since independence.

Administrative Reforms is as old as administration. But it is re-gaining importance recently. The gross inadequacies in administration in the fast changing globalised environment make it an indispensable need of our times. *Administrative Reforms* is a political attempt to bring about dramatic change or transformation in public administrative structure, procedures, attitudes and behavior in bureaucracy, rationality, effectiveness and efficiency, service delivery to citizens etc. so as to have economic, political and social development in the country. It is a conscious attempt and activity to improve our public services.

Administrative Reforms presupposes reforms in

- administrative structure

- budgetary process
- executive functioning
- income and expenditure assignment
- accounting procedures
- personnel recruitment and management
- computer applications etc.

Administrative Reforms should be a continuous process and never be periodic or episodic events. The three stages in administrative reforms at a particular point of time are:-

- Analysis of current situation
- Formulation of reform strategy and
- Implementation of reforms

No other country in the developing world might have witnessed such a spate of administrative reforms as India did. Even the British period was not devoid of attempts in this direction. All those attempts brought to us a lot of improvements that interspersed with continuing disappointments arising out of constant failures.

The inordinate administrative delays, mounting corruption and shortfalls or failures in development projects in our country make our administration so weak in spite of ever continuing efforts in administrative reforms.

Some of the important milestones in A*dministrative Reforms* in India are:-

- Gopalaswami Ayyangar Committee Report in 1949
- A D Gorwala Committee Report in *1951 to assess the capability of existing public administration to undertake development planning.*
- Paul H Appleby's survey on Public Administration in India in 1953
- Paul H Appleby's Report of Reorganisation of Indian Administrative System in 1956

- V T Krishnamachari's Report on India and State Administrative Services and Problems of District Administration in 1962
- K Santhanam Committee Report on Prevention of Corruption in 1964.
- First Administrative Reforms Commission (chaired by Shri. Morarji Desai) Report 1966.
- Report of the Commission on Review of Administrative Laws chaired by Shri. P. C. Jain in 1998.
- P C Hota Committee Report in 2004.
- Second Administrative Reforms Commission (ARC) chaired by Shri. Veerappa Moily in 2005.

2. About Second Administrative Reforms Commission

The Second Administrative Reforms Commission (ARC) was set up on 31st August 2005 to prepare a *detailed blue print for revamping the public administration system*, with Shri. Veerappa Moiley as chairperson. The Commission was expected to suggest measures to achieve a proactive, responsive, accountable, sustainable and efficient administration in the country at all levels of government including local self government system.

The Commission submitted six reports so far and they are as follows:-

Report

No	*Date of Submission*	*Subject*
1.	June 2006	Right to Information
2.	July 2006	Unlocking Human Capital
3.	Sept 2006	Crisis Management
4.	January 2007	Ethics in Governance
5.	June 2007	Public Order
6.	October 2007	Local Governance: An Inspiring Journey into the Future

The following section provides an overview of the sixth report titled *Local Governance: An Inspiring Journey into the Future.*

3. The Structure and Content of the Report

The purpose of the **Sixth Report of the Second Administrative Reforms Commission** titled ***Local Governance: An Inspiring Journey into the future*** was to examine the issues that would help evolve a vibrant rural and urban local governance system in India as we have been cherishing for long.

The Report has five dominant sections or Chapters as follows:-

1 Introduction

2 Core principles

3 Common Issues

4 Rural Governance

5 Urban Governance

4. Sixth ARC Report on Local Governance: Recommendations

4.1 The Introductory Chapter: Contents

In the introductory chapter, the Report outlines the evolution and growth of local governance and the need to empower it in the context of economic reforms in the 1990's that paid the dividends well. Local governance is deep rooted in India since Vedic period and the British rulers had made several attempts to make it vibrant. The chapter outlines the local attempts, essential recommendations of numerous committee reports and programmes that we had witnessed after the independence to make local governance a key theme culminating in the much cherished Constitutional Amendments in 1992.

The local governments are conceptualized as inherent part of 'government' or 'state' consequent to the amendments and Supreme Court ruling in this regard. But the structure of the district administration under the District Collector remained somewhat anachronistic in the modern democratic framework with district Collector as the kingpin. The creation and existence of large number of functional bodies in the form of development authorities, housing boards, slum development agencies and sanitation boards inherently weakened the growth of stable local governance.

Local governance is purported to concentrate on improving the quality of life of citizens by providing amenities in sectors such as water supply, solid waste management, sanitation etc as they are remaining closer to the people and are concerned about citizens' needs better. But they were performing poorly over the years as against their counterparts in developed countries.

So the report says that there is a need to make substantive reforms in local government institutions by creating an autonomous space, with solid environment as part of the governance system with non overlapping jurisdiction for local governments with other bodies and devoid of bureaucratic control by the State government.

4.2 Core Principles: A Descriptive Account

India is a Union of States and the devolution of the State functions to local governments has become the norm. Since empowerment of States due to the rise of regional parties, emergence of coalition politics, evolution of fair and non-discriminatory fiscal devolution etc. has not weakened the Union. On the contrary it has strengthened the State and has made the Centre-State relation more harmonious. The strengthening of local governments should also have the same effect and hence need to be done. So the State governments should continue to play an effective role in devolving more functions and improving local governance.

The six core principles relied on by the Commission as the basis of the recommendations are as follows:-

Principle of Subisidiarity

Subsidiarity defines that the central authority in governance should have a subsidiary function, performing only those tasks that cannot be done by the lower levels. In governance, the citizens are the final decision makers. They are sovereign and stake holders of governance. They are consumers of governance services too. They delegate the functions upwards, to the community, to the local government, to the State and so on. The delegation is determined by economies of scale, technologies and managerial ability. The citizen should exercise as much authority as practicable and delegate the rest upwards. Like wise, the smallest closer local government should perform all they can do and delegate the rest upwards.

Application of the subsidiarity principle has three great advantages such as improvement in local decision making, promotion of self reliance, encouraging competition and nurturing innovation. It should promote greater responsibility, enlightened citizenship and maturing of democracy.

Principles of Effective Democratic Decentralisation

Effective decentralisation of functions from the States to the local governments should be a cardinal principle as the Seventh Schedule of the Constitution remains unaltered.

It should be on the basis of four guiding norms such as:-

- there is a link between the citizens votes and consequent public good it may bring
- there should be a link between the generation of resources and the outcomes in the form of better services
- the existence of asymmetry in power and the imbalances in the society due to the employment of only a mere 8 percent of our work force in our organized sector with a secure monthly wage and associated benefits.

- the need to make the locus of governance closer to the people to have direct participation, constant vigil and timely intervention.

Governance in the local government sector should have a twin focus that it should satisfy people's needs and aspirations and should lead to economic growth of the nation as a whole in which there should be an improved role for the State Government.

Principle of Delineation of Functions

Our country is a federal democracy working with a detailed Constitution. The subjects under the jurisdiction of each tier of government and the specific role assigned to each tier needs to be clearly spelt out.

The sectors devolved to local governments are now defined as inherent part of the State subjects. There should be a clear delineation in the specific roles of the State and the local governments. As well, within local governments, there is a need for clear functional delineation amongst different tiers.

Principle of Devolution in Real terms

In order to make the devolution to be real and meaningful, the local governments should be empowered to frame regulations, take autonomous decisions and enforce their will.

In finance, the local governments should be able to meet their statutory obligations. There must be sufficient flexibility through untied resources, sufficient opportunity and incentive to mobilize the local resources through local taxes.

For this, there is need to give more voice for local governments to negotiate with the State. So there should be an upper house – a Legislative Council - for legislature in each State and that should reflect the voice of the local governments.

Building the capacity for local governance to discharge their functions is highlighted as very important aspect to be attended to. Empowered legislative committees to bring in more transparency and accountability are also suggested in the section.

Principle of Convergence

Governance is possible only through compartmentalized structures. But citizen's needs are indivisible. Isolated functioning of disparate government agencies as water tight compartments can make citizens' life miserable. So there is a need for convergence of services in local governance.

Convergence at the district and below levels is essential to overcome the problem of rural -urban divide. The existence of parastatals run counter to the principle of subsidiarity and precludes effective citizen's participation. Access to the multiple agencies is difficult for the citizens unless having convergence of services. Citizens must have access to all the service providers though a single-window as far as possible.

Empowered stake holder groups should be converged with local government activities to improve the management of institutions and service delivery.

Principle of Citizen Centricity

Citizen satisfaction is the core aspect of local governance, for which mechanism should be created to give him voice. There should be mechanisms for measuring citizen's satisfaction through various mechanisms including social audit. Citizen's participation in decision making is not practicable in large structures. So create smaller structures at the local community level. Stakeholders should be empowered as part of application of principle of subsidiarity and the process should be seen as a continuum.

4.3 Common Issues: Recommendations

The chapter on Common Issues examines the issues that are common to both urban and rural areas.

An analysis of the functioning of local governments indicates that there is a strong case to revisit the basic Constitutional scheme relating to local governance. A strong constitutional provision mandating effective empowerment of local governments seems both desirable and necessary. The incongruity between eleventh and twelfth schedules need to be removed, even though they are illustrative items of functions. So the Constitution should include provisions mandating States to enact proper laws for local governance in accordance with the principle of subsidiarity and by ensuring local government at the appropriate level vested with adequate powers and authority to function as *institutions of self governments*.

Each State should have a Legislative Council as upper house of the legislature and it should be a council of local government. The legislative council should have members elected solely from the elected representative of the local bodies.

There shall be District Council in every district with representation from both urban and rural areas. District Collector shall function as the Chief Officer of the District Council. The appointment of the Collector should be in consultation with the District Council.

The number of tiers of local government should be left to the discretionary decision of the State government. The States governments are free to decide the manner of election of members in the intermediate and district panchayat either as direct or indirect. But it should be ensured that either Chair Person or members in each tier should be directly elected.

The delimitation and reservation of constituency should be entrusted to the SEC. The Assembly electoral rolls should be used for local governments and the building block approach should be followed in electoral roll making. In case of reservation, either there should be at least 2 terms of 5 years or the list system with multi-member constituency should be followed.

There should be a clear delineation of functions for each tier of local government based on detailed activity mapping.

Each new law in the State should contain a *local government memorandum.* The memorandum should indicate whether any function as per the new piece of legislation is to be attended to by local governments as we include a *financial memorandum* which indicates the financial implications in each piece of legislation.

Union Government should enact a Framework Law for Local Government. It should lay down the broad principles of devolution of powers, responsibilities and functions to the local governments and communities.

Regarding devolution of funds, SFC should evolve objective and transparent norms such as area wise indices for backwardness for devolution and distribution of funds. Action taken report on SFC report must compulsorily be placed in the State legislature within six months. SFC should evolve formula for staffing of local bodies.

Capacity development in local governance should concentrate on organization building and individual skill up gradation. Local governments should outsource their activities to private agencies whenever needed, on the basis of specific guidelines from the State. The training institutions should be networked and continuous training should be envisaged. Academic research should have a prominent role in the capacity building for decentralization.

District Council should be created and district planning should be entrusted to them. Each state should develop the methodology for participatory local level planning and provide support for decentralised planning.

Audit Committees must be constituted in each district. The Audit Committees must have independence, access to all information, ability to communicate with technical experts and accountability to the public. There should be a separate standing committee of the State legislature for local governments in the manner of Public Accounts Committee. Local Ombudsman, for conflict resolution between citizen and local governments, should be constituted for one or more district. An in house mechanism for grievance redressal should also to be established.

Urban local governments should follow National Accounting Manual. An Auditor, in addition to the Local Fund Auditor/CAG, should audit the accounts, as per the guidelines of CAG. CAG should provide guidelines to the local fund auditor. A Committee of the State Legislature should discuss the audit report placed in the State Legislature.

4.4 Rural Local Governance: Recommendations

The issues regarding rural local governance were comprehensively examined by the commission.

The States should ensure appropriate size for the panchayats duly considering the geographical condition and the possibility of popular participation. When Grama Panchayat is large, Ward Sabhas should be constituted to exercise the powers and functions.

Panchayat should have power to recruit personnel and to regulate their services. If it is not possible, staff from other departments can be drawn on deputation during the interim period.

The provision of approval of the budget of the lower tier panchayat by an upper tier panchayat should be disposed of. The State government should not hold the power to suspend or rescind any resolution. If any action is needed, it should be as per the recommendations of the Local Ombudsman.

Parastatals should not be allowed to work in parallel to local governments. DRDA and similar other agencies should be discontinued. If any agency has to be set up, it should work under direct control of the panchayat.

States should undertake comprehensive activity mapping with regard to all matters transferred to local governments. Union governments should undertake activity mapping with regard to the Centrally Sponsored Schemes.

Rural policing, enforcement of building bye-laws, birth & death registration, residence certificates, voters identity cards, regulation relating to weight and measures etc. should be kept under the domain of panchayats. There should be continuous devolution of regulatory functions to the panchayats.

The revenue base of the panchayats should be broadened and deepened. All common property resources should be made productive. The tax domain of panchayats should be expanded. The higher level panchayats should be enabled to run or manage transport, water supply, power distribution and such other utilities. The State governments should fix a band of rates for taxes and levies. Village panchayats should have primary authority over taxation. But upper tiers of local governments should get a portion when there is inter-panchayat ramification.

Except a few specific purpose programmes, all allocation to the panchayats should be untied. There should be a separate budget. The State government should release the funds sufficiently early to ensure effective use of it.

Panchayats should be allowed to borrow funds within the limits fixed by the State. All flow of funds to the public development schemes such as MPLAD, MLALAD etc should be routed through Panchayats. The Local Area Development schemes of MP and MLA should be stopped. There should be focused efforts to use all mass media for creation of awareness on panchayati raj. Rural radio programme should have panchayati raj content. The elementary education, preventive health care, water supply, sanitation, environment and nutrition should be immediately transferred to panchayats. Information technologies should be used to more in panchayati raj activities and in information dissemination relating to it.

4.5 Urban Governance: Recommendations

The report examines the complex urban governance which poses a formidable challenge to planners.

There is an urgent need to constitute a new National Commission on Urbanisation to bring about a balanced and smooth urbanization in the country.

In municipalities there should be Municipal Council, Ward Committees and Area Committees. The same functionary should chair the Municipal Council and function as the Chief Executive. The Chairman/Mayor should be directly elected by popular mandate. In Municipal Corporation, the Mayor should appoint a Mayors Cabinet. Mayor should choose the members of the cabinet from among the members of the Council.

Mayor should be the Chief Executive of the Municipality and the Commissioner should perform all delegated function. The Directorate of Municipal Administration should be abolished and the employees should be absorbed in to municipal governments through a due process.

All local governments should ensure that property tax should be derived on the basis of objective unit area method. Levy of tax on any unauthorised building should not confer any right of ownership and that should be provided for in the law. A computerised database of all properties using GIS mapping should be prepared for all municipal areas. Transparent taxing procedures based on self declaration should be followed. There should be a monitoring cell for taxes and a quasi-judicial appellate authority for taxes.

The grants to the municipalities should be linked with their own efforts in resource sharing. Municipal authorities should have power to impose fines for violation of civic laws and the fines for civic offences should be enhanced.

The SFC should determine and State government should formally fix the limit of borrowings by various municipal bodies.

Municipalities should have an updated database of all their properties. The lease or renting out of municipal property should be based on a fair competitive process.

Each State government should start a prorgramme for updating and simplification of all regulatory provisions in local government laws relating to urban local governments. Citizen's Charter should be published by all urban local governments and it should specify the time limit of providing service and about relief in case of non-adherence of the stipulations in the Charter. The local governments should provide civic amenities and the parastatals of the State government, if exist separately, should be accountable to the municipalities in respective areas.

Water supply should be the responsibility of the urban local government in collaboration with the parastatal. SFC should determine the tariff structure. All water connection should be metered. Incentives for rain water harvesting should be adopted. Sanitation and public health should be given due priority. Sewerage facility in slum areas should be provided in a time bound manner. A separate user charge for sanitation and sewerage need to be introduced. Public-Private Partnership projects for waste management can be taken up in all towns and the cities above one lakh. Solid waste management charges should be levied on the units generating high amounts of solid waste. Municipalities should be encouraged to take up distribution of powers after building up their capacity to do so.

Education and health sector should be subject to decentralised reform activities. Within next two years, all schools should be made self sufficient in infrastructure. Help from NGOs should be sought for this. Municipalities should focus on preventive aspect rather than curative aspects. Third party assessment should be made in schools and hospitals to fix the basic standards. Convergence of health systems, sanitation facilities and drinking water facilities should be made. Performance indicators for services should be fixed.

Integration of land use, with transparent planning, should be done in all urban local governments. Management of traffic should be done by imposing congestion levies, pedestrianisation of roads in certain zones and earmarking of some areas for public transport.

There should be sectoral allocation for sanitation and solid waster management. Measures should be taken to regulate the real estate sector. The public private partnership for re-development of inner city areas need to be encouraged through bringing in more regulatory measures.

An exhaustive survey for identifying poor should be done within one year. Then a mission mode approach should be followed to alleviate urban poverty. The poverty alleviation should be based on skill development and training. Self Help Group (SHG) based activities should be promoted. Slums should be redeveloped. City Development Plan should be valid for ten years and it should contain all infrastructure development. Enforcement of building regulation should be done through licensed architects and engineers.

Municipal governments should have full autonomy over function/activities devolved to them. The State government should take any punitary action on local governments only after due recommendation of the Local Ombudsman.

5 The Recommendations that have long term Implications

Almost all suggestions, recommendations or observations put forth in the report, in a neo-liberal perspective, are laudable. But some of them are brighter than the rest. It would be ideal to have a look at them.

The report proposes a **Framework Law for Local Governments** at the national level to be formulated with the consent of the States, in order to ensure mandatory - not optional- devolution of functions, funds and functionaries. It may put pressure on the reluctant States to divest with powers to the lower levels of governance.

The proposal for creation of a third tier representative government at the district –as **District Council**- by adding the strength of historically important office of the District Collector to the District Council, is an excellent recommendation. Putting the District Collector inside the system is the right thing as per the experience in Kerala too.

The report proposes greater **autonomy in personal management and in management of local resources by local governments**. It proposes to have crystal clear mapping of activities, before devolving those functions to the local governments, in order to have better clarity of the roles to be played by each tier of governance. This would enable the local governments to have better control over the functions, functionaries and finance that they are expected to manage.

The proposal to create a **Legislative Council** in each State consisting of members elected by local governments alone is a very important recommendation having long term implication in strengthening the voice of local governments in public governance. The option available for local government functionaries in stepping into a State's Legislative Council will motivate many to involve in local democracy and the council can draw wider attention to the issues of decentralization and local governance through its focused deliberations.

Another positive proposal in the report is the need to **devolve the law making authority to local**

governments in possible areas to uphold the autonomy. The report beautifully mixes the market dynamism and the public domain decision making in setting the basic standards aiming at improving the efficiency and effectiveness of local government services. The stress on continuous devolution of regulatory powers such as rural policing is another good step.

The **prominent drawback** of the report is that it does not deal much with the transfer of powers now with central governments, down to the State governments in possible areas even. The full exercise of principle of subsidiarity and creation of organically linked local governments in our public governance system requires re-examination of the power balance between Centre and the States. More powers from the Center needs to be devolved down to the State governments and further down to the local governments.

The enunciation of Principle of Subsidiarity, as the core principle for devolution of authority, is good and it will work in a well evolved lower level system. But we should be careful that unless the capacity of the local governments and their functionaries are not developed simultaneously, anyone can deny the real devolution of powers citing the incapability and invoking the principle itself. So there is urgent need to go ahead with proper capacity building as a simultaneous exercise.

Unfortunately the report speaks less emphatically on capacity development and its strategies. This is a notable lapse in a context when many of our well acclaimed capacity development attempts are becoming a mere farce or a ritual by focusing it on good stay, tasty food and entertaining lectures. There is urgent need to focus more on the capacity development for decentralization.

Conclusion

Public Administration in Indian was not directly or consciously planned for independent India and was a legacy of policies and procedures followed by the British rulers. When the third tier of local governments emerged, it was not much discussed even by the framers of our Constitution. So we have to build our own public administration or governance system by reforming all inter-related segments including local governments. The sixth report of ARC mentioned above is a blue print or agenda for further discussion and action.

The report stresses that empowerment of local governments requires careful nurturing, abundant patience and institutional design that ensure constant self-correction. Transfer of power in any form is painful and difficult. Giving up power is never easy and is usually resisted. There will be tendency to hold on to power and resist any kind of decentralisation. So there is need to have strategic moves to empower local governments. It should also be ensured that the decentralisation of powers should lead to greater efficiency and accountability in local governments rather than resulting in decentralised corruption.

A casual look at the report will reveal that the best minds available in India on local governance have associated in the formulation of the report. There is urgent need to carry it forward to bring administration, powers and welfare closer to the people trough a vibrant local government system.

References

1. Chaturvedi T.N: *Administrative reforms*. New Delhi. Indian Institute of Public Administration. 1984.
2. Dubhashi P.R.: *Administrative reforms*. New Delhi. B.R Publishing. 1986.
3. Kistaiah M.: *Administrative Reforms in a Developing Society*. New Delhi. Sterling Publishers. 1990.
4. *The Report of the Administrative Reforms Committee: 1958*. (Chairman E M Sankaran Namboothirippad) Thiruvananthapuram, The Government Press, 1958.

5. Singh Amita. : *Administrative Reforms: - Towards Sustainable Practices*. New Delhi. Sage Publications. 2005.

6. Government of India. : *Second Administrative Reforms Commission - Right to information: Master key to good governance*. New Delhi. Government of India. 2006.

7. Government of India. : *Second Administrative Reforms Commission - Unlocking Human Capital: Entitlements and Governance - A case study*. New Delhi. Government of India. 2006.

8. Government of India. : *Second Administrative Reforms Commission - Crisis Management: From Despair to Hope*. New Delhi. Government of India. 2006.

9. Government of India. : *Second Administrative Reforms Commission - Ethics in Governance*. New Delhi. Government of India. 2006.

10. Government of India. : *Second Administrative Reforms Commission - Public Order*. New Delhi. Government of India. 2006.

11. Government of India: *Second Administrative Reforms Commission - Local Governance: An Inspiring Journey into the Future*. New Delhi. Government of India. 2007.

16

Making Democracy Inclusive : Panchayats as Conduit

Toms K. Thomas

Prologue – Struggles for Inclusion – Real stories

Jagrani Devi belongs to a SC family. She is Gram Pradhan of Hamirpur gram Panchayat in Kasmanda development block of Sitapur district in U.P. She was elected as gram Pradhan for the first time in the year 2000, and has subsequently taken several initiatives for development in the Panchayat. Jagrani share her struggle in the following lines; there were numerous difficulties I had to face during the election phase. The family members of the previous Pradhan made an all out effort to stop me from contesting. Just a week before the election some other contestants framed a false case against my husband for illegal possession of ganja (type of narcotic), and he was imprisoned. I had to run from pillar to post to resolve the matter. Besides being a psychological shock, this incident has severe financial implications; I had to take a loan from my relatives and friends to bail him out.

On July 25, 2000 Lata Sahu was branded as witch and forced to parade naked in the village Bijili in Raipur district. Her crime; she had dared to stand for the post of Sarpanch against the wife of powerful clan leader Ramesh Yadav.

Sukhiya Bai (Madhya Pradesh) - a tribal Sarpanch of Gubrail Panchayat in Betul district. A year ago, she died in a hospital in Bhopal with 80 per cent burns. Sukhiya tried to struggle against the corrupt officials who demanded a cut for releasing money for development work. Simultaneously, she was under pressure from the villagers who demanded the money due to them for their labor. She had even borrowed Rs. 4,000 from a relative to pay the Panchayat secretary who had been demanding a bribe for releasing the money for a well that had been constructed by the villagers. Unable to bear the constant tension, she set fire to herself.

In Tamilnadu, Leelavathi contested the Madurai municipal elections in 1996, promising to bring water to the ward. She was elected as councilor and within six months water came to the area. This threatened the mafia of the water tanker owners, who had a flourishing business in the area. Within days of her victory to get water in the area, Leelavathi was murdered by those who lost their water business.

1.0. Introduction

Democracy is one of the best forms of governance where people have been put first in the ladder of governments. In democracy a lot of powers have been given to the people and elections are a very important part of the democratic system. Democracy itself is an inclusive form of governance where people are given the prime priority in the governance in democracy. It is a system of governance;

- For the people
- By the people
- Of the people

However the power relations and the caste and ethnic division in the country significantly excluded the majority of the population from the mainstream governance and the public governance became a business of few. The common men, the majority, who are at the lower layer of the population, are not often given an opportunity to voice their concerns.

The last 10 years have witnessed a steady progress as far as the governance inclusion of the excluded sections of

Indian population in the decision-making process from the village to the district level is concerned. The government over the years has set up various constitutional mandatory requirements to make the democratic system in our country more inclusive. Some of the examples are;

- Reservation for women
- Reservation for SC and ST
- Protection of minorities

Amartya Sen, the Nobel laureate economist considers development as freedom; in fact, that is the very title of one of the books (Sen, 1999) written by him. Democracy as he suggests is the best form of governance to ensure citizens freedom. Democracy should make serious and sincere effort to ensure that it gives opportunity to voice the concerns of all with equal importance.

1.1. History of Indian Democracy

The word democracy comes from the Greek words - demos meaning 'the people' and cratos meaning 'power' - in other words it means 'people power'. Democracy ensured the voices of the majority / the people are safeguarded while making decisions. Elections are one of the very important features of democracy and these elections are a means to ensure that the elected representatives act for the good of the society and the citizens and are made accountable for their doing during the governance at the time of next elections. India is a democratic country.

Switzerland is a country which maintains certain systems similar to that in a direct democracy. Some of the examples are

• **Referendum**

People can express their opinion on government policy or decision.

• **Recall**

People could call back a representative before completion of term if he / she go against public interest.

• **Initiative**

People can take preliminary steps to suggest a legislation which they think is necessary

• **Plebiscite**

People express their opinion on specific political issues.

India follows a representative democracy. The features of the representative democracy include

Rule by representatives: In India we have representatives at the state level and at the central level called Member of Legislative Assembly and the Member of Parliament. The 73rd amendment of the constitution instituted Panchayats as an integral part of the government structure and consequently, Panchayat members also have become people's representatives.

Existence of definite representative mechanism: We have the parliament at the central level which has a Lok Sabha and a Rajya Sabha and at the state level we have a Legislative Assembly. In some states the state Legislature has two tiers. Apart from this we have a Gram Sabha at the village level which is more or less like a direct democracy component where the citizens are made a part of the decision making at the local level. There are also various councils at the district level Panchayats and in the Municipalities and Corporations.

- Political parties compete for political authority
- Existence of interest and pressure groups
- Practice of universal adult franchise
- Elections and Voting Systems: Election as well as a definite voting system is very important for the representative democracy to function effectively. A

fool proof electoral system to elect the representatives is very important. In India there is an Election Commission at the centre as well as at the state level which are primarily responsible for conducting elections and formulating election policies and regulations.

1.2. Electoral system in India

India is the largest democracy in the word and is one among the very successful ones. India has a system of elections at every five years and there are different mechanisms of accountability. In every five years, elections are conducted for choosing the members for the parliament and the legislative assemblies. 543 members to Lok Sabah and roughly about 4500 members to the state legislatures are elected every five years. All Indian citizens above the age of 18 years have the right to vote. The number of representatives from each state is dependant on the size of population. In addition to this there are 250 members in the Rajya Sabha. Rajya Sabha MPs remain in office for 6 years. Rajya Sabha is a permanent body and is never dissolved. One third of its members retire every second year and thus the continuity is ensured.

Running cost of Legislatures

According to an assessment made by Common Cause, an NGO, the cost of running both the houses of parliament works out to be Rs.17000 per minute. This amounts to Rs.10 lakh per hour and Rs.75 lakh per day. Similar figures for state legislatures are not available. However if we assume that running expense of each state assembly cost a modest Rs.35 lakh the bill for running all the legislature in all 28 states for the whole day would be close to 10 crore. Some states like Karnataka and Jammu and Kashmir have two houses – an assembly and a legislative council, which pushes up the bill further. All these expenses are ultimately borne by the citizens through various taxation.

1.3. People's Participation in Governance

It has been observed that there has been a conspicuous decline in participation as indicated particularly by the lower voter turn outs in the recent local body elections *viz-a-viz* election to the state assembly and the parliament (Harilal 2005). The participation of the citizens is very crucial for the best functioningl of any democratic system. However, the structural deficiencies within the system 'regulate', to a certain extent, the participation of all the citizens and there is a declining trend in the percentage of voters which suggest the loss of interest of the public to be included in the over all democratic process. The citizen's participation in the central and state legislatures is limited significantly to the election of its members. Post election accountability to citizens is not largely available in both these two tiers of the governance. However the Panchayat Raj significantly allows citizens not only to participate in elections but also to post election monitoring of the elected representatives. Since most of the elected candidates are known very personally to all the electorates the accountability is much higher in this tier of the governance when compared to the other two. The following table suggests the same.

Table 1. Functional Participation of Governance Levels

Level of Governance	Constitutional Mechanism	Type of Participation		If answerable to the Electorate Directly
		Indirect (Electorate/ Voter)	Direct (Influence Decisions)	
National Level	Parliament	Yes	No	No
State level	Legislative assembly	Yes	No	No
Panchayat Level	Gram Sabha (Peoples Assembly)	Yes	Yes	Yes

Participation is viewed as a process rather than a single act at a particular point of time (Mohanan 2005). The election trend also suggests that there is declining trend in the voter turn outs which suggest that the people at large are loosening the interest in the democratic decision making process. Votes gained by the major parties have declined over years that are from 45% to 36.6% in 1991. The percentage of seats also declined from 74% to 46% over the last 10 years.

Table 2. Summary of election results 1952 – 1991

Year	*Party*	*Votes %*	*Seats %*
1952	INC	45	74.4
1957	INC	47.8	75.1
1962	INC	44.7	73
1967	INC	40.8	54.4
1971	INC	43.7	67.9
1977	JNP	41.3	54.4
1980	INC	42.7	65.1
1984	INC	48.0	76.5
1989	INC	39.5	37.2
1991	INC	36.6	45.6

Source: Electoral Reforms in India, Anjoo Sharan Upadhyaya

The national and state governments in the past two election rounds suggest that no single party gets majority in the elections. Entering into alliance after elections has been seen as the trend both at the national as well as in the centre to get in to power. This is the case even in the case of some of the municipal elections. This suggests that the preferences of the electorate are changing and there is no majority rule and the democracy currently practicing is a coalition one which may not be the desired outcome of the electorate. This could be one of the reasons for the declining trend in the voting turn outs in various elections.

1.4. The case of Kerala

The Kerala case though is a bit different. The voter participation in the various elections and the democratic process is encouraging. However, the over all rate has declined since 1987 from 81% to 72% though there is an increase in the voting percentage from 67% to 72%. The following table provides the details of the polling status of Kerala state from 1957 to 2001.

Table 3. Votes polled in the Kerala Legislative Assembly elections 1957-2001

Years of Election	*No of seats*	*Electorate*	*Votes Polled*	*Percentage*
1957	126	8851443	5899822	66.62
1960	126	9601601	8228812	85.70
1965	133	8557716	6428937	75.12
1967	133	8613658	6518272	75.67
1970	133	10168467	7634451	75.07
1977	140	11462487	9078459	79.20
1980	140	13263837	9587663	72.28
1982	140	19117012	9649083	73.56
1987	140	15944280	12839457	80.53
1991	140	19646607	14433354	73.45
1996	140	20667409	14706806	71.16
2001	140	21690331	15664511	72.45

Source: Kerala Election Commissions

1.5. Cost of Elections and Electorate Accountability

The conducting of elections as stated earlier is very expensive and the money is spending from the tax saving of the state. The fall of a government before maturity therefore increases the financial burden of the state and so it affects the over all fund allocation since the reallocation probably might be necessary in the light of the anticipated election cost. This spending from the public treasury for election makes the elected representatives to be accountable and transparent. Electorate and the citizens should have a right to be adequately informed of the democratic decision making process. The following table suggests the Lok Sabha election expenses over the years.

Table 4. Election Expenses over years

Year of Election	*Expenditure in Rs.*
1952	10450000
1957	59000000
1962	73200000
1967	107969000
1971	106087450
1977	230368000
1980	547739000
1984	815134000
1989	1542200000
1991	3591024679
1996	5973441000
1998	6662216000
1999	8800000000
2004	13000000000

Source: Election Commission of India

1.6. Participation of Women in Governance

The participation of women in the national governance seems to be declining and not up to the level of expectation of the constitution. In most states, except in local governments, women are not adequately represented in the government. The representation of women in national and state governments is very minute and this is against the constitutional expectation of provision of equal opportunities to all. The table below suggests the trend of participation of women in governance at various levels.

The trend over the past years suggests that there is no significant progress made on this line. The women representation in both the Lok Sabah and the Rajya Sabha seems to be very minimal and this is the case in most of the legislative assembles of the various states. The following table suggests the voter turn out of both men and women and the representation of women in the state legislative assemblies in the various state assemblies. Even for the literate states like Kerala the percentage of women legislators is very insignificant. Tamil Nadu and Delhi comes to be the highest with more than 10% of women in the state legislature.

Table 5. Representation of women in Lok Sabah and Rajya Sabha

Year	*Lok Sabha*			*Rajya Sabha*		
	Seats	*Women MP*	*% of Women MP*	*Seats*	*Women MP*	*% of Women MP*
1952	499	2	4.41	219	16	7.31
1957	500	27	5.40	237	18	7.59
1962	503	34	6.73	238	18	7.56
1967	523	31	5.93	240	20	8.33
1971	521	22	4.22	243	17	7
1977	544	19	3.49	244	25	10.25
1980	544	28	5.15	244	24	9.84
1984	544	44	8.09	244	28	11.48
1989	517	27	5.22	245	24	9.8
1991	544	39	7.17	245	38	15.51
1996	543	39	7.18	223	19	8.52
1998	543	43	7.92	245	15	6.12
1999	543	49	9.02	245	19	7.76
Average	528	33	6.15	238	22	9.00

Source: Election Commission of India

Table 6. Women's Participation and Representation in State Assemblies

State	*Election Year*	*Turnout Men*	*Turnout Women*	*Percentage of Women in the State Legislature*
Andhra Pradesh	1999	72.07	66.24	9
Arunachal Pradesh	1999	72.38	73.58	3
Assam	2001	77.23	71.82	8
Delhi	1998	50.89	46.41	13
Bihar	2000	70.71	53.28	6
Goa	2000	69.90	68.23	3
Gujarat	1998	63.34	55.03	2
Haryana	2000	69.97	67.85	4
Himachal Pradesh	1998	70.26	72.21	9
Jammu & Kashmir	1996	60.57	46.08	2
Karnataka/Mysore	1999	70.62	64.58	3
Kerala	2001	74.39	70.67	6
Madhya Pradesh	1998	66.45	53.53	8
Maharashtra	1999	63.62	58.03	4
Manipur	2002	90.09	91.07	2
Meghalaya	1998	74.20	74.83	5
Mizoram	1998	76.42	76.22	0
Nagaland	1998	80.65	7.07	0
Orissa	2000	63.63	54.25	9
Punjab	2002	65.92	64.27	7
Pondicherry	2001	69.51	70.70	0
Rajasthan	1998	67.45	58.88	7
Sikkim	1999	84.36	79.10	3
Tamil Nadu	2001	61.30	56.83	11
Tripura	1998	81.96	79.65	3
Uttar Pradesh	2002	56.75	50.33	6
Uttaranchal	2002	55.96	52.89	6
West Bengal	2001	77.83	72.53	9

Source: www.ec.gov.in

1.7. Women in Panchayat

An alternative system of larger representation and accountability has been seen as the local self government and the three tier Panchayat governance structure. The Panchayat Raj was mainly intended at making the governance more inclusive through wider participation of the people. A look at the statistics of the Panchayat elections suggests that the Panchayat has more accountability mechanisms and transparency in the decision making. There is a better mechanism for back and forth interaction with the community through the Gram Sabha meetings.

The over all trends in the women turn out in the elections in the national level elections suggest that there is a very clear growth in the voter turn out of women but the gap between the women and men voter turn out is still persistent at the average range of 5%. The total women voters also increased from 38 to 46 percent over the past 10 years. The following table provides the detaisl of this growth and changes in electorate over the past few decades since independence.

Table 7. Women turnouts and their proportion to total votes in the Loksabha elections 1957-98

Year	*Women percent turnouts*	*Men percent turn outs*	*Women percent of total voters*
1957	38.8	55.7	38.3
1962	46.6	62.1	39.8
1967	49	61	42
1971	49.2	61.2	42.4
1977	54.9	65.4	43.6
1980	51.2	62.2	43.1
1984	59.3	68.4	44.5
1989	57.5	66.4	44.1
1991	50.5	60.7	42.9
1996	53.4	62.1	44
1998	61.0	65.9	46.9

Source: www.eci.gov.in

2.0 Panchayat Raj – Towards Larger Inclusion

Local Self Government is one of the pioneering initiatives of the government to transfer the power to the people. It gave more transparency and accountability of the public governance. It is in fact a realization of the dream of the father of our nation, Mahatma Gandhi. The 73rd and 74th constitutional amendments gave constitutional backing to the local self government institutions and made them an integral part of the over all governance. Many of the local public institutions have been re-routed to the Panchayats to make them more transparent. Kerala, though a pioneer in many areas of development, was a bit slow in making Panchayat Raj into effect. Kerala Panchayat Raj Act was brought into effect in 1994 and it gave tremendous inspiration to the local governments since it made them as an integral part of the over all state governance structure. The first elections to the three tier Panchayat Raj set up were held in September 1995 and the Panchayats came into being on the 2nd of October. A significant event was the issue of a comprehensive government order in September 1995, transferring various institutions and staff to the three tier PRIs (see Annexure I). Panchayat has been provided with various powers at the grass root which make grass root governance more transparent and participatory. Another noteworthy event was the budget of 1996 which had a separate document known as Annexure IV, which detailed the grants-in-aid, and the schemes transferred to the local bodies. Thus the allocation for the local bodies was seen as an independent subset of the State Budget giving it the stamp of legislative approval and protecting it from the vagaries of executive decision-making.

2.1 Objectives of Decentralized Governance

The objectives of Decentralization are many. The introduction of the Panchayat Raj system also has been thought of keeping these objectives in mind:

- Promotion of more balanced development in the country: Decentralization significantly helps a country like India with vast diversity and development differences to achieve a balanced development. The areas that lag behind shall get more focused attention because of the decentralization. Similarly the voices of the people at various levels would also get voices through decentralized governance.
- Design of more realistic projects and programs which takes in to account local potentials and constraints: Decentralization facilitates identification of the needs of the localities and formulate program that are most appropriate to address the problems. This facilitates a significant amount of participation of the majority of the citizens specially the beneficiaries in decision making in relation to the future.
- More effective coordination of development activities at various spatial levels through aggregation of planning functions: people have been given a role as a monitor in the plan and program implementation.
- Strengthening local political institutions and increasing people's participation in development; and
- Boosted mobilization of local resources: Mobilization of local resources and the optimum use of it are very important objectives of decentralized governance. This helps identifying unexplored potentials at the various local levels through the decentralized governance structures and this would improve the over all resource base of the localities.

2.2. Principles Guiding Local Governance

Some basic principles that govern the transfer of functions and powers to the LSGIs and their exercise by them are explained below.

(i) ***Autonomy*** - The LSGIs should be left to function freely and independently. Government supervision should be limited to the obligatory and regulatory functions of the LSGIs. In development matters only national and state priorities and general guidelines need be indicated to help them take their own decisions.

(ii) Subsidiarity - It means what can be done best at a particular level should be done at that level and not at a higher level. If this principle is applied, the process of transferring functions and powers should start from the level of the Grama Sabhas and Wards Committees and go up to the Union Government.

(iii) Role clarity – This would govern the exercise of autonomy. Decentralized development implies unity of vision and diversity of means. This calls for a clear perception by the various levels of their role in the developmental process so that the sub-systems can support each other and do not work at cross-purposes. There must be clarity at the conceptual and operational level about what each tier of local self-government can do in each area of development.

(iv) Complementarity – This is closely related to the principle of role-clarity. While functions should not be overlapping and repetitive they should merge into an overall unity through a process of horizontal integration.

(v) Uniformity – This implies that the norms and criteria for selection of beneficiaries, sites or prioritization of activities and pattern of assistance within a given LSGI would be the same for all programs implemented within its area irrespective of the agency sponsoring such a program.

(vi) People's participation – It is necessary to involve the people fully, particularly those sections who were hitherto excluded from the development process. And participation should not be limited to mere information giving or consultation or contribution or even seeking prior concurrence. It would reach the level of empowering the people to take their own decisions after analyzing their situation.

(vii) Accountability – The LSGIs are accountable to the people within their jurisdiction and in certain respects, to the whole nation. The accountability to the people is not to be left to the elections alone to be settled.

(viii) Transparency – Every decision taken has to be based on norms and criteria evolved on the basis of social consensus and the rationale behind each decision has to be made public.

2.3. Gram Sabha – Making Governance Participatory

People's assembly (Gram Sabha) is an instrument at the local level for direct democracy. This traditional Instrument of democracy gets a prominent place in the Gandhian concept of self sufficient village republic. Article 243(G) of the Indian constitution suggests that Gram Sabha means a body of persons registered in the electoral rolls relating to a village comprised within the area of Panchayat at the village level.

The Kerala model of decentralization aims at empowerment of the people particularly the common men. It envisages power flowing to the people through the Panchayat Raj Institutions, which are to serve as a vehicle for participation. The policy aims at giving not only voice to the people but the power of choice as well. Though Kerala does not have traditional villages which are natural sociological units marked by a compact spatial cluster of settlements with a social pattern in their lay out. It has made a bold attempt to induce people's participation by creating a fourth tier in the form of Grama Sabhas equated with the electoral constituency of a Village Panchayat Member, as all the electors of the Ward are members of the Grama Sabha. In the modern period, meetings of the village have been very rare and what is now being attempted is a kind of Socio-political engineering to create an entirely new set up for direct democracy. It is because of this that the Kerala Act dwells at length on the powers and responsibilities of the Grama Sabha so that these fledgling institutions are able to develop with a clear idea of their role.

2.3.1. Responsibilities of Grama Sabha

The major responsibilities of the Panchayat include the following;

(i) Dissemination of information regarding developmental and welfare activities;

(ii) Participating in and canvassing of programs of health and literacy and such other time bound developmental programs.

(iii) Collecting essential socio-economic data;

(iv) Providing feed back on the performance of development programs;

(v) Resort to moral suasion to pay taxes, repayment of loans, promote environmental cleanliness and to maintain social harmony;

(vi) Mobilize local resources to augment resources of the Panchayat;

(vii) Supervising development activities as volunteer teams and

(viii) Make arrangements for reporting urgently incidence of epidemics, natural calamities etc.

Apart from these, various powers of local importance are also given to the Panchayats. Kerala is also unique in providing special opportunity for the people living in tribal areas. Though the state has only a very small tribal population (just about a percent of its total population) it provides for separate Grama Sabhas for tribals wherever their population is 50 or more in a ward. Such Grama Sabhas have the same powers and responsibilities of the general Grama Sabhas.

2.4. Panchayat Raj and Participatory Governance

Panchayat compared to the state legislature and the parliament has better participation of citizens in the governance process. The Grama Sabha is one of the best ways to ensure the participation of the people in the governance process. This facilitates the accountability of the elected Panchayat leaders to the electorate. The regular meeting of the Grama Sabha and the various powers given to the Grama Sabha even make it much more electorate friendly compared to the other tiers of the governance like state legislative assembly and the parliament. The members need to be more transparent and accountable in decision making since they also have a moral and social obligation to the electorate. However it is unfortunate that in many places especially in states like Bihar, UP, Chhattisgarh and Madhya Pradesh the participation of people in the Grama Sabha is very poor. In many places it is even less than 10 % of the total electorates. There are though trends in change in this because of the large scale awareness building and campaigns done at the village and Panchayat level by the government as well as civil society organizations. The following table suggests the Grama Sabha membership in various districts in Kerala. The table suggests that the literate Kerala also lag behind in people attending the Grama Sabha meetings.

Table 8. People's Participation in Gram Sabha in Kerala

District	*Av. Participation in Grama Sabha*	*Average Women Participation in Grama Sabha*	*Average SC/ST Participation in Grama Sabha*
Trivandrum	183.17	34.95	3.45
Kollam	178.21	25.14	4.13
Pathanamthitta	156.57	29.88	3.85
Alapuzha	205.26	29.35	3.45
Kottyam	148.36	23.85	2.60
Idukki	205.21	19.26	2.37

District	*Av. Participation in Grama Sabha*	*Average Women Participation in Grama Sabha*	*Average SC/ST Participation in Grama Sabha*
Ernakulam	189.79	19.04	1.94
Trichur	150.60	26.95	3.17
Palaghat	168.11	20.09	3.38
Malappuram	193.40	26.69	2.32
Calicut	214.18	27.72	0.41
Wayanad	215.58	19.99	2.40
Kannur	166.57	21.24	4.58
Kasargodu	148.41	20.96	0.87
State	179.67	24.82	2.75

Source: Kerala State Planning Board 2005

It is though encouraging that local government structures in the state has comparatively better representation of women. This suggests that the Panchayats are more inclusive and democratic than the other two higher layers of governance. The following table suggests this. This is however not the same in many of the other states. In many North Indian states though the reservation exists the actual Panchayat functions are performed by either their husbands or brothers.

Table 9. Distribution of Elected Representatives of Local Bodies in Kerala 1997

Type of local Bodies	*Number of bodies*	*Number of Males*	*%*	*Number of Females*	*%*	*Total*
Gram Panchayat	990	6842	63.8	3878	36.2	10720
Block Panchayat	152	1002	64.9	541	35.1	1543
District Panchayat	14	196	65.3	104	34.7	300
Municipality	58	1055	34.7	555	34.7	1610
Total	1214	9095	64.2	5078	35.8	14173

Source: State Election Commission

However, it is not of much difference in case of the highest voted party and their share in the total votes which in most cases is less than 50% in most of the cases. An analysis of the recent Panchayat election suggests that except in one district the highest score of the largest party is less than 50% of the total votes polled. The following table suggests the same.

Table 10. District wise voting status in Panchayat Elections

District	*Party*	*Votes Secured*	*Total Polled*	*Percentage*
Trivandrum	LDF	653557	1541124	42.41
Kollam	LDF	572694	1352376	42.35
Pathanamthitta	UDF	242986	666643	36.45
Alapuzha	LDF	493836	1232257	40.08
Kottyam	UDF	404275	1061633	38.08
Idukki	UDF	225606	612412	36.84
Ernakulam	UDF	600798	1679757	35.77
Trichur	LDF	639286	1655770	38.61
Palaghat	LDF	682119	1375701	49.58
Malappuram	UDF	746818	1808898	41.29
Calicut	LDF	679494	1598644	42.50
Wayanad	UDF	144814	405833	35.68
Kannur	LDF	710328	1320844	53.78
Kasargodu	LDF	243337	639907	38.03

Source: Kerala State Election Commission

3.0 Conclusions and Way Forward

There is a clear need for finding means to address the issue of inclusion through innovative governance reforms at the various levels. The present structure seriously lacks the participation of women and the general public. Women are not represented adequately in relation to their total population figure of the country at the higher levels of governance like the parliament and state legislative assembly. However it is encouraging to note that there is significant progress on women inclusion in the lower tiers of governance like Panchayat. There are needs of capacity building of the women Panchayat leaders to make them more functional.

There is also need to raise the total voter turn out rate to an acceptable level to make democracy more functional and practical. Though the current voter turn out is good in some states like Kerala there is a need to improve on to the extent of complete inclusion. The electoral reforms should be made adequately practical accommodating all the segments of the population. There is also a need to ensure that the elected candidates secure a reasonably good percentage of votes to make the winning more democratic. Innovative mechanisms in elections and representation shall be thought on these lines to ensure that the percentage of vote they secure is more democratic.

Strengthening of Panchayat and inclusion of the Panchayat Raj in to the larger democracy is very important to have wider inclusion of the lower tiers in to over all governance. The direct democratic principles applied in the Gram Sabhas could be a model which probably the state and union parliament could think of incorporating in those tiers of governance. It could be also advisable to think of the ways and means to incorporate Gram Sabha as an extension of not just Panchayat Raj but even a very strong layer of state legislature.

17

Gram Sabhas and Democratic Deepening : Evidence from a Village Panchayat in Kerala

Nisha Velapan Nair

Introduction

Development has a trajectory of its own. There is now a common understanding that development should ultimately lead to all round human development and that sustainability should be the key issue in it. The top-down approach divorced from the realities of the lives of people often led to failure. The people's campaign for the 9th plan was launched in Kerala in 1996, and as a result, the Gram Sabhas received definite functional tasks with respect to planning and beneficiary selection.

Deepening local democracy means involving citizens more in local decisions that affect their lives. It means seeking a balanced involvement of both genders and citizens of all ages. It means adequate scrutiny, accountability and information flows. It also means putting effective strategies in place for increasing and deepening citizen's participation in decision making process in the local sphere (CPSU, 2004).

The Balwant Rai Mehta committee, which was appointed in January 1957, had suggested a three-tier system of decentralization (Sundaram, 1999). There would be village panchayats at the village level, panchayat samithis at the block level and Zilla Parishads at the district level. The 73rd Amendment of 1992 which came into effect on April 24, 1993 is a major land mark in the transition of political power to the grass root level in the country.

Decentralization as it is being attempted in Kerala is informed by some clarity of vision about the nature of local governments and the process of empowering them. "Local Self Governments", in the words of the Sen Committee, is essentially the empowerment of the people by giving them not only the voice, but the power of choice as well, in order to shape the development which they feel is appropriate to their situation. It implies maximum decentralization of powers to enable the elected bodies to function as autonomous units with adequate authority and resources to discharge the basic responsibility of bringing about "Economic Development and Social Justice" (John, 2002).

The people's campaign was inaugurated on 17th August 1996. The people's campaign can also be seen as an outcome of the long drawn out and extensive development dialogue in Kerala, sparked off as it was by the crisis faced by the 'Kerala Model of Development' (Thomas and Harilal, 1999)

The theoretical basis of decentralized planning initiated by the Left Democratic Government (LDF) is that due to deficiencies and defects of market mechanism, one cannot achieve socio-economic development which will ensure social justice and reduce social and economic disparities and poverty. It is pointed out that investment decisions taken on the basis of the profitability criterion are not socially desirable and won't take into consideration long term interest and sustainable development. Hence it is argued that intervention of the state through decentralized public investment decisions by delegating more administrative and financial powers to local bodies will safeguard the interest of the poor and weaker sections and ensure social justice (Prakash, 2005).

Panchayati Raj envisages total democratic decentralization. The Constitution of India in Article 234 (A) makes the Gram Sabha an integral part of the Panchayati Raj system. Gram Sabha is seen as the best vehicle for achieving genuine people's participation. Gram Sabha is the fourth tier system at the village/ward level and decision taken by it is expected to act as an input in local governance. An effective Gram Sabha is possible only with the willing co-operation of the representatives of the people, after the panchayat has been invested with sufficient powers. Although there is a relation between sincere efforts made by a panchayat member to increase participation and the achievement of real participation, good local governance may induce greater participation as it has a cumulative or spiraling effect (John and Chathukulam, 1999).

Participation in development

Participation has often been used in the normative sense, whereby anything participatory is assumed to be synonymous with 'good' and 'empowering'. Some critics have also likened it to a Trojan horse that can hide manipulation and even coercion under a cloak of social palatability (Slocum and Thomas Slaytes, 1995). An instrumental approach views participation as a means to achieve better cost-effectiveness, living standards, etc. While an empowerment approach values the process of increasing participation as an important end in itself (Gujit and Kaul Shah, 1999).

Chambers (1995) feels that participation, as a concept, has experienced a renaissance in the 70s and identifies three main ways in which participation is used in the context of development. First, it is used as a cosmetic label to take whatever is proposed appears as good. Second, it is used as a method for co-opting local labour to reduce the cost of maintenance of projects. Thirdly, it is a way of empowering people by enabling them to take decisions on the problems they encounter and the possible ways of getting out to them.

Participation is in its highest form when there is self organization, self responsibility and self actualization. Participation is an essential part of human growth, development of self confidence, pride, initiative, creativity, responsibility and co-operation (Burkey, 1993).

Quality of deliberation

Participation has no direct relationship with deliberation. When a large number of people participate in a forum we cannot say that it is a deliberative forum, by looking at the numbers alone. John Stuart Mill (1861) commented that the success of democratic arrangements can be measured in two ways - by the quality of its decisions and the quality of citizens it produces. There are, however, significant limitations to the deliberative character of Gram sabhas. To begin with, they are too large and unwieldy for meaningful deliberation. This does not allow for serious discussion of the large number of complex issues that are normally included in the agenda of the Gram sabha. (Issac and Heller, 2003). Rational choice perspectives emphasize the trade off that individuals face between the costs and opportunities associated with participation, where the costs and opportunities are influenced by a range of features of the socioeconomic environment in which individuals are located. The opportunity costs of participation could be correlated with the nature of the local economy – for example, in areas with a higher percentage of non-agricultural workers (who, in Kerala, are likely to have higher incomes) one might expect to find less participation (Chaudhuri and Heller, 2002). It has been that a majority of the people go to the Gram sabha out of expectation of benefits. There is no overt caste domination of the body in Kerala and where it exists, it always takes cover behind its secularist variant – the party. The tendency to cook up figures to create an impression on high levels of people's participation is not widespread in the study area unlike in the southern part of Kerala. (Kurian, 2002).

A study based in Northern Kerala reveals that the participants in the sabha attended the body purely out of expectation of personal benefits rather than out of a civic sense. Many participants also were persuaded to attend the Gram sabhas by the party leadership, especially that of the leftist parties. It was seen that some participants disappeared when the session of the Gram sabha was adjourned for group discussions stating that the transactions were beyond their comprehension. Those who did not participate in the sabha alleged that individual interest and party interest played a big role in shaping the projects and selecting the beneficiaries, and even if they had participated, it would not have made any difference (John and Kunhambu, 2005).

The ordinary people who often participate in the public forums enthusiastically may find that participation is increasingly burdensome and less productive than they had imagined, leading to a kind of disillusionment and disengagement. Deliberative democracy cannot be a substitute for the poor way in which the overall social and political institutions are functioning since it cannot have an existence and style of functioning independent of these institutions (John, 2006).

Objectives and Methodology

This paper makes an effort to study the role of Gram Sabhas and its impact through people's participation by focusing on two wards of Nattakom Panchayat in Kottayam District. It also looks at the patterns of women's participation in the Gram Sabha.

Nattakom Panchayat is located in Kottayam Taluk of Kottayam district. It has an area of 2004 hectares and a population of 41,702 as per the 2001 census. There are 20,488 males and 21,214 females in the panchayat. It has 19 wards (22 after the most recent delimitation of electoral constituencies). Of all the panchayats in Kottayam district, Nattakom panchayat stands second in income from non-agricultural sector.

The main objectives of the study are to understand the nature of people's participation in the Gram Sabhas, the motivating and constraining factors of participation, the extent of women's involvement in the Gram Sabhas, the degree to which the Gram Sabha acts as a democratic support structure and the perceptions of the Panchayat members to the prospect of greater participation in the Sabha.

The approach taken in the study also sought to incorporate some elements of an ethnographic approach wherever it was possible. Primary data and secondary data were used for the study. Primary data for the study has been collected mainly through questionnaire from 100 voters (50 male and 50 female) of the panchayat, interview with panchayat members, former members, panchayat staff, and through focus group discussion. Secondary data were collected from books, journals and e-sources.

Table 1. Respondents who attended the Gram Sabhas

No of times attended	*Male*	*%*	*Female*	*%*
1-5	14	77.78%	11	35.48%
6-10	1	5.56%	7	22.58%
11-15	1	5.56%	3	9.68%
16-20	2	11.1%	10	32.6%
Total	18	100%	31	100%

Source: Field Survey

Table (1) shows the frequency of attendance in the Gram Sabha. This figure shows that females had attended more Gram Sabhas than males. The females who had attended the Gram Sabhas 16-20 number of times is 32.6% while that of males is 11.1%. Kudumbashree is an important factor which has increased the participation rate of women in the Gram Sabha as 28 out of 31 female respondents belong to Kudumbashree.

Table 2. Respondents who do not attend the Gram Sabha

	Reason	*Male*	*%*	*Female*	*%*
1.	No time to participate	12	37.5%	9	47.37%
2.	Not interested	7	21.88%	2	10.53%
3.	Do not know about it	0	-	1	5.26%
4.	Do not know about it and not interested	0	-	2	10.53%
5.	One member of the family is participating	0	-	5	26.32%
6.	It will never give any benefit	8	25%	0	-
7.	It is all party politics	3	9.37%	0	-
8.	Others	2	6.25%	0	-
	Total	32	100%	19	100%

Source: Field Survey

Table 2 depicts the factors constraining participation in the Gram Sabha. Lack of interest, time and benefit, and the feeling that one member of the family alone needs to particpate in the Gram Sabha are the major constraining factors of participation. Majority of Males (37.5%) and females (47.37%) do not attend the Gram Sabha because they have no time to participate. The males do not attend Gram sabha because of lack of perceivable benefits, partisanship and other reasons while females do not participate because of knowledge gaps, lack of interest and due to the fact that one member of the family is already participating.

Table 3 shows that the participation of people in Gram Sabha is showing a declining trend. It also shows increase in the rate of participation of women compared to men. In 2003 – 2004 the total percentage of attendance was below 10%. But we can see that the female participation was 87.3% while that of the males was only 12.7%.

Table 3. Strength of Participation in Gram Sabha (Ward A) 2001 - 2007

Year	*Total % attendance*	*Male %*	*Female %*
2001-2002	14.84%	44.72%	55.28%
2002-2003	13.69%	26.43%	73.57%
2003-2004	9.05%	12.7%	87.3%
2004-2005	10.01%	32.53%	67.47%
2005-2006	10.01%	36.75%	63.25%
2006-2007	11.03%	36.22%	63.78%

Source: Estimated from the office records of Nattakom Gram Panchayat

Table 4. Strength of Participation in Gram Sabhas (Ward B) 2001 - 2007

Year	*Total % attendance*	*Male %*	*Female %*
2001-2002	9.70%	53.68%	46.32%
2002-2003	11.04%	58.25%	41.75%
2003-2004	10.7%.	60.56%	39.44%
2004-2005	11.02%	55.79%	44.21%
2005-2006	10.14%	44.55%	55.45%
2006-2007	10.11%	36.47%	63.53%

Source: Estimated from the office records of Nattakom Gram Panchayath

Table (4) shows that the people's participation in the Gram Sabha of Ward 2 is somewhat constant. It also shows that there is an increase in the participation rate of women.

The field study reveals that the official data regarding the Gram Sabha attendance are all cooked up. The panchayat members, Panchayat staff and the voters of the ward say that Gram Sabha attendance figures are all fabricated, by adding extra names and signature to keep all records in order. This does not reflect the real level of participation. The panchayat members do not see the achieving of the quorum in the Sabha as a problem since they are known to add additional names after the Sabha to fill the gaps in the required quorum. The general motivation of the people to participate in the Gram Sabhas is beneficiary oriented and not due to a civic sense and responsibility. The quality of discussion in the Gram Sabha is generally poor.

Pancyahat members are of the opinion that participation of people in the Gram Sabha is beneficiary-oriented and therefore they see it essentially as a mechanical forum where the list of beneficiaries prepared by them is authenticated. Since the body is unlikely to challenge the authority of the member and the panchayat in its present form, they generally are not keen to strengthen the sabha. Women's participation in Gram Sabha is greater than that of males and it is due to the emergence of Kudumbashree, a state-supported project of women self-help groups functioning in close relationship with the village Panchayat. Power changes and the arrival of new representatives after the elections also impact on participation. The new member may not have the motivation, interest and skills to marshall more participation in the sabha.

A novel method of enhancing participation in the Sabha was witnessed in one of the adjoining wards not covered under this study. In this case the ward member announced a one gram gold coin to the winner of a draw from all the participants in the sabha. This served as an incentive for people to attend the sabha, and the participation improved remarkably.

The study reveals that as years pass, the participation of people in the Gram Sabha is declining in absolute terms. Feminization of the Gram Sabha has increased in quantitative terms, but this increase is not accompanied by greater activism in the sabha, even for causes that women consider important. The increasing participation of women has made the body more a pliable instrument in the hands of members in which conflicts and contestations are generally not found.

Conclusion

This study of two wards shows a general trend of declining participation in absolute terms and a feminization of participation in relative terms. The early gains in participation, especially that of the socially engaged sections, witnessed during the commencement of the people's plan campaign in late 1996 is no longer visible in the Sabha. Hence the potential of Gram Sabhas to serve as a mechanism of democratic deepening in our rural areas is severely limited. At the same time we witness considerable enhancement in participation in other exclusive community forums, which people find more attractive.

References

1. Burkey. S (1993): *People First, A Guide to Self Reliant Participatory Rural Development*, London: Zed Books, London.
2. Chambers. R (1995): 'Paradigm Shifts and the Practice of Participatory Development', *IDS Working Papers* No.2, Institute of Development Studies, Sussex.
3. Chaudhuri, Shubham and Patrick Heller (2002): 'The Plasticity of participation: evidence from a participatory governance experiment' *ISERP working paper*; New York. Columbia University.
4. Commonwealth Policy Studies Unit (2004): 'Deepening Local democracy in the common wealth', prepared for the *Common Wealth Local Government Forum*; November. www.cpsu.org.uk
5. Gujit. I and M.K. Shah (1999): 'Waking upto Power, Conflict and Process' in I. Guijt and M. Kaul Shah (eds.), *The Myth of Community: Gender Issues in Participatory Development,* London: Intermediate Technology Publications.
6. Issac, Thomas T.M and Patrick Heller (2003): 'Democracy and Development: Decentralized Planning in Kerala' in

Archon Jang and Erik Olin Wright (eds.), *Deepening Democracy: Institutional Innovations in Empowered Governance*. The Real Utopias Project, IV, London: Verso.

7. John, M.S and Jos Chathukulam (1999): The Relationship between Gram Sabha and Gram Panchayat, *Kurukshetra*, Vol. 48, No. 1, October.
8. John, Moolakkattu Stephen and V. V. Kunhambu (2005): "People's participation in Gram Sabha: Evidence from Three Village Panchayats in Malabar" (Kerala), *Man and Development*, Vol. 27, No. 2, June.
9. John, Moolakkattu Stephen (2006): 'Musings on Deliberative Democracy and the Gram Sabha', *Gandhi Marg*, Vol. 27, Nos. 3 and 4.
10. John, Oommen (2002): 'Performance Audit in Local Bodies Kerala's Experiment', *Kurukshetra,* March.
11. Kurian, Luciamma (2002): 'The Structure and Function of Gram Sabha. A study focused on the District of Kottayam', Kottayam: Mahatma Gandhi University (Unpublished Ph.D Thesis).
12. Mill, John Stuart (1861): *Consideration on Representative Government,* Indianapolis, Bolilis – Merrill.
13. Prakash B.A. (2005): 'Decentralised Planning in Kerala' in D. Rajasenan and Gerard de Groot (eds.), *Kerala Economy: Trajectories, Challenges and implication,* Cochin University of Science and Technology: Directorate of Publication of Public Relations.
14. Slocum, R. and B. Thomas-Slayter (1995): 'Participation, Empowerment and Sustainable Development', in Slocum, L. Wichart, D. Rocheleau and B. Thomas – Slayter (eds.) *Power, Process and Participation: Tools for Change*, London: Intermediate Technology Publications.
15. Sundaram Sataya. I. (1999): *Rural Development*, New Delhi: Himalaya Publishing House.
16. Thomas T. M and K. N. Harilal (1999): 'Democratisation of the Planning Process' in M.A Oommen (ed), *Kerala Development Experience* Volume II. New Delhi: Concept Publishing Company.

Index

D